ARISTOTLE
POLITICS

Translation, Introduction,
and Glossary

THE FOCUS PHILOSOPHICAL LIBRARY

The Focus Philosophical Library is distinguished by its commitment to faithful, clear, and consistent presentations of texts and the rich world part and parcel of those texts.

Thanks to our series advisors:
Peter Kalkavage, St. John's College
Maureen Eckert, University of Massachusetts-Dartmouth
Dustin Gish, College of the Holy Cross

Aristotle: De Anima • M. Shiffman
Aristotle: Nicomachean Ethics • J. Sachs
Aristotle: Poetics • J. Sachs
Athenian Funeral Orations • J. Herrman
Descartes: Discourse on Method • R. Kennington
Empire and the Ends of Politics (Plato/Pericles) • S. D. Collins and D. Stauffer
Four Island Utopias (Plato, Euhemeros, Iambolous, Bacon) • D. Clay and A. Purvis
Hegel: The Philosophy of Right • A. White
Liberty, Equality & Modern Constitutionalism, Volume I • G. Anastaplo
Liberty, Equality & Modern Constitutionalism, Volume II • G. Anastaplo
Lucretius: On the Nature of Things • W. Englert
Plato and Xenophon: Apologies • M. Kremer
Plato: Euthydemus • M. Nichols
Plato: Gorgias • J. Arieti and R. Barrus
Plato: Gorgias and Aristotle: Rhetoric • J. Sachs
Plato: Meno • G. Anastaplo and L. Berns
Plato: Parmenides • A. K. Whitaker
Plato: Phaedo • E. Brann, P. Kalkavage, and E. Salem
Plato: Phaedrus • S. Scully
Plato: Republic • J. Sachs
Plato: Sophist • E. Brann, P. Kalkavage, and E. Salem
Plato: Statesman • E. Brann, P. Kalkavage, and E. Salem
Plato: Symposium • A. Sharon
Plato: Theatetus • J. Sachs
Plato: Timaeus • P. Kalkavage
Socrates and Alcibiades: Four Texts • D. Johnson
Socrates and the Sophists • J. Sachs
Spinoza: Theologico-Political Treatise • M. Yaffe

ARISTOTLE
POLITICS

Translation, and Glossary

Joe Sachs

with an Introductory Essay by
Lijun Gu

focus *an imprint of*
Hackett Publishing Company, Inc.
Indianapolis/Cambridge

Aristotle *Politics*: Translation, Introduction, and Glossary
© 2012 Joe Sachs

Previously published by Focus Publishing/R. Pullins Company

Focus an imprint of
Hackett Publishing Company
P.O. Box 44937
Indianapolis, Indiana 46244-0937
www.hackettpublishing.com

Cover drawing by Cindy Zawalich, based on a sketch by Robert Abbott envisioning Aristotle's description in Book VII, Chapter 12.

ISBN: 978-1-58510-376-8

19 18 17 16 15   2 3 4 5 6

Library of Congress Cataloging-in-Publication Data
Aristotle.
  [Politics. English]
  Aristotle Politics : translation, introduction, and glossary / Joe Sachs.
   p. cm.
  Includes index.
  ISBN 978-1-58510-376-8
  1. Political science—Early works to 1800. I. Sachs, Joe, 1946– II. Title. III. Title: Politics.
  JC71.A41S28 2012
  320.01'1—dc23   2012014290

Contents

Contents

TRANSLATOR'S PREFACE

It is now more than twenty years since this series of translations of works of Aristotle began, and the scope of that project has grown far beyond anything that was originally envisioned. I once told someone that I had no intention of translating the *Nicomachean Ethics*; I had accomplished my purpose, I thought then, by showing that Aristotle's principal theoretical works—the *Physics*, the *Metaphysics*, and *On the Soul*—could be read without any of the Latin-based jargon that centuries of tradition had imposed upon them. After I had in fact added the *Nicomachean Ethics* to the list, I told someone else that was the last work of Aristotle I would translate. I was always telling the truth as I saw it at the time, but, as Aristotle has said, human things are variable and cannot be known with complete precision. The publication of the present work may be seen, at the moment anyway, as completing a series of translations of Aristotle's principal works on human life—the *Ethics, Poetics, Rhetoric,* and *Politics*. In one case after another, I was persuaded, or persuaded myself, that I had something to contribute to the understanding and appreciation of these books. The close study involved in translating them has continually revealed more to me of connections among them. And in the case of the *Politics*, a book that many people have devoted their lives to studying while my own primary interests have led me elsewhere, one argument that was finally persuasive was simply that I ought not to leave this one conspicuous gap in a group of Aristotle's major writings.

Getting a handle on any of Aristotle's inquiries is a challenging task. My own experience with them is that they usually begin to come together when one finds a direction of dialectical motion. Typically, Aristotle's arguments move from starting points that are widely believed, by ordinary people or by those who have studied previous thinkers, and arrive at conclusions that leave those initial opinions behind. Readers who praise Aristotle as the philosopher of common sense often do not notice that his reasoning can end up in some uncommon places, and other readers who admire him only as a master logician fail to see that he always has more respect for the complex ways of the world we perceive than for the logical arrangements anyone might seek to fit them into. The common claim that he writes "treatises" cannot be sustained by anyone who has allowed himself to be taken on the whole ride that any of these inquiries contains. But each of those rides takes its own course, and the *Politics* is an especially confusing ride to take. Aristotle always lets his subject matter determine his approach, and we in turn need to let each of his books teach us how it needs to be read. The parts of the *Politics* do not display a motion from beginnings to conclusions, but seem instead to build up a whole that remains everywhere in balance.

Political life is a realm in which practical judgment takes precedence over theoretical reasoning, and that is equally true within Aristotle's study of political life. Much can be determined dialectically about better and worse ways of ordering human communities, but carrying out any such measures in practice depends on the customs, habits, and circumstances of people as one finds them. Kingship and aristocracy may have been viable forms of government at early stages in the formation of cities, but Aristotle regards them as impossible in his own time. What remains from the three forms he considers rightly directed is the form he calls constitutional rule, which he describes as a mixture of democracy and oligarchy. But since he classes the latter two forms along with tyranny as deviations from the aims of government, constitutional rule seems to be a case in which two wrongs make a right. And much of the task of the *Politics*, and of the political art, is to develop the judgment to make that unlikely result come true. In practice, according to Aristotle, political life is a tug-of-war between the rich and the poor. He concludes that every time one or the other side decisively gets the upper hand, everybody loses. If the conflict between the rich and the poor could be resolved once and for all in favor of one side, or superseded altogether by some new order of things, then there could be a dialectical science of politics that laid out the best way for everyone to live. But while the *Politics* that Aristotle wrote does have a dialectical side, and while it does contribute to the practical political task, that dialectic does not and cannot replace or override the variety of practical arrangements that circumstances call for. This is true not only because the political art, like that of the doctor, must be applied to human beings who vary, so that there can never be a single right approach to curing their ills; in the case of political life, some strong traditional human opinions will necessarily guide and limit the organization of political communities from the outset. This is what Aristotle means on those occasions in Book I when he declares he will take his bearings for political inquiry by following the usual course, or beaten path, of popular opinion. Here in the *Politics*, popular opinion is not just a point of departure but the road along which the whole journey has to be made.

Most of the topics Aristotle discusses in the *Politics* come up more than once, and it can be difficult to put together the things he says about them. I am suggesting that this is not an inquiry in which provisional beginnings are gradually refined into dialectical conclusions. And I certainly do not believe that Aristotle speaks differently to different classes of readers, concealing his inmost thoughts from those of us who are unfit to hear them, or that he changed his mind over time and his youthful thoughts somehow got lumped in with his mature ones. The *Politics* contains a number of statements and images that capture Aristotle's approach to differences of political opinion. On the subject of democratic and oligarchic arguments about justice, he says the claims on both sides are true while neither alone is adequate (III, 9). About food, he says that dinners are better when many people contribute dishes, and that a diet is more nourishing when it contains a mixture of pure and impure food than either alone; about works of art, he says that the multitude is generally a better judge of music and poetry than experts are, and that the user is always the best judge of items made for use (III, 11). And he says that Socrates went off-course in the *Republic* by assuming that a community ought to sing in unison rather than in harmony (II, 5). Perhaps the best summary of his way of thinking is his extended comparison of fellow citizens to shipmates (III, 4): we are all in the same boat, and we sink or swim together. And if this is only one strand among many in Aristotle's political thinking, its contribution to the meaning of the whole becomes all the more important. Whether we choose to think of the *Politics* itself as something like a voyage, a symphony, or a feast, here too, the preponderance of images suggests that everything that goes into the whole ought to be regarded as remaining intact in the whole.

One topic about which Aristotle speaks a number of times in the *Politics* is the government of Sparta, and this might provide us with a brief illustration of the way the work hangs together. In Bk. II, Chap. 9, Aristotle examines that government in some detail, and he finds serious faults in every Spartan law and political arrangement he mentions. Still, two chapters later, he concludes that Sparta belongs within a small handful of governments that are "justly highly regarded." There is a similar pair of passages near the end of the *Politics*; in VII, 15, Aristotle criticizes the Spartans' form of education as seriously misguided, but three chapters later, in VIII, 1, he judges them worthy of praise for having a public education at all. From these bookends, one might conclude that Aristotle views Sparta as being on the right track, without in fact having found the most successful ways of carrying out any of its policies. But the situation is worse: in VII, 14, Aristotle blasts the whole design of the Spartan government as based on a misunderstanding of the ends of human life. It has not only missed the mark but failed even to aim at the right target. And yet, if one is starting to catch on to the kind of work I am proposing that the *Politics* is, one might be on the lookout for an "and yet" somewhere in the middle. And there is one: in IV, 9 Aristotle finds Sparta to be one of those places that can seem both oligarchic and democratic because it is neither. The Spartans pulled off the rarest accomplishment in the whole political world (see 1296a 36-38) by minimizing, and in many ways eliminating, the difference between the lives of the rich and the poor. The *Politics* may be said to balance around a point somewhere between democracy and oligarchy, and whatever Sparta's faults and failures may have been, it found and spent centuries at a spot very near that point.

So I am claiming that, whenever you find conflicting statements in the *Politics*, the most fruitful question to ask is not the dialectical one—How does he get from *a* to *b*?—but the organic one: What is the whole body of which those statements are limbs? For this sort of discernment, Aristotle recommends, the best preparation is not a training in logic but lessons in drawing (1338a 40-b 2). It follows that you should not trust anyone who singles out part of what Aristotle says about anything as his political opinion. To any question such as "Does Aristotle endorse aristocracy?" the answer has to be "Yes... and no," followed by some explanation and qualification. Even in the case of tyranny, which he condemns repeatedly in the strongest terms, Aristotle also makes the point that a tyrant capable of listening to reason about his own long-term self-interest can end up being a halfway-decent sort of ruler (1315b 7-10). On the other hand, you should not trust my advice either. I am a recent convert to the view of the *Politics* I am now advocating. For much too long, I was content to concentrate on Books I and III and treat the rest as a collection of loosely related essays. But even if it were true that the *Politics* is not a coherent whole, it will do you no harm to try first to let its parts come together for you. To this end, this volume contains a number of aids. The index is selective in its choice of entries, but tries to include an adequate span of occurrences under those that Aristotle looks at from differing angles. Proper names of people and places are included only when Aristotle's references to them stand out as memorable or remarkable. And there is a summary of contents to provide something like a map of the whole terrain. The footnotes sometimes contain cross-references or note connections, and there is a glossary meant to guide you to the primary instances in which Aristotle's language does not entirely match the expectations to which our own language might lead. Of scholarly or historical background for its own sake, there is none here. There are plenty of books, easy to find, to which you may turn for that sort of thing. Everything here is chosen with the aim of immersing the reader more fully in what Aristotle wrote.

Lijun Gu's introduction can help launch you into such a reading. He has both practical and academic qualifications for political study, and a passion for the subject. It was he who kept urging me for years to make this translation, and I am grateful to have his partnership in a project he has been in on since before it began. His introduction is a model of how to approach the task of assembling and comparing, weighing and assessing, to which the *Politics* invites the reader. And speaking of gratitude, my thanks go once again to Eric Salem, who has again found a way to slow down the turning of the celestial sphere enough to permit him to read through this translation for errors and lapses of judgment. Needless to say, he found quite a few, and raised the quality of this translation as he has done with so many before it. The translation is made from the 1973 printing of Sir David Ross's Oxford Classical Text; departures from his readings are few and noted. The standard pagination of the two-column Bekker edition, used in all modern versions, is carried in the margins, with the line numbers of the OCT edition between them. References in the index are to these Bekker pages. Though the glossary will be found with the back matter, it will do the reader no harm to look over it before reading the text.

Annapolis, Maryland
Fall, 2011

INTRODUCTION

Among the works of Aristotle, the *Politics* unexpectedly proves to be more difficult in some ways than the others. Part of the blame can be laid on the work itself; for compared to many other works by Aristotle, and especially to its cousin, the *Nicomachean Ethics*, the *Politics* is looser in structure and less polished in style. For example, much has been made of the disjointedness between the end of Book III and beginning of Book IV (so much so that Werner Jaeger claims that Chapter 18 of Book III is an interpolation of a different author).[1] In addition, the similarity between this chapter and the beginning of Book VII has led many to believe that Books III and VII belong to one unit, whereas Books IV-VI belong to a different unit and were inserted at a later date.[2] These and other apparent inconsistencies have caused much trouble in our attempts to interpret the *Politics*. They also help explain why so much of the literature is about the question of whether the work is a coherent whole, and, if not, whether the contradictions and incoherencies are in the form, the "doctrine," or both.[3]

The rest of the blame, however, probably lies with us. Since such complaints are not limited to the *Politics*, but are leveled, to various degrees, against almost all of Aristotle's works, they perhaps reveal a deeper discomfort. That is, it may well be that the *Politics* appears disjointed and confused not because *it* is so itself, but because *we* are so accustomed to a certain way of seeing politics—a way that

---

1   Werner Jaeger, *Aristotle, Fundamentals of the History of His Development*, translated with author's corrections and additions by Richard Robinson, 2nd Ed, (Oxford University Press, 1968), 267-268.

2   For a more detailed account, see: *Aristotle, The Politics*, translated and with an Introduction, Notes, and Glossary by Carnes Lord, (University of Chicago Press, 1984), 8-17.

3   Peter L. Phillips Simpson, *A Philosophical Commentary on the Politics of Aristotle*, (the University of North Carolina Press, 1998), xviii.

thinks of politics as a "common power" that "overawes" us, as a tool for purposes beyond itself, and ultimately as a "science" that is based on "clear and distinct" things that have their roots in our perceptive faculties. In addition, contrary to Aristotle's other works (particularly the *Physics* and *Metaphysics*), the terminology in the *Politics* seems relatively familiar to us. This often convinces us—usually without our even realizing it—that Aristotle thinks about politics in the same way that we do today; as a consequence, we come to expect a similar familiarity in the reasoning and structure of the book. Therefore, if the *Politics* does not conform to that expectation but instead appears disjointed, we think it must be because the manuscript has been damaged, altered, mis-edited, or interpolated; or because there are some "hidden teachings;" or because Aristotle himself gradually "developed" and "matured" in his thinking on politics.

There may well be merit to some of these claims. But pursuing them would lead us down a path which I am not prepared to take. A different approach is to ask: Can we engage the Politics in a fruitful way by taking the text as given, thereby avoiding the traps of exegetical expertise and modern prejudices? Let us begin such an inquiry by first considering Aristotle's approach to politics in general and then investigating some of the key issues in the text.

I. Politics as an Organic Growth

Despite using familiar terms to describe politics, Aristotle actually sees it in a rather different light. To begin with, since politics is the affairs of the city, to understand politics, one must first understand the city. At the beginning of Book I, Aristotle describes how the city comes into being. This description of the transition from the household to the village and then to the city actually bears a resemblance to Machiavelli's description of the emergence of political rule in his *Discourses on Livy*.[4] It should be noticed, however, that Aristotle characterizes this movement toward the city as a *growth*, and in so doing separates himself from Machiavelli and other modern thinkers. For Machiavelli describes a city as an alliance for safety and security, whereas Aristotle describes it as a growth toward an organic whole with its end in full self-sufficiency. From plowing the field and reproducing children to forming colonies and attending assemblies, the city comes into being as our activities expand and grow. Therefore, alongside the growth of our body, there is another

---

4   Niccolo Machiavelli, *Discourses on Livy*, translated by Harvey Mansfield & Nathan Tarcov, (University of Chicago Press, 1996), p. 11.

growth—the growth of our *activity*. Just as the growth of the body produces a physical whole, the growth of our activity produces an organic whole of its own—the city.

That our activity is not random and extraneous but rather forms an organic whole may sound odd to our modern ears. Yet it may seem less so if one reflects upon the following example: If someone walking down the street trips over a rock and falls, we would tend to call this an "accident" (since no one plans on tripping over things and there is no real reason or logic behind such random occurrences). But if one thinks about it more carefully, it becomes clear that this so-called "randomness" never occurs to a whole class of beings—worms. Therefore, this "tripping over" is something that belongs a particular type of being, namely those that raise their bodies above the ground, particularly those that walk on two legs. Hence, one may say that a particular being brings along with it particular types of "accidents" and at the same time eliminates others. In this sense, there are no "accidents"—each being's activities fully conform to its nature and form a whole.

To Aristotle, political activity seems to be of such a nature. It is not some random activity that we happen to do, but an organic growth in itself that conforms to our being: Just as the city is the end of human associations and forms a whole with the household and village, so too is politics the end of all types of rule and forms a whole with the types in the household and village. Therefore, contrary to the Hobbesian notion that politics causes human beings to be less complete (since through it we lose some of our rights), politics according to Aristotle is just the opposite: it is the very activity that completes us. Those who do not need a city cease to be human beings—they are either beasts or gods.[5]

In keeping with the city's similarity to organic growth, politics is an ordered activity, but it is not an order derived from logical deduction. Likewise, Aristotle's *investigation* of politics has a guiding principle, but it is not one long logical sequence with one single beginning. It may involve multiple beginnings and follow along multiple paths. These multiple beginnings and paths are meant to be grasped and understood as a whole, even though the presentation of this understanding has to be broken up and arranged on pages in a sequence. This inherent tension between the understanding of the whole and its presentation in parts may be at the root of much of

---

5   Aristotle, *Politics*, 1253a 27

the discontent over the organization of the book. But if one takes a step back and looks at the book as a whole, one might see that these "inconsistencies" are the result of Aristotle's unique way of thinking about politics. For, as mentioned earlier, the most natural beginning of politics is always the *living* human being already in real life—being in a household, being a son or a father, a wife or a mother—not a fragmented being reduced to his perceptive faculties and placed in an imaginary "state of nature." This is a beginning that is familiar to us both in experience and in opinion, and that is easily spoken about by many. But as Aristotle points out elsewhere, what is most familiar to us is not always what is most clear in itself. The former may serve us well as the beginning of investigation, but the latter is prior in its intelligibility.[6] While the city as a compound being is further away from us and is made of parts, it is at the same time the place where human beings become more intelligible because in it we fully realize ourselves. To investigate the city, Aristotle has to "uncompound" it. However, this "uncompounding" into its smaller parts is not the same as modern analysis, nor are the smaller parts analytical units. This can be seen in the claim that although the city is preceded by the household and village, it is in another sense actually *prior*. Each of these parts does not exist in isolation but already aims at the city. Otherwise, it would be like the stone hand, which has the looks of a real hand, but is in fact dead.[7]

Within this general approach to politics—that the city is a whole whose parts contain an image of that whole, the discussions of various specific topics follow a similar path. For example, the *Politics* ends more or less with a discussion of the best forms of government in Book VII. Yet this issue is already present at the very beginning as the forms of rule in the household. Our experiences in a household—and the different accounts of and opinions about these experiences—serve as the beginning of our thinking about the best form of political rule. But, because of the various forms of inequality in the household, its different types of rule are only images of the true forms in the city. If one stays only at the level of the household without moving toward the city (which is exactly what happens to the barbarian tribes), one cannot hope to understand the best forms of government. Hence, investigating the city, its origin, its components and its citizens will ultimately require a new start. Yet, this is not a separate investigation. The question of forms of government

---

6   For example, Aristotle, *Metaphysics*, 1029b 3-13; and *On the Soul*, 413ab 13

7   Aristotle, *Politics*, 1253a 22.

is embedded in each of the stages of a city's growth and is present throughout. The end of Book III raises the question about the best form of government: Book IV begins with a broad discussion of this question from the view of one single knowledge; Book VII makes a fresh start on the same question, but with an eye to how the best governments are related to the best life. Viewed separately, these appear disjointed because each looks like a new beginning along a different path. But if they are read together, they each contribute to the inquiry and are parts of a whole. It is this dialectical thinking that weaves together the parts and the whole, the more familiar and the more intelligible, the opinions and the philosophic inquiries. This back-and-forth between various parts may appear sloppy, confusing, and even disorienting; but it ultimately pushes us to read the *whole* investigation carefully before deciding upon what the best form of government is.

Before ending this section and turning to the book itself, a few words on another important aspect of Aristotle's thinking on politics are needed. In Books IV through VII, Aristotle mentions two types of best government: the "best simply" and the "best possible." This language is familiar and perhaps reminds us of the distinction made by Machiavelli between the "real" and the "imaginary" republics.[8] Yet it seems that Aristotle's "best simply" and "best possible" regimes are much more nuanced and complicated, especially in the case of the latter. In the general articulation, the "best possible" is a type of middle regime based on a "mixing." But this mixing can mean different things: In one sense it may be understood as the mixing of degrees of wealth; in another, of wealth and freedom; in yet another, of wealth and virtue. There is no formula because the "best possible" is not based on a rigid claim about the inherent flaw in our nature and its failure to measure up against some theoretical ideal. Rather, it is based on the fact that political associations are real *living* communities. As such, they are inevitably conditioned by their separate histories, traditions, customs, geographies, etc., all of which will tend to give rise to sets of unique professions and temperaments. These in turn will affect the political behaviors of their citizen bodies. This brings us to the important aspect of Aristotle's thinking on politics—practical judgment. Since the "best possible" is not based on a universal formula of human nature, one cannot really get it from book learning. It thus falls to those who have the experi-

---

8   Niccolo Machiavelli, *The Prince*, a new translation with introduction by Harvey C. Mansfield, (University of Chicago Press, 1985), 61.

ence and prudence to study it and inquire about it. A true politician, therefore, not only has to have the knowledge about the best form of government, but also the long and wide experiences that are necessary to make a sound judgment on how to make the right mixture (what to mix and how to mix them) for his own city. This is why Aristotle famously claims at the beginning of his *Ethics* that politics is not a suitable subject for the young.[9]

Now that we have looked at Aristotle's general approach to politics, let us turn to some of the key issues in the *Politics*.

II. "A human being by nature is an animal meant for the city"— *Politics* I, 2

It has been said that passages at the end the *Nicomachean Ethics* subordinate the *Politics* to the *Ethics*. Is this really true, or does the *Politics* stand on its own and have its intrinsic value separate from the *Ethics*?

A comparison of two passages is a good place to start. The first one is from the *Ethics*:

"And what is referred to as *self-sufficiency would be present most of all in the contemplative life*, for while the wise and the just person, and the rest, are in need of the things that are necessary for living, when they are sufficiently equipped with such things, a just person still needs people toward whom and with whom he will act justly, and similarly with the temperate and the courageous person and each of the others, but the wise person is able to contemplate even when he is by himself, and more so to the extent that he is the more wise. He will contemplate better, no doubt, when he has people to work with, but he is still the most self-sufficient person." (1177a 27, italics added)

Compare it to the following passage from the *Politics*,

"The complete association made of more than one village is a city, since at that point, so to speak, *it gets to the threshold of full self-sufficiency*, coming into being for the sake of living, but being for the sake of living well... For it is their end, and nature is an end; *for what each thing is when it has reached the completion of its coming into being is that which we say is the nature of each, as with a human being, a horse, a house*. And that for the sake of

9   Aristotle, *Nicomachean Ethics*, 1095a 3.

which, the end, is also the best, and self-sufficiency is both an end and what is best." (1152b 35, italics added)

There is something curious about there being two completions for man. Since a complete being cannot be further completed, how can both the contemplative life and the city be said to complete man? With the help of a passage in Aristotle's *Metaphysics*—namely, that the end of every being is work and activity[10]—we can further refine the question: what activity does contemplative life lack? Or, to put the question in a slightly different way, what is the activity which, though present in the contemplative life, cannot be fully explored in the *Ethics* and, therefore, must be articulated again in the *Politics*?

If we think through how the completion described in the *Politics* differs from that in the *Ethics*, we will gain a better understanding of the *Politics*. Since Aristotle never directly discusses exactly how the city completes us or what exactly the deficiency is that cannot be overcome by the other types of associations, one has to trace his argument back to Chapter 2 of Book I to see what it entails:

> "Now it is necessary that there first be a pairing together of those who do not have the power to be without each other, such as a female and a male for the sake of generation (and this not out of choice but just as in the other animals and plants, by a nature striving to leave behind another like itself), and something naturally ruling and ruled for preservation." (1252a 25-31)

Since as individuals we are incomplete in two ways—we cannot generate or preserve ourselves—then, by necessity, there are two types of pairings we require for completion: that of male and female for generation, and that of naturally ruling and ruled for preservation. Until the coming into being of the city, Aristotle doesn't introduce any other types of pairings. This may lead one to conclude that the city completes us because it contains these two types of pairings.

Of these two, it is clear that the first type is of only secondary importance; for although human beings choose particular mates, the male-female pairing itself is not the result of a deliberate choice and is therefore not special to being human, but is shared with other animals and even plants. This may also explain why, when referring to human generative pairings, Aristotle uses a word meaning "cou-

---

10   Aristotle, *Metaphysics*, 1050a 21

pling" (*sunduazesthai*) instead of one meaning marriage. Therefore, however it completes us, it does so for those parts of us that we share in common with animals and plants, and hence does not complete us *as humans*.

What is left then is the second type of pairing, the naturally ruling and ruled. Hence, let us for now proceed with the assumption that the activity whose lack renders us incomplete is that of the ruling and ruled. Indeed, the second half of the above quote leads us one step further in this direction,

> "For that which has the power to foresee by thinking is naturally ruling and naturally mastering, but what has the power to carry out those things with the body is ruled and is naturally slavish; hence the same thing is advantageous to a master and to a slave. *And by nature, the female and the slave are distinct.* (For nature does nothing stingily, the way the bronze-workers make the Delphic knife, but one thing for one job, since in that way, by serving not for many jobs but for one, each of the instruments accomplishes its working in the most beautiful manner)." (1252a 30-b 5, italics added)

A careful reading of this passage shows that what were originally presented as two types of pairings are not, strictly speaking, two *separate* kinds at all, for the comparison between the female and the slave implies that the second pairing actually underpins both kinds: at the root of the male-female pairing lies the pairing of ruling and being ruled. The female, who was initially presented as being for the sake of generation, is now shown to have a much different role; she is subject to a type of rule which differs fundamentally from that to which a slave is subject. On this view, one might say that there is only one type of pairing, that of the ruling and ruled, but it takes different forms because of the different types of work that each pairing accomplishes, generation for that of a male and female, and daily necessity for that of a master and slave.

Therefore, it is by the fulfillment of the need to rule and be ruled that the city completes us, and hence "a human being by nature is an animal meant for the city" because he/she has *by nature* the need to rule and be ruled.[11]

One may raise a question at this point: If it is the ruling and

---

11   One can clearly see the difference between this translation and those which render this sentence as "a human being by nature is a *social* animal."

being ruled that complete us, and if this is also present in other associations (such as the household) why cannot the full completion be achieved in the household? In other words, why must there be a city? One obvious difference between the rule in the city and those in the other associations is that only the former is a rule among equals, while the rest are rules among unequals. These latter include rules between the parent and the child and between the master and the slave, and they are based on natural distinctions between the ruling and the ruled. For, compared to the adult citizens, "the slave wholly lacks the deliberative capacity...and the child has it, but incomplete."[12] If it is the city which completes us, the rule among unequals which exists in the household and village must be of secondary importance. A little reflection on what Aristotle says in the following short sentence shows us why:

> "Why a human being is an animal meant for a city, more than every sort of bee and every sort of herd animal, is clear. For nature, as we claim, does nothing uselessly, and a human being, alone among the animals, has speech." (1253a11)[13]

Since we are not the only animals that are deemed political by Aristotle, and since nature does nothing uselessly, the passage seems to be saying that nature has also privileged certain members of these other "political" animals and endowed them with foresight. For example, a new queen bee seems to have the foresight of picking a suitable place for a new hive, whereas worker bees do not. Hence, when the time comes, she will lead and the workers will follow. Among these animals, therefore, the rule is fundamentally unequal and naturally so because in essence it is a kind of rule whose excellence is not based on an *excellence in work* but on a natural endowment and a natural distinction that cannot be overcome. Hence, when we look to the kinds of rule among human beings, the same reasoning can apply: any forms of rule that are based on natural distinctions—such as those between master and slave, and those between parents and offspring—are similar to that between the queen and the worker and should be deemed inferior. Aristotle makes this clear in another passage:

---

12   Aristotle, *Politics*, 1260a 15.

13   Aristotle has made similar claims about "political animals" in some of his other works, including the following from *History of Animals*:

> "Political creatures are such as have some common object in view; and this property is not common to all creatures that are gregarious. Such political creatures are man, the bee, the wasp, the ant, and the crane." (488a 8)

"The kind of rule is always better when those ruled are better, as when the one ruled is a human being rather than a beast, since the work is better that is carried out by those who are better, and wherever one rules and another is ruled there is something that is *their* work" (1254a 25, italics added)

Unequal rule therefore is an inferior rule because it is over inferior subjects, and it consequently produces inferior work. The rule in the city is better because it is a rule over better subjects, and with the rule over better subjects comes *better work*. It is particularly important to notice that the above passage starts with the better work only on the part of those ruled—a ruled human being can do better work than a domesticated animal—but it ends with the *implied* better work *on both parts*, the ruling and the ruled. Aristotle does not say directly in this passage what the better work of the ruler is, but one can get a very good idea by considering two other passages from Books I and III:

"And while the voice is a sign of pain and pleasure, and belongs also to the other animals on that account (since their nature goes this far, having a perception of pain and pleasure and communicating these to one another), speech is for disclosing what is advantageous and what is harmful, and so too what is just and what is unjust. For this is distinctive of human beings in relation to the other animals, to be alone in having a perception of good and bad, just and unjust, and the rest, and it is an association involving these things that makes a household and a city." (1253a 11)

"Hence in the case of political offices too, whenever they are organized on a basis of equality and similarity among the citizens, they expect to take turns ruling. In former times, in a way that was natural, they expected to take turns doing public service, while having someone look after their good in return, just as, when that person was ruling before, someone had looked after his advantage." (1279a 10)

If one looks at these two passages in relation to each other, it becomes clear that the second one is predicated on the first: namely, that a citizen can convince another citizen to take care of his own interests is based on the capacity for speech and the ability to persuade in making clear what is advantageous and just. Therefore, while the rule among unequals is based upon force or natural distinctions, the rule among equals (that is, rule in the city) is based upon persuasion. Therefore, whereas the former rule relies on inborn foresight or brute strength (natural and often insurmountable differences), the latter relies on reason and speech (our highest capacities). Since the better capacity yields the better work, rule among equals is better and more properly human. In this sense, Aristotle's take on the city is different from Plato's, who claims that a good man does not want to rule because the proper rule aims at the interest of the ruled. To Aristotle, the city is precisely the place where, through its political rule, both the ruler and the ruled can do their best work—something that is impossible within the confines of the household or village.

In addition, the rule in the city and rules in the household or village do not just differ in degree along a continuum, but in kind. That is, it is not that the rule in the household, without the city, can complete us partly, and the city, when it comes along, picks up from where the household leaves off and completes us fully. In fact, it is just the opposite:

> "For every household is under kingly rule by the eldest, and so their colonies are too, through their family connection. And this is what Homer is talking about when he says 'each one is a law unto children and wives...'" (1252b 23)

> "...one who is cityless as a result of nature rather than by choice is either insignificant or more powerful than a human being. He is like the person reviled by Homer as 'without fellowship, without law, without a hearth," for someone of that sort is at the same time naturally bent on war, since he is in fact like an unpaired piece on a checker-board...and one who is no part of a city, either from lacking the power to be in an association or from needing nothing on account of self-sufficiency, is for that reason either a beast or a god." (1253a 5-29)

Without the city, then, the rules in the household and village actually become destructive to human beings; for just like the relationship between the growth of the whole and that of the parts, where the latter is beneficial only in relation to the former (without respect to which it can be cancerous and harm the body) so too is the relationship between the rules in the household/village and that in the city. If the unequal rules in the household do not aim at the rule among equals in the city, the inferior work produced by them will turn human beings into Cyclopes with a natural bent toward war and cannibalism. Only in the city, then, are we completed *as humans*, because our fundamental need to rule and be ruled (though present in different forms in the other associations) gets *transformed* in the city, so that it is fulfilled in a way that is beneficial to us, rather than turning us into Cyclopean beasts.

At this point, a question may be raised about an issue that has not been explored thus far—the rule of husband over wife. For Aristotle does mention that this rule is political, which seems to mean that in essence it is a rule among equals. If this is *unqualifiedly* true, then, it would seem that one would not need the city, for all aspects of the need to rule and be ruled could be fulfilled in the household.

There is indeed a longstanding debate over what Aristotle truly thinks about this rule. The source of this difficulty comes partly from various claims by Aristotle that seem rather ambiguous,[14] but primarily from an example that Aristotle uses to describe the relationship between husband and wife in Book I, Chapter 12, which involves the story of the Egyptian King Amasis,[15]

> "Now in most instances of political rule there is an interchange among those who rule and are ruled, since they tend by nature to be on an equality and have no difference; nevertheless, whenever one rules and another is ruled, the former wants there to be a difference in formalities, words, and tokens of respect, as Amasis said in the story about the footpan. The male is always related to the female in this manner." (1259b 5)

Many have argued that this example shows that, to Aristotle, the difference between male and female is really a matter of convention, just like the difference between the footpan and the statue (for the underlying material is the same). If, however, one looks carefully into the Amasis story, this conclusion becomes questionable. The details of this story are in Book II, Section 172 of Herodotus' *History*:

> "Now at the first the Egyptians despised Amasis and held him in no great regard, because he had been a man of the people and was of no distinguished family; but afterwards Amasis won them over to himself by wisdom and not willfulness.

---

14   For example, Aristotle, *Nicomachean Ethics*, 1160b 33: "The relationship between husband and wife *appears* to be aristocratic in nature." (italics added)

15   There are a few other examples of this sort in the *Politics*. For instance, the quote from Sophocles' play *Ajax* at 1260a30.

Among innumerable other things of price which he had, there
was a foot-basin of gold in which both Amasis himself and all
his guests were wont always to wash their feet. This he broke
up, and of it he caused to be made the image of a god, and set
it up in the city, where it was most convenient; and the Egyptians went continually to visit the image and did great reverence to it. Then Amasis, having learnt that which was done by
the men of the city, called together the Egyptians and made
known to them the matter, saying that the image had been produced from the foot-basin, into which formerly the Egyptians
used to vomit and make water, and in which they washed their
feet, whereas now they did to it great reverence; and just so,
he continued, had he himself now fared, as the foot-basin; for
though formerly he was a man of the people, yet now he was
their king, and *he bade them accordingly honor him and have regard
for him*." (italics added)[16]

The story indeed conveys the connotation that there is no inherent difference between high birth and low birth, just as there is
no inherent difference between the gold made into a footpan and the
gold made into a statue. When Aristotle applies this story to the relations of male and female, the moral does appear to be that there is no
inherent difference between the members of either pair and that the
apparent difference is the product of convention.

Although this interpretation is reasonable, it relies on only one
of the two (if not more) possible readings of the story (the one which
locates the analogy between the husband and wife, and the footpan
and statue). If one really reflects upon it, however, it becomes clear
that the logic behind this interpretation risks rendering the story un-
intelligible by turning Amasis into a fool rather than the wise person
that Herodotus claims him to be – for if the respect paid to the statue
is essentially conventional (because, the argument goes, the statue is
made of the same material as that of the footpan), then would it not
be dangerous for Amasis to expose it? For, after all, how can he expect any respect from the Egyptians if it is publically acknowledged
that he is composed of the same "material" as they are?

An alternative (and perhaps more plausible) way of relating
the story to what Aristotle says is to compare the husband and wife
to the 'footpan-Amasis' and the 'statue-Amasis;' for although these

---

16 Herodotus, *History*, translated by David Grene, (University of Chicago Press,
    1987), p. 206.

two Amases are composed of the same "material," they have different desires. This reading, which takes into consideration the difference between human beings and inanimate objects, helps bring to
light two crucial points about the political world and the world of
inanimate objects. First, the inanimate gold is indifferent to whether
it is made into a footpan or a statue, but Amasis is not indifferent to
whether he is a commoner or king. Second, in the political world,
the statue-Amasis' desire for "tokens of respect" from the Egyptians
does not automatically fulfill itself. For while the Egyptians come
of their own will to pay respect to the statue, it is not clear at all
whether they would do the same for Amasis. It seems that Amasis
understands the situation rather well: He does not just sit there like
a statue and wait for the Egyptians to come; he *bade* them to honor
him.

It might be interesting to note that the bidding does not just occur at the end of the story. In fact, it is clear that the very unfolding of
Amasis' design—which Herodotus calls "wise"—consists of a series
of biddings: from having the footpan broken up, to having it made
into a status and then moved to a very public place. Without the
ability to bid and command, Amasis' wisdom and foresight would
not have come to fruition. In this sense, these biddings themselves
become the embodiment of Amasis' wisdom.

Viewed in this light, Aristotle's reference to the story takes on a
different meaning. Rather than hinting at a true equality between the
husband and wife, Aristotle may actually be implying that the true
foundation for equality in political rule is not "material." Just like
Amasis, all political rulers desire "tokens of respect," even though
they are composed of the same "material" as those ruled. Although
these tokens of respect may create apparent differences among
citizens, the situation is equalized in the city as citizens take turns
ruling and being ruled. In the household, however, the situation
is different; the female, for whatever reasons—be they physical or
otherwise—cannot command. Therefore, although the rule between
husband and wife is political, the equality that underlies this rule is
not *unqualified*, since the tokens of respect in this situation are not
reciprocated.[17] In the following two passages, we can come to further

---

17   A question might be raised as to whether to command itself belongs to the realm
      of the convention, since who can command and what to command appear to
      be conditioned by different histories, cultures and customs. Yet, this argument
      seems to assume that to Aristotle, there are such things in the political world
      that are not thus conditioned, and it is against these that commanding is called
      conventional.

understand Aristotle's distinction between male and female:

> "For this is distinctive of human beings in relation to the other animals, to be alone in having a perception of good and bad, just and unjust, and the rest, and it is an association involving these things that makes *a household and a city*." (1253a 11, italics added)

> "The slave wholly lacks the deliberative capacity, while the female has it, but without authority." [18]

The first passage is particularly important since it reveals that the household, just like the city, is not merely a place for necessities, but also a place where there exists the perception of good and bad and just and unjust. Through these two passages, Aristotle clearly indicates that the female has the deliberative capacity, and nature places her on the same footing with the male in terms of the perception of good and bad as well as just and unjust. Yet, the difference between the two is not just conventional, but real—though, again, not in the material sense. The "without authority" in the second quote immediately reminds us of the "bidding" in the Amasis story. Without the authority to command, certain types of work are not available to the female, and consequently, neither is the opportunity to rule and be ruled in turns.

Whatever one might think of Aristotle's view about women, it is worth mentioning that the lower (political) position of women does not necessarily lead to their diminished role in Aristotle's thinking. In Book I, Chapter 2 Aristotle says,

> "Among the barbarians, though, the female and the slave have the same rank. The reason is that they do not have that which by nature rules, but their association becomes that of a female slave and a male slave." (1252b5)

Taken by itself, this passage seems to show that the cause for the low status of women among the barbarians is that their men by nature cannot rule. However, it does not explain why if the men cannot rule, *both* men and women are in a slavish condition. If one reads this passage in conjunction with the aforementioned one about the rulers being better when the ruled are better,[19] the direction of the

---

18   Aristotle, *Politics*, 1260a 14.

19   Ibid, 1254a 25

causality of the social degradation is circular — it is just as possible to read Aristotle as saying that the barbarian men cannot rule because they have a naturally flawed way of treating their women. It is the degrading of their women that ultimately leads to the degrading of the barbarian men.

III. The Best Form of Government

If ruling and being ruled in the city completes us, then what role do different forms of government, especially the best ones, play? In Book VII, Aristotle gives two "definitions" of the best forms of government:

> "Now it is manifest that the best regime must be that arrangement in which anyone might act best and live blessedly." (1324a 23)

> "And since our proposed task is to get a look at the best form of government, and this is the one by which a city would be best governed, and the one governed best is that in which there is the greatest possibility for the city to be happy, it is clear that the question of what happiness is must not be passed over." (1332a 5)

Straightforward as these definitions may seem, they do not readily lead to a clear understanding of the issue. This is in large part due to various things that Aristotle says in Book III and IV about the best forms of government, where it is not clear how they are related to one another or to the notion of best rule discussed earlier.

At first glance, Aristotle's discussion of the best forms of government can be put into two categories, each of which has difficulties. The first category is what Aristotle calls the "best simply:" kingship and aristocracy in the true sense. Part of the reasoning is presented toward the end of Book III:

> "And since we claim there are three right forms of government, the best of these would necessarily be the one managed by the best people, and this is the sort of government in which one person, or a whole family or multitude, would turn out to be surpassing in virtue compared to all the rest together, the latter capable of being ruled while the former are capable of ruling with a view to the life most worthy of choice...it is clear that one would organize a city under an aristocracy or kingship in

the same manner and by the same means that a man becomes excellent." (1288a 33)

Since it is not possible for a large number of people to each have the best virtues (except those related to military excellence) it is natural that the "best simply" governments be aristocracy and kingship. In addition to the discussions of aristocracy in Book III, there are others in parts of Book IV. But despite this, it is unclear how seriously Aristotle takes these "best simply" forms of government. There are obviously some practical concerns: these "best simply" require a large amount of resources which many cities cannot afford.[20] And with regard to aristocracy in particular, Aristotle says:

"For it is only just to refer to the form of government made up of those who are the best people simply on the basis of virtue, and not by some particular assumption about good men, as aristocracy, for in it alone the same person is a good man and a good citizen." (1293b 5)

Of course, how plausible it is to have a city composed of all good people is the question—one which Aristotle appears to have rejected elsewhere.[21]

But Aristotle also seems to indicate that beyond these practical concerns may lie an even deeper reason for the impossibility of the "best simply" regimes. In Book II, Aristotle criticizes Plato's *Republic* for giving exclusive rule to the guardians and for having the citizens hold all property in common:

"For a city is by nature a certain kind of multiplicity; by becoming more of a one it would turn from a city into a household and from a household into a human being. For we would claim that a household is more of a one than a city is, and a single person than a household; *so even if someone were capable of doing this, it ought not to be done, since it would abolish the city. And a city is made up not only of a multiplicity of human beings, but also of human beings differing in form, for no city comes about from people all alike.* For a city and an alliance are different." (1261a 18, italics added)

Yet what Aristotle here criticizes is precisely what the "best simply," as discussed in the *Politics*, resemble. By excluding other

---

20   Aristotle, *Politics*, 1288b 42

21   Ibid, 1276b 38

citizens from ruling, these governments move the city toward unity, and turn it into something like a household in the sense that the rulers in these regimes are so far above the rest in virtue that they are like fathers to their children. It seems, then, that in these "best simply" governments, there is an inherent tendency to transform the city (and, thereby, itself) into what it is not.

In Book IV, Aristotle elaborates upon this point by comparing the city to a living animal;

> "For we are agreed that every city has not just one part but more than one. It is the same as, if we intended to get a grasp of the species of animals, we would first separate out the things it is necessary for every animal to have (such as certain sense organs, something suited to work on and absorb food, such as a mouth and digestive tract, and in addition to these, parts by means of which each of the kinds moves)." (1290b 25)

This comparison shows that the city is made of diverse parts that are different in kind, and these parts have to fit so that the "animal" can be a real living animal. But the "best simply" governments seem to violate this:

> "For it is surely not appropriate to kill or exile or ostracize such a person, or to claim he deserves to be ruled in his turn. *For while it is not the natural thing for the part to exceed to the whole, this is what has happened with someone who has such a great superiority.*" (1288a 25, italics added)

In this view, the "best simply" governments—by containing within themselves far superior parts (their rulers)—destroy the very proportionality that is necessary for the city (if it ought to resemble the living animal). There is something monstrous about undoing the very being from which one has sprung. Amongst human beings this is called patricide, one of the most heinous of crimes. Perhaps this is why Aristotle acknowledges in the above passage that the "best simply," when considered with a view to the best rule—the rule among equals—are "unnatural." If the best rule in the city is the one which completes us to the highest degree, it is difficult to see how this can be achieved through these "best simply" governments as these threaten to alter the nature of rule in the city to the point of its undoing.

The second category—the "best possible" governments for most cities and most people—also presents difficulties. Many have claimed that by the "best possible" Aristotle means a mixed regime with a large "middle class." This argument is based on passages from Book IV, especially the following two:

> "It is evident, though, that the middle form is best, since it alone is free of faction. For where the middle range is large, factions and schisms among the citizens occur least. And large cities are more free of faction for the same reason, because the middle part is large." (1296a 5-10)

> "And in a place where the number of those in the middle group exceeds either both extremes together, or even just one of the two, it is possible for there to be lasting constitutional rule. For there is no fear that the rich would ever conspire with the poor against them, since neither side would ever want to be subject to the other one, and if they were looking for a more communal arrangement, they would not find any other besides this one. They would not put up with ruling by turns because of their distrust of one another; but the most trusted person everywhere is a neutral arbiter, and the one in the middle is a neutral arbiter." (1296b 38-1297a 8)

From these passages and several others, it is quite obvious that Aristotle has an apparent preference for a city with a large "middle group." What this "middle group" means, though, is not entirely clear. For if the "middle group" is really the same as the middle class in the modern sense, and the middle regime is the best regime, then the most important thing that a city can do would be to develop its economy and form a large middle class—in other words, to become a modern liberal democracy. If this does not sound right, then the meaning of the "middle group" in Aristotle warrants a more careful examination.

In all relevant passages of Book IV, various forms of the word *mesos* (the word that for Aristotle denotes a "middle group") are used to describe the "middle," and indeed it does carry the meaning of a middle position between two extremes. However, the word can also mean "impartial," "moderate," and "undetermined." Whereas the first meaning is a middle in a spatial sense, the rest have the connotation of a middle in attitude and thinking. Likewise, Aristotle uses the same word to describe the "mean" condition between two extremes in moral virtues. Taking all this into account, it seems plausible that when Aristotle uses *mesos* to describe the middle he intends something more complex than simply a "middle class" in the sense of property possessions.

Let's look at Aristotle's description of the "middle" regime. By definition, the "middle" regime, or constitutional rule, is "a mixture of oligarchy and democracy."[22] In Book IV, Chapter 8, Aristotle adds,

> "For since there are three things disputing over equality in the government—freedom, wealth, and virtue...it is clear that the mixture of the pair consisting of the well-off and the needy ought to be called constitutional rule, while the mixture of the three, compared to the others, most deserves the name aristocracy, aside from its true and primary form." (1294a 20)

One can see two things from this. First, the middle form of government is based not on a homogeneous middle but on a "mixture," the coming together of two. Second, whereas this coming together at first appears to consist of two groups, the wealthy and the needy, when we recall Aristotle's emphatic condemnation of the redistribution of wealth in Book III, it seems that the coming together of the wealthy and the needy cannot be a mixture of property possessions simply. In fact, we have seen Aristotle making it clear that the relevant mixture is not of property, but of *principles*—namely, wealth and freedom. Just how wealth and freedom—which seem to differ in kind—can be mixed is a rather perplexing question.

At first, Aristotle seems to indicate that it can be accomplished by mixing offices in the same way as one might fit together the pieces of a broken coin.

> "For in oligarchies, they assess a fine against the well-off for not doing jury services and do not assign a fee for the needy, while in democracies, they assign a fee for the needy and no fine for the well-off. To have them both is a common ground and mean between these forms, and hence is suited to constitutional rule, since it is a mixture of both." (1294a 38)

However, in Book IV, Chapter 9, Aristotle offers a short but intriguing new way of thinking about mixing. Having just discussed how to mix offices from one regime with those from the other, he says,

> "This, then, is the manner of mixing them, and what marks

22   Aristotle, *Politics*, 1293b 35.

out democracy and oligarchy as having been well mixed is that it is possible to speak of the same form of government as democracy or oligarchy, since it is clear that it is because they are beautifully mixed that people who speak that way are led to do so. The mean also has this character, since each of the extremes is evident in it, which is exactly what happens in the Spartan form of government. For many people try to speak of it as being a democracy, since its arrangement includes a number of democratic features. *First of all, for example, in regard to the bringing up of children, those of the rich are brought up like those of the poor, and the manner in which they are educated is one for which the children of the poor also have the means. And likewise in the next stage of life, and once they become men, the same is true, since there is no way in which a rich person is distinguished from a poor one; what pertains to food is the same for everyone at the common meals, and the clothing rich people wear is of such a sort as any poor person whatever is capable of providing.* What is more, of the two highest offices, the populace chooses the one and takes part in the other (since they choose the elders and participate in the ephorate). But others call it an oligarchy because it includes a number of oligarchic features; for instance all ruling offices are elected and none chosen by lot, and a small number have authority over penalties of death and exile, and there are many other such things." (1294b 15-35, italics added)

This passage is worth quoting at length since, in the italicized portion especially, it is clear that the mixing Aristotle is interested in is less of offices and properties than of actions; namely, it is about how two extreme groups, the rich and the poor, can come together by *acting* toward a middle in their *everyday life*—from raising and educating their children, to taking their daily meals. And not only does it extend horizontally to cover nearly all aspects of daily living, it also extends vertically to cover one's entire lifespan. It is rather telling that although there is no mention of a middle with respect to property in Sparta, Aristotle still considers this a "beautifully mixed" *middle* regime. This must mean that Aristotle thinks that a middle regime can be composed of a middle not of property possessions, but of actions - through two "extremes" (i.e., the poor and the rich) *acting* toward the middle. From this perspective, then, the middle regime would not result from *having* similar properties and offices (a "middle possession") but from similar actions (a "middle doing").

A middle in this sense is consistent with a reference Aristotle makes to the *Ethics* in his discussion of the middle regime:

> "For if it was beautifully said in the *Ethics* that the happy life is one in accord with unimpeded virtue, and that virtue is a mean, then the mean in life, consisting of a mean condition every person is capable of attaining, would necessarily be best, and these same terms would necessarily also apply to the virtue and vice of a city and a government, since a form of government is one sort of life of a city." (1295a 37)

The mean condition of virtue is not a middle point on a line between its two extremities, since human action is not a static line upon which one can stand. The virtue courage, for example, is not in its true sense a fixed point between two extremes (cowardice and recklessness),because what ought to be feared is not always the same: charging the enemy could be deemed courageous in one situation but reckless in another just as retreating could be deemed cowardly in one situation but courageous in another.[23] Therefore, simply reading books and "possessing" a definition of courage are of no help at all. Real courage involves a right knowing of what to fear and when to fear, and this can only be achieved through repeated actions concerning fearful things while aiming at becoming courageous. Hence, Aristotle says that in one sense—and the truest sense—courage is what a truly courageous man does.

The discussion of the middle regime likewise emphasizes doing and acting. Even when there is no "middle possession" of property present in a city, the middle regime can still be formed through long and repeated actions by the two extreme groups, as illustrated by the example of Sparta. And this acting toward the middle, since it involves two extreme groups, will inevitably involve a constant deliberation and making of choices on the part of these groups, affecting the thinking and attitude of each. Hence, the activity itself, by constantly aiming at the middle, becomes the middle regime.

In this sense, the "middle possession" of property becomes incidental in the same way that numbers are incidental in relation to the more fundamental principles like wealth. In his discussion of oligarchy in Book III, Chapter 8, Aristotle defines oligarchy in terms of wealth, not the number of rulers. The characteristically smaller number of rulers is incidental to, or an external sign of, the principle because it just so happens that wealth is usually concentrated in the

---

23   It is rather telling that the ultimate example of courage in Plato's works is the brave retreat described by Alcibiades in the *Symposium*.

hands of the few. Similarly, acting toward the middle can be thought of as the essential principle of the middle regime, while a "middle possession" of properties is incidental to it (as a small number of rulers is to wealth in an oligarchy). If we indeed accept this middle action as the essential characteristic of the middle regime, then it is by this—and not its incidental quality of a middle property possession—by which we ought to understand such a regime.

The middle activity also serves as a link between the best rule and the best form of government. In Book IV, chapter 11, Aristotle says,

> "Also, those in the middle range are least likely to avoid ruling or be eager to rule, and both these things are harmful to cities. And in addition to these things, those who have an overabundance of the goods of fortune—strength, wealth, friends, and other things of that sort—do not want to be ruled and do not even know how to....But those who suffer from an extreme state of neediness in these things are too broken in spirit. Consequently, the latter sort of people do not know how to rule, but only how to be ruled under a slavish rule, while the former sort do not know how to be ruled in any way at all, but only to rule the way slavemasters rule." (1295b 12-22)

As one can see, the obstacle to the best kind of rule (citizens taking turns ruling and being ruled) is the habitual—often hostile—attitude of the different groups toward one another: envy, arrogance, pettiness, and slavishness. Aristotle's depiction of the Spartan form of government shows how the middle activity provides remedies for these animosities: Though lacking a "middle possession," the rich and poor in Sparta come together in the activity of sharing food, clothing, education and child-rearing, *all while the poor remain poor and the rich remain rich*. Since the middle activity is the result of active and deliberate choice by two non-middle groups rather than something simply *allotted* to the members of a materially homogenous bloc or to a small number of office holders, it imparts a greater effect upon the souls of its participants, and hence, more effectively alleviates the overbearing attitude of the rich and the broken spirit of the poor, and thereby eliminates factions that can be so harmful to the city. It is in this sense that the full meaning of *mesos* becomes clearer: It is not merely (or perhaps not even) characterized by a large middle class, but, more essentially, by its moderation, impartiality and "undetermined" appearance—one cannot tell whether the city is under an oligarchy or a democracy because, although there are rich and poor people, it is hard to tell who's who since in their everyday life, all *act* toward the middle.

Hence, one perhaps should not be surprised by Aristotle's seemingly odd claim that the "best possible" government actually has not often existed.[24] For just as the mean condition which constitutes virtue is attainable by every person[25] though rarely achieved, so too is it with every city and the middle regime.

IV. The *Politics* and Its Relations to the *Ethics* and the *Rhetoric*

Where the *Politics* stands in relation to the other works of Aristotle is always an interesting question. For the purpose of this introduction, though, the discussion will be limited to how the *Politics* is related to its two closest cousins, the *Ethics* and the *Rhetoric* (as all three deal with human affairs).

Let's begin by considering the relation of the *Politics* to the *Ethics*, which Aristotle explicitly addresses toward the end of the *Ethics*. The discussion seems to have two parts: First, since virtue does not come from nature, and habituation is unpleasant to the young, politics—especially lawmaking—prepares people for virtue by giving force and strength to good habituation, just as the soil has to be worked on first if it is to foster the seed.[26] Second, since one needs not only knowledge but also experience to become virtuous, politics provides the "practical life" in which experiences can be gained and virtues fostered and exercised.[27] Both of these aspects seem to subordinate the *Politics* to the *Ethics*: the first makes it preparatory for virtue, the second useful for it.

A parallel can be drawn to the way Aristotle talks about the relation of the *Politics* to the *Rhetoric*. Consider the following two passages in Chapter 8 of Book I of the *Rhetoric*:

> "The greatest and the most decisive of all things that contributes to being able to be persuasive and to do a beautiful job at giving advice is to have a grasp of all forms of government." (1365b 20)

---

24   Aristotle, *Politics*, 1293a 39

25   Ibid, 1295a 39

26   Aristotle, *Nicomachean Ethics*, 1179b 25

27   ibid, 1179b 1-5

"So the future or present things we need to strive for in making exhortations, and the things among which we need to find persuasive arguments having to do with what is advantageous, and also the means and manner for us to be equipped to deal with the kinds of character and customary practices in the various forms of government, to an extent commensurate with the present occasion, have been stated; these things are investigated with precision in the *Politics*." (1366a 18)

In the first passage, Aristotle states that the understanding of various forms of government is the greatest and most decisive contributor to being able to make persuasive arguments. In the second, he says that the study of various forms of government (along with other things) are investigated "with precision" in the *Politics*. Therefore, just as the *Ethics* treats issues related to virtue with more precision than the less theoretical *Politics* (which describes a political life through which virtues can be fostered and exercised), so too does the *Politics* treat the political life with more precision than the *Rhetoric* (which describes practical activities in the political life such as making persuasive arguments). This resembles a proportion in which degree of 'practicality' defines the equal relationships: as the *Ethics* is to the *Politics*, so is the *Politics* to the *Rhetoric*. Ordered from most to least practical, then, it appears the *Politics* stands in the middle, with *Ethics* on the one side and the *Rhetoric* on the other.

But if one looks to other places in these books, their relations seem less orderly, more complicated and yet, in a way, more reciprocal. Whether the *Politics* is still in the middle among these complex relations is worth exploring. Let's first revisit the *Politics'* relation to the *Ethics* and then its relation to the *Rhetoric*. At the beginning of the *Politics*, Aristotle states that since the city aims at the most sovereign goods, it is therefore the most sovereign of all associations and encompasses all others. In Book VIII, Chapter 9 of the *Ethics*, he expands on this idea:

"But all communities are like parts of the political community, for people come together for some advantage, and to provide for something that contributes to life, and the political community seems to gather together from the beginning, and to remain together, for the sake of what is advantageous...So the other communities aim at what is advantageous in a partial way; for example, sailors aim at what results from a voyage for making money, or something of that sort, and fellow soldiers aim at what results from warfare, grasping at money or victory or a city...But all of these appear to be under the political community, since the political community aims not at a present advantage but one that extends to all of life." (1160a 9-25)

These passages seem to place the relationship between the *Ethics* and the *Politics* in a different light. For the city now is the entity that encompasses not only all communities, but also what is advantageous for all of life. In a passage quoted earlier, Aristotle goes even further in linking politics to the soul.

"And this leads straight to a consideration of the soul, for there is in it by nature something ruling and something ruled, of which we claim there are different virtues, as of the part having reason and the irrational part. It is evident, then, that things are the same in the other cases as well, so that most things are ruling or ruled by nature. For it is in different ways that the free rules the slave, the male the female, and the man the child, and while the parts of the soul are present in them all, they are present in differing ways. For the slave wholly lacks the deliberative capacity, while the female has it, but without authority, and the child has it, but incomplete." (1260a 5-15)

Compared to similar passages regarding the soul in the *Ethics*, this is a much more forceful description in the sense that it makes politics the pattern of the human soul. According to this passage, politics is not an external activity that we do "out there," but an internal activity among parts of the soul. This relationship of the soul is exhibited externally by various types of rule—one can therefore tell the condition of a man's soul by looking at the type of rule in which he is engaged. Politics, then, is the soul writ large and is the most fundamental work of a human being. A human being is a political animal who needs to rule and be ruled because the human soul is of such a nature. And this need becomes more complex as one matures. One will need to know whom to rule and by whom to be ruled, as well as at which time and in what manner each of these is fitting. As this ruling-ruled relationship becomes more complex, virtue also becomes more complex. What was simply "courage" now branches out into different types of courage. The mean in moral virtues, which changes according to different circumstances, must also be affected by ruling and ruled relations. What is truly at work is not *courage*, but the courage that belongs to one who is ruling, or one who is ruled, to a man or a woman.[28] Therefore, "those who speak in general terms are fooling themselves, saying that virtue is the good condition of the soul, or acting rightly, or anything of that sort."[29] For the general terms do not make clear what the *appropriate* work is for each human being, and politics is that which gives the moral virtues their *appropriateness*. Therefore, politics is the underpinning activity through which moral virtues become real and achievable. For moral virtues imply the proper ordering of the soul, which in turn implies the proper ruling-ruled relationship among different parts of the soul. If we return to the metaphor of the soil preparing for the seed, we can now see that the soil is not merely a physical platform upon which the seed grows; it also "nurtures" the seed, as Aristotle says. The same can be said about politics—it "nurtures" ethics. It is the living force that allows and assists the seed to grow and flourish. In this way, the relationship between the *Ethics* and the *Politics* is perhaps similar to that of the household and city—for in one way the household is prior, but in another city is prior. Similarly, in one sense the *Ethics* is prior, but in another it must presuppose the *Politics*.

We now turn to the second two terms in the aforementioned proportion, the *Politics* and the *Rhetoric*, with a special attention to one type of rhetoric—the advisory rhetoric. It has been said that Aristotle's *Rhetoric* is a refutation of Socrates' view of rhetoric as expressed in *Gorgias* and *Phaedrus*.[30] Whether this is true or not—and if it is true, to what extent they disagree—remains a question. However, the following passages from the *Rhetoric* seem to show that Aristotle differs from Socrates in at least some respects:

> "To the extent one tries to make either dialectic or this art [rhetoric] into a kind of knowledge rather than a power, he will unwittingly obliterate their nature by the transformation, remaking them into knowledge of some underlying subject matter rather than of arguments only." (1359b 15)

> "Even though the same proceeding applies to speaking to public assemblies and to lawcourt, the business of the public assembly is of greater beauty and greater civic importance than that involved in private transactions (1354b 25)

---

28   This is discussed in detail in Book I, Chapter 13 of the *Politics*.

29   Aristotle, *Politics*, 1260a 25

30   One articulation of such a view is at the end of *Phaedrus*, 271D-E.

In the first passage, Aristotle appears to contradict Socrates' claim that true rhetoric should be grounded in knowledge;[31] in the second, he seems to disagree that true rhetoric can only be practiced in private settings, claiming instead that public rhetoric has a greater beauty and a rightful place. Together these form a general view of rhetoric: namely, that it is not knowledge but a power of seeing what is persuasive broadly (that is, in any subject matter). If it were made a proper knowledge, it would cease to be rhetoric in the strict sense of the word, since it would no longer be characteristically broad in scope, but restricted to a particular subject matter. Rhetoric, then, has a very special place among arts: despite being an art, it is not grounded in knowledge and is not restricted to one particular type of expertise; rather, it remains open to a wide range of issues in the realm of human action. Within this general sphere, advisory rhetoric is particularly important because its beauty lies precisely in the public arena.

One may wonder what ground there is for Aristotle to make such claims. Since the current inquiry is about the relationship between the *Politics* and the *Rhetoric*, we will approach the question from this perspective, considering here a passage from each:

> "For nature, as we claim, does nothing uselessly, and a human being, alone among animals, has speech. And while the voice is a sign of pain and pleasure, and belongs also to the other animals on that account...speech is for disclosing what is advantageous and what is harmful, and so too what is just and what is unjust."(1253a 9)

> "The end is different for each of these... For the advisory speaker, it is what is advantageous or harmful, since someone who exhorts is advising something as best, and someone who warns is warning against something as worse; other things, that it is just or unjust, beautiful or shameful, they take as side-issues to that." (1358b25)

In the passage from the *Politics*, Aristotle claims that human beings *alone* are endowed with the power of speech for the purpose of disclosing what is advantageous and harmful, and we see in the passage from the *Rhetoric* that this is exactly what is said regarding the end of advisory rhetoric. Clearly then, rhetoric—especially advisory rhetoric—is a *uniquely human* activity and has its source in

---

31   Plato, *Phaedrus*, 271D

nature. From the *Politics'* point of view, advisory rhetoric is a better cause in the realm of human action because it moves human beings to act by employing reason and persuasion rather than something extraneous like force or coercion. In a public speech, this use of reason and the power of speech is an expression of the foresight to see what means of persuasion are available for any given issue[32] and the ability to present alternatives and articulate the advantages and disadvantages of each.[33] This ability to present alternatives is in turn related to another uniquely human quality—the sense of time.[34] Advisory rhetoric is specifically linked to the future, for, when it comes to this type of persuasion, it is meaningless to present alternatives and opposites that were in the past or are in the present because only alternatives in the future can be acted upon and therefore deliberated and advised about. This inherent connection to our sense of time further illuminates why rhetoric occupies a rightful place in human arts, since it involves a kind of foresight and seeing of which no other animals are capable.

Ultimately, however, the legitimacy of advisory rhetoric and rhetoric in general has its justification in one extraordinary ability that underlies all the others mentioned above—our ability to reason to opposite conclusions. This ability is so unusual that it goes beyond not only animal instinct but also most of the human arts. According to Aristotle dialectic is the only other art with this ability,[35] which is the reason why rhetoric is said to be analogous to it.

Yet, as discussed earlier, certain types of human associations— the private domains of household and village—do not encourage this extraordinary human activity. This is because the forms of rule in the household and village are for the most part based on inequalities and natural distinctions, and these tend to transform these private interactions into either instructions (between parents and children), or coercion (between masters and slaves). Even the rule between husband and wife is not favorable to the exercise of rhetoric because of the lack of authority on the part of women. For rhetoric to be fully exercised, there has to be a place where individuals can be taken out of their narrow and private domain and placed with others who are like them. It is here that the crucial role of politics becomes

---

32   Aristotle, *Rhetoric*, 1355b 10

33   Ibid, 1357a 8

34   Ibid, 1358b 15

35   Aristotle, *Rhetoric*, 1355a 35

apparent: It is only in the city that people meet one another as equals (as citizens). Furthermore, of the two primary public institutions where rhetoric is commonly exercised – the public assembly and the court – the former surpasses the latter because it is there that the citizens' interests and the common public interests intersect.[36] In a properly functioning public assembly, all members are equal, physical strength plays no role, both the future of the city and the private interests at hand are discussed, and decisions will affect both others and oneself. To move other members on any given issue, one has to be able to present what he sees as the alternatives and opposites, the reasons and justifications that lead to each, and how they are related to the common interest as well as to one's own. It is only in the city, therefore, that rhetoric as a uniquely human activity can be fully at work. It is then reasonable to say that if nature does nothing in vain and she endows human beings with the power of speech to disclose advantage and harm, and if an important part of rhetoric (advisory rhetoric) is aimed at such disclosures, then the city is the place where nature's work comes to full fruition. Without the city, nature would have done something in vain.

It is worth noticing that among different forms of government, public assembly plays the most important role in the "best possible" government (constitutional rule), since in it citizens take turns ruling the city, making decisions by coming together for discussion and debate. It is interesting to note that rhetoric, the counterpart to dialectic, finds the best place for its practice in the "best possible" form of government. If the contemplation described in the *Ethics* is primarily a private activity, and rhetoric a kind of beholding,[37] then rhetoric is perhaps an imitation of contemplation in the public arena. If this is true, then the city in general—and the constitutional rule in particular—provides the ground where private contemplation and its public counterpart meet. The *Politics*, then, would indeed be the middle term of the *Ethics* and *Rhetoric*, for through it the two types of contemplation—theoretical and rhetorical, private and public—connect.

V. About This Translation

Joe Sachs is well-respected for his studies and translations of

---

36 Ibid, 1354b 30

37 The word is *theôrêsai*. For a detailed explanation of this word, see Joe Sachs, *Plato Gorgias and Aristotle Rhetoric* (Focus Publishing, R. Pullins Company, 2009), p. 137, footnote 11.

Aristotle. He taught for thirty years at St. John's College before his retirement in 2005. He has translated all the major works of Aristotle, including the *Physics* (1995), the *Metaphysics* (1999), *On the Soul* (2001), the *Nicomachean Ethics* (2002), the *Poetics* (2006), and the *Rhetoric* (2009). In addition, he translated Plato's *Theaetetus* (2004), *Republic* (2007), and *Gorgias* (2009). I have seen in my own classroom how much students have been helped by the Sachs translations. I'm frequently approached by students and asked why there isn't a Sachs translation for Aristotle's *Politics*. This translation will undoubtedly be welcome news to many students and scholars of Aristotle.

Many have lauded Mr. Sachs' other translations for their use of simple and lucid language, which frees the texts from the long Latin tradition. In so doing, they bring the reading experience as close to the original as possible. The same can also be said about this translation. However, to this general sentiment I would like to add two things. First, as Mr. Sachs points out elsewhere, the Latin influence is less serious in the less theoretical works of Aristotle, such as the *Ethics*. A quick reading affirms that this is also the case with the *Politics*: it too contains less jargon. In fact, my own experience with the *Politics* leads me to believe that the crucial consideration in translating the *Politics* is actually the opposite of the usual difficulty with translating Aristotle: as pointed out earlier in this introduction, if our understanding of Aristotle's more theoretical works is impeded because the language in those works is too *alien* to us, then that of his *Politics* is so because the language is sometimes too *familiar* to us. A primary example is the famous statement by Aristotle in Book I: *kai hoti ho anthropos phusei politikon zoon*. The standard translation of this sentence is the well-known "and a human being by nature is a political animal." Although there is no jargon in this translation, it has a modern sound which is all too familiar and smooth. This familiarity tends to produce a false confidence that the meaning of the sentence is self-evident, and that no further inquiries and reflections are necessary. This can be seen from that fact that some translators even go as far as to render this sentence as "and man by nature is a *social* animal." The effect of this and similar translations is to facilitate a premature conclusion about Aristotle's view of human nature that is very difficult to shake. In contrast, the current translation renders the sentence as "and a human being by nature is an animal meant for the city." This translation is faithful to the original, but it loses the smoothness. It gives the reader pause, which opens up opportunities for further reflection, for if one is to understand this sentence, he/she must first look into what a "city" is, and this can lead in all kinds of fruitful directions.

Second, although many scholars have already commented on the value of notes and glossaries in the Sachs translations in general, I still would like to say a few words about the notes in this particular translation. One of the difficulties in reading Aristotle is that many of his key ideas are present in all of his works, but not all of them are fully articulated or referenced each time they appear in different places. It is as if Aristotle assumes that the reader is familiar with all of his writings. Hence, the reader is often left to figure out how to make the right connections on his own. It is in these places that I find Mr. Sachs' notes to be much more than just explanations or cross-references. They often help a passage whose meaning may appear clear at first acquire an even deeper significance. In this sense, Mr. Sachs' notes themselves merit their own separate standing as scholarly commentaries. A good example is the note to the following passage from Book I:

> "So similarly for those that have come into being, it is clear that it is appropriate to assume that plants are for the sake of animals and the other animals for the sake of human beings, the tame ones both for use and for food, and if not all the wild ones, at least most, for the sake of food and other assistance, so that clothes and other kinds of gear might come from them." (1256b 18)

The text as it is may seem uncontroversial: no beings in nature have ends in themselves; they all exist for the sake of others. However, if one reads Mr. Sachs' footnote to this passage, its meaning becomes more interesting:

> "It is a central claim of Aristotle's theoretical works that living things are for their own sake. He invented the word *entelecheia* as a fusion of the notions of completeness and activity, or being-at-an-end and being-at-work. That word is the heart of the definition of the source of life in *On the Soul* (412b 4-6), of the discovery of the primary instances of being in the world of experience in the *Metaphysics* (1028b 9-10, 1050b 2-3, 1050a 21-23), and of the intelligibility of motion in the *Physics* (201a 9-11). The question whether living beings also have ends external to themselves is raised in *On the Soul* in relation to their offspring (415a 26-b3), and in the *Metaphysics* in relation to the organization of the cosmos as a whole (1072b 1-4). The positive statement here that living things exist for our sake follows the beaten path of popular opinion of which Aristotle reminds us

at the beginning of this chapter. In the *Physics* (194a 34-35), he says instead: 'we treat everything there is *as though* it is for our sake.'" (italics added)

With this footnote, Mr. Sachs not only provides a fuller explanation of the sentence, but also gives it a much broader context. The second reference to the *Physics* is particularly important as it suggests a reading that contradicts the most immediately apparent meaning. This passage appears at an important moment in Aristotle's discussion of property and its acquisition, because slaves turn out to be a kind of property. If one goes with the first reading of the text, then Aristotle seems to suggest that, as with some animals that exist for the sake of other animals and human beings, some human beings also exist for the sake of other human beings. If one instead goes with the second reading suggested by the *Physics*, then, it is quite plausible to conclude that some human beings *may appear as though* they are for sake of others, but in fact they are not. One can readily see how the broader context furnished by Mr. Sachs' note adds layers of complexity that greatly enrich our understanding of Aristotle's thinking on this issue.

This translation abounds with clarifying and enriching renditions and notes like the ones just mentioned. However, I would like to close by quoting what Mr. Sachs says about the beautiful in the preface to his translation of the *Ethics*. The beautiful, says Mr. Sachs, "is not an object of contemplation simply, but the source of action." I believe that this insight can be equally applied to the *Politics*. Long Latin influence and textually inattentive reading have pushed Aristotle deeply into the purview of a few scholars and specialists while excluding "amateurs." By employing plain and thoughtful language, this translation closes the distance between the reader and the book, and in so doing, reminds us that Aristotle's *Politics* is not political science in our understanding of the term. While it is a theoretical reflection on the affairs of the city, it is equally a book on *praxis*: Politics is a kind of being-at-work that is part of the overall human thinking and doing.

Acknowledgements

I owe much gratitude to Joe Sachs for both offering me the opportunity to write this introduction and for all the thought and care that he has given to it. It is through his translations that Aristotle first became a living thinker to me. I consider myself fortunate for having taught with him in the same classroom. His profound knowledge and insight have deepened my interest in Aristotle and enriched my understanding of him. All the conversations I have had with him over the years prove to be not only a source of enlightenment, but also of pleasure.

My thanks also go to Timothy J. Reilly who has given meticulous care in reading through this introduction. His many stylistic as well as substantive comments have brought great improvement to this introduction.

Lijun Gu
Annapolis, MD

Book I

Chapter 1

Since we see that every city is some kind of association, and every association is organized for the sake of some good (since everything everyone does is for the sake of something seeming to be good), it is clear that all associations aim at something good, and that the one that is most sovereign and encompasses all the others aims at the most sovereign of all goods. And this is the one called the city, the political association.[38]

Now those who assume that the same person is skilled at political rule as at kingship, household management, and mastery of slaves do not speak beautifully.[39] (For they regard each of these as differentiated with respect to manyness or fewness but not in form—a master being over few, a household manager over more, and a political ruler or a king over still more, as if a large household were no different from a small city; as for the political ruler and the king, when one has control himself, they regard him as a king, but as a political ruler when he rules and is ruled by turns in accordance with the propositions of this sort of knowledge. These things, though, are not true.) What is being said will be clear

---

38   "Political" (*politikon*) means "of or pertaining to a city (*polis*)." The latter word refers not to a place but to people (see Herodotus, *History*, Bk. VIII, Ch. 61), and it does not carry any of the connotations of our word "urban" (see Thucydides, *Peloponnesian War*, Bk. I, Ch. 10). The word *politikon* is translated literally at 1253a 2-3 and 7-8, and 1278b 19 below, where Aristotle states the fundamental principle of his study of political association, but elsewhere its English derivatives are used.

39   This is the assumption made by the Eleatic Stranger at the beginning of Plato's *Statesman* (258E-259C).

to those who investigate it along the usual path,[40] for just as
it is necessary in other cases to divide a compound thing up
20   into uncompounded ones (since these are the smallest parts
of the whole), so too with a city, it is by examining what it
is composed of that we shall also see more about these rulers, both in what respect they differ from one another and
whether it is possible to get hold of anything involving art[41]
applicable to each of the things mentioned.

Chapter 2

So if one could observe the things from the beginning
as they grow, then just as in other cases, so too in these, one
could study them most beautifully by that means. Now it is
necessary that there first be a pairing together of those who
do not have the power to be without each other, such as a
female and a male for the sake of generation (and this not
out of choice but just as in the other animals and plants, by
30   a natural striving to leave behind another like itself), and
something naturally ruling and ruled for preservation. For
that which has the power to foresee by thinking is naturally
ruling and naturally mastering, but what has the power to

---

40   This phrase (*hê huphêgêmenê methodos*) is virtually always translated as
"*our* usual method" or words to that effect, but in fact it means "the
beaten path" of popular or received opinion. There is a clear example
of this meaning at 643b 11 of the *Parts of Animals*, where Aristotle uses
the same verb to say it is better to follow the lead of the common distinctions among groups of animals used by ordinary people than to
try to make a neatly logical classification on one's own. According to
the first chapter of the *Physics*, the smallest parts of the whole are the
things any philosophic inquiry is seeking, and are not available to us
as starting points. Here, the uncompounded parts would be human
beings who have not grown up in political associations. Imagining a
pre-political human condition was commonly indulged in by poets
(Aeschylus, *Prometheus Bound* 441-470; Sophocles, *Antigone* 354-364)
and sophists (Protagoras in Plato's *Protagoras*, 322A-D), and was adopted by Socrates in Plato's *Republic* (369B-371E) to see what justice is
by watching a city come into being in speech.

41   The word art (*technê*) refers to a broad range of practical skills, from
horse riding to shoemaking to mathematical calculation, all understood as rooted in some form of theoretical knowledge that guides the
reliable—artful—production of some artifact or result.

carry out those things[42] with the body is ruled and is naturally slavish; hence the same thing is advantageous to a master and to a slave. And by nature, the female and the slave   **1252B**
are distinct. (For nature does nothing stintingly, the way the
bronze-workers make the Delphic knife,[43] but one thing for
one job, since in that way, by serving not for many jobs but
for one, each of the instruments accomplishes its work in
the most beautiful manner.) Among the barbarians, though,
the female and the slave have the same rank. The reason is
that they do not have that which by nature rules, but their
association becomes that of a female slave and a male slave.
That is why the poets say "it is reasonable for Greeks to rule
barbarians," [44] on the grounds that a barbarian and a slave
are by nature the same thing.

A household of the primary sort is made of these two   10
kinds of association, and Hesiod spoke rightly in composing
the verse[45] "first and foremost a house, a wife, and an ox for
plowing," since for poor people an ox takes the place of a
servant. So the kind of association organized in accord with
nature for everyday life is a household, the people whom
Charondas refers to as fed on the same bread, and Epi-
menides of Crete as fed on the same crops. The first kind of
association composed of more than one household, to serve
purposes not of a daily sort, is a village. And the village
seems to be most of all a natural colony of the household,
the children and children's children whom some refer to as
fed on the same mother's-milk. And this is why cities at first

---

42   Ross emends "carry out those things" (*tauta poiein*) to "work" (*ponein*),
     but it seems better to stay close to the manuscripts for Aristotle's ref-
     erences to natural slavery. It is only in the next clause that Aristotle
     shifts from neuters (for something that fits its possessor to rule or be
     ruled) to the words for a master and a slave. It is the need for another
     person, and hence the lack of one of those "somethings," that makes
     a human being naturally a master or slave. It should be noted too that
     the qualification for mastery given here is foresight by thinking (*dia-
     noia*), not foresight by "the mind" as many translations have it; Aristo-
     tle makes clear in Bk. III, Ch. 11 of *On the Soul* that he regards animals
     as having foresight by way of imagination.

43   Nothing is known about this implement, but animals sacrificed at the
     temple at Delphi would presumably have ranged from pigeons to
     bulls.

44   Euripides, *Iphigenia at Aulis* 1400.

45   *Works and Days* 405.

20   were ruled by kings, and nations[46] still are even now, since they came together out of people under kingly rule. For every household is under kingly rule by the eldest, and so their colonies are too, through their family connection. And this is what Homer is talking about when he says "each one is a law unto children and wives," since they were scattered, the way people dwelt in ancient times as well.[47] For this reason all people claim the gods too are under a king, because they themselves were ruled by kings, some even now, others in ancient times; just as human beings copy the looks of the gods from their own, so too with their lives.

The complete association made of more than one village is a city, since at that point, so to speak, it gets to the threshold of full self-sufficiency, coming into being for the sake of living, but being for the sake of living well. Hence every city is by nature, if in fact the first forms of association are as well. For it is their end, and nature is an end; for what each thing is when it has reached the completion of its coming into being is that which we say is the nature of each, as with a human being, a horse, a house.[48] And that for the sake 1253A of which, the end, is also what is best, and self-sufficiency is both an end and what is best. From these things, then, it is plain that the city is one of things that are by nature, and that a human being is by nature an animal meant for a city; one who is cityless as a result of nature rather than by chance is either insignificant or more powerful than a human being. He is like the person reviled by Homer as "without fellowship, without law, without a hearth," [49] for someone of that sort is at the same time naturally bent on war, since he is in

---

46   A nation or a "people" (*ethnos*), which could be large and subsume conquered nations under its empire, was the typical form of sovereign association in the non-Greek world.

47   The quotation, *Odyssey* IX, 114-115, refers to the Cyclopes, who were monsters and cannibals. Homer points out that there is no law (*themis*) where each lays down the law.

48   In the *Physics*, 193a 28-b 18, Aristotle argues that in any natural process of growth it is not the materials from which but the form into which it grows that discloses the nature of the growing thing. Hence the beaten path of an imaginary genesis of a city was only a scaffolding that can now be kicked away. At the threshold of self-sufficiency the association attains its natural form.

49   *Iliad* IX, 63.

fact like an unpaired piece on a checker-board. Why a human being is an animal meant for a city, more than every
sort of bee and every sort of herd animal, is clear. For nature,
as we claim, does nothing uselessly, and a human being,   10
alone among the animals, has speech. And while the voice
is a sign of pain and pleasure, and belongs also to the other
animals on that account (since their nature goes this far, to
having a perception of pain and pleasure and communicating these to one another), speech is for disclosing what is
advantageous and what is harmful, and so too what is just
and what is unjust.[50] For this is distinctive of human beings
in relation to the other animals, to be alone in having a perception of good and bad, just and unjust, and the rest, and it
is an association involving these things that makes a household and a city. And a city is more primary by nature than a
household, and more primary than each of us, for the whole   20
is necessarily more primary than its parts. For if the whole is
done away with, there will not be a foot or a hand, except in
an ambiguous sense, as if one were to speak of a hand made
of stone (for once it has been disabled it will be like that); but
all things are defined by their work and potency, so when
they are no longer of the sort defined they cannot be called
the same things except ambiguously. So it is clear both that
the city is by nature and that it is more primary than each
person, for if each person is not self-sufficient when separate, he will be in a condition similar to that of other parts in
relation to the whole, and one who is no part of a city, either
from lacking the power to be in an association or from needing nothing on account of self-sufficiency, is for that reason
either a beast or a god.

---

50 Aristotle calls the vocal communication of some animals a language (*diale-
    ktos*) in Bk. IV, Ch. 9 of the *History of Animals*. This discussion of the distinc-
    tion of cities from hives and herds shows that he regards speech (*logos*) as
    a power not primarily for communicating but more deeply for disclosing
    the intelligible connections among things. He says in *On the Soul* that ani-
    mals behave intelligently (406b 24-25), but he ascribes this not to the power
    of *logos* but to a deliberative imagination (434a 5-10), though he says that
    where perception and imagination are concerned it is hard to draw a sharp
    line between irrational and rational (*alogon ou logon echon*, 432a 30-b 2). The
    transition to justice and injustice seems to refer to corrective justice, which
    Aristotle describes as redressing harm by restoring some advantage of
    which one person has deprived another (*Nicomachean Ethics*, 1132a 6-19).
    Any consideration of right and wrong in such inequities could only begin
    among beings capable of recognizing their existence.

30   So the impulse toward this sort of association is in all people by nature, but the first person to have organized one was responsible for the greatest of goods. For just as a human being in a state of completeness is the best of the animals, so too, one who is separated from law and a judicial process is the worst of them all. For injustice is the most severe when it has weapons, and a human being is born having weapons for good judgment and virtue which are capable of being used to their utmost for their opposites. This is why he is the most impious and savage animal, and worst where sex and food are concerned.[51] And justice belongs in a city, for a judicial process is the source of order for a political association, and justice is a judging of what is just.

Chapter 3

1253B   And since it is plain what the parts are out of which a city is organized, it is necessary to speak first about household management, since every city is composed of households. And the parts of household management repeat those out of which a household is organized, while a complete household consists of slaves and free people. And since each thing is to be sought out first in its smallest instances, and the first and smallest parts of a household are a master and a slave, a husband and a wife, and a father and children, it would be appropriate to examine, with regard to each of these three parts, what it would be and of what sort it ought to be. And these are skill at mastery, skill at marriage

10   (since there is no name for the married woman and man as a couple), and third, skill at child-rearing (since this too has no special name given to it). So let there be these three that we mentioned. But there is a certain part which seems to some people to be household management, and to others to be the greatest part of it, and how that stands needs to be looked at. I am talking about what is called provisioning.[52]

---

51   In Bk. VII, Ch. 5 of the *Nicomachean Ethics*, Aristotle argues that certain animal-like extreme and aberrant indulgences go beyond vice and unrestraint to a bestial condition, blameable in human beings who are capable of choosing otherwise.

52   The Greek word is *chrêmatistikê*. It is usually translated by phrases such as "money-making" or "skill at business" but Aristotle will distinguish that form of it from a more primary kind of know-how at securing the usable or consumable goods (*chrêmata*) a household needs.

But first let us speak about master and slave, so that we may see both what has to do with necessary service and whether we might be able to get hold of anything having to do with knowing about them that is better than the things currently accepted. For it seems to some that mastery of slaves is a certain kind of knowledge, and that household management, mastery of slaves, political rule, and kingship are the same,   20 as we were saying at the beginning. But to others it seems contrary to nature to be a master of slaves (since it is by convention that the one is a slave and the other free, while they are no different by nature), and that it is consequently not just either, since it is by force.

Chapter 4

Now since property is part of a household, skill at acquiring possessions is also part of household management (for without the necessities it is impossible both to live and to live well); so just as it would be necessary in the various arts for their appropriate instruments to be available if one is going to carry the job to completion, so too does that apply to a household manager. And among instruments, while some are soulless, others are ensouled. (For instance, for a helmsman, the tiller is a soulless instrument, but the lookout man is an ensouled one, for in the arts, a person in a subordinate role   30 is in the form of a instrument.) A possession too, then, is an instrument for life, and property is an assortment of instruments; and a slave is an ensouled possession, and like every subordinate, is an instrument over instruments. For if each of the instruments had the power to carry out its job when commanded or in anticipation of the command, the way people say those of Daedalus did, or Hephaestus's tripods, which the poet says "came into the gods' assembly on their own," [53] so that shuttles would ply the loom and picks play the lyre, there would be no need of subordinates for master-craftsmen or   1254A slaves for masters. Now the instruments mentioned are productive instruments, while a possession is meant for action, for some other thing comes into being from the shuttle apart from the use of it, but the use alone comes from clothes or a bed. And further, since production and action differ in form, and both have need of instruments, it is necessary for these

---

[53]   *Iliad* XVIII, 376.

too to have the same difference. And life is action and not production. Hence a slave is also a subordinate for things having to do with action.

A possession is meant in the same sense as a part. For a part is not only part of something else but also belongs wholly to something else, and similarly too with a possession. Hence, while the master is only a master of the slave and does not belong to him, the slave is not only a slave of the master but does wholly belong to him. What the nature and capacity of the slave are, then, is clear from these things. For one who, though a human being, belongs by nature not to himself but to someone else is by nature a slave; and a human being belongs to someone else who, though a human being, is a possession; and a possession is a separate instrument for action.

Chapter 5

Whether there is anyone of that sort by nature or not, and whether it is a better thing and a just thing for anyone to be a slave, or not, but all slavery is contrary to nature, needs to be examined next. And it is not difficult either to have insight into this through reason or to observe it from what happens. For ruling and being ruled are not only among the necessities but also among things that are advantageous, and some things diverge right from the moment of birth either toward being ruled or toward ruling. And there are many forms of ruling and of being ruled. (The kind of rule is always better when those ruled are better, as when the one ruled is a human being rather than a beast, since the work is better that is carried out by those who are better, and wherever one rules and another is ruled there is something that is their work.) For in cases in which anything is organized out of a number of things, whether continuous or separated, and becomes some one thing in common, something that rules and something that is ruled become apparent in them all, and this carries over from nature as a whole into beings with souls. For there is a kind of ruling even in things that do not share in life, as in harmony; but these things probably belong to a more popular sort of inquiry. And an animal is the first thing organized out of a soul and a body, of which the one is by nature the ruling part and the other the ruled.

And it is preferably in things having their natural condition that one ought to examine things that are by nature, and not in defective ones; so the appropriate sort of human being to study is one who is best disposed in both body and soul, in whom this is evident. For in those who are corrupt or in a   **1254B** corrupt condition, it would seem that the body often rules over the soul, from being in an inferior condition that is contrary to nature.

So as we are saying, the first place to get an insight into the rule of a master and political rule is in an animal. For the soul rules over the body with the rule of a master, while intellect rules over desire with political or kingly rule. In these cases it is evident that it is an advantageous thing in accord with nature for the body to be ruled by the soul, and for the part that operates by feeling to be ruled by the intellect, the part that has reason, while an equal or reversed relation is harmful to them all. And it is the same way again   **10** in the case of a human being and the other animals; the tame animals are better in nature than the wild ones, and it is better for them all to be ruled by a human being, since in that way they attain preservation. Also, the relation of male to female is by nature that of a superior and inferior, and ruler and ruled. And it is necessary that it be the same way in the case of all human beings. So those who stand as far removed as soul is from body or a human being from a beast (and those for whom the use of the body is their work, and for whom this is the best that comes from them, are situated in this way) are slaves by nature, and for them it is better that   **20** they be ruled by this sort of rule, if indeed it is better for the things that have been mentioned. For someone is by nature a slave if he is capable of belonging to another person (and hence also does belong to another person), and if he shares in reason only to the extent of perceiving it but not of having it.[54] For the other animals are subservient not to reason but to feelings. And their usefulness is only slightly different, since assistance with necessities by means of the body comes from both, from slaves and from tame animals.

---

54   This formulation makes it clear that Aristotle is not speaking of people with a passive demeanor but of those with only a passive intellectual capacity. Modern law contains the notion of being "mentally incompetent" to own property, enter into contracts, or otherwise be permitted to control one's own life.

And nature intends to make the bodies of free people and slaves differ, one sort strong for necessary service, the
30 other upright and useless for labors of that kind, but useful for a political life. (And that comes to be divided as well, into service in war and in peace.) But things often turn out the opposite way, with some having the bodies of free people and others the souls. This at least is obvious, though, that if people were born surpassing others in body only as much the images of the gods do, everyone would claim that those who fell short of that deserved to be their slaves. And if this is true in the case of the body, it is a much more just thing for this distinction to be made in the case of the soul; but it
1255A is just not so easy to see the beauty of the soul as it is with that of the body. It is clear, then, that some people are free and others slaves by nature, and that for the latter it is both advantageous and just for them to be enslaved.

Chapter 6

But it is not difficult to see that those who say the opposite are in a certain way speaking rightly. For "being enslaved" and "slave" are meant in two different senses. There is a sense in which a slave or one who is enslaved is a matter of law, the law being a certain agreement by which people assert that things conquered in war belong to the conquerors. But many of those experienced with the laws charge those who say that, the way they would charge a rhetorician, with urging measures that violate the law, on the grounds that it would a terrible thing if what is overcome by force is going
10 to be a slave and be ruled by what is capable of force and predominant in power. And even among the wise, it seems that way to some, but the other way to others. What is responsible for this dispute, and what makes the tug-of-war of arguments keep going, is that in a certain way virtue, when it happens to have resources, is also best able to use force, and what predominates is always in excess in some sort of good; consequently, it seems that there is no force devoid of virtue, but what is disputed has to do only with what the just thing is (since in this matter it seems to some that the just thing is

kindness,[55] but to others that this very thing is just, namely for the conqueror to rule). At any rate, though, when these arguments are set out separately, the one set of arguments   20 has nothing strong or persuasive in it to say that what is better in respect of virtue ought not to rule and be master. But some who cling entirely, as they assume, to a sort of justice (since the law is a sort of justice) set down the slavery resulting from war as just, but at the same time they deny it. For it is possible for the origins of wars not to be just, and there is no way to say that someone who does not deserve to be enslaved is a slave. Otherwise it will turn out that those held to be of highest birth are slaves and descended from slaves, if they should happen to be captured and sold. For just that reason people do not want to call them slaves, but do say so about the barbarians. And yet when they say that, they are   30 looking for nothing other than the natural slave which we were speaking of from the beginning, for it is necessary to say there are some who are slaves everywhere and others nowhere. And it is the same way with being high-born, for they consider themselves high-born not only among themselves but everywhere, but consider barbarians high-born only at home, as if there were something high-born and free simply, and something not simply so. It is as Theodectes's Helen says

> Sprung from divine roots on both sides as I am,
> Who would think it right to call me a serving-maid?

When people say that, it is by nothing other than virtue and vice that they are distinguishing slave from free and   40 high-born from base-born. For they think that good is born   1255B from good the same way that a human being is born from a human being and a beast from a beast. But while nature intends to do this, it is often not able to do so.

It is clear, then, that there is some reason for the dispute, and there are not always natural slaves on the one side

---

55   This (*eunoia*) is the reading in all the manuscripts, but Ross emends it to *anoia* (nonsense). Ross's version presumably makes everyone agree with enslaving the conquered, some saying that it is just, the others that it makes no sense to think justice has anything to do with it. The manuscript reading seems to mean that the conquerors always intend to do justice but differ over what that is. That version keeps the tug-of-war going, and focuses it on the just thing (*to dikaion*) as distinct from the virtue of justice.

and free people on the other. It is also clear that there is a distinction of such a kind in some people, among whom it is advantageous for the one to be enslaved and the other to be master, and that the one ought to be ruled and the other to rule by that form of rule by which it is natural to rule, and therefore to be a master, though to do so badly is disadvan-

10 tageous to them both. For the same thing is advantageous to the whole as to the part and to the soul as to the body, while the slave is a certain part of the master, like an ensouled but separated part of his body. Hence for a slave and a master who deserve to be regarded as such by nature, there is both a mutual advantage and a friendship toward one another, but when it is not that way, but they are slave and master by law and by force, it is the opposite.[56]

Chapter 7

It is also clear from these things that mastery of slaves and political rule are not the same, and that all forms of rule are not the same as one another, as some claim. For one sort is over people free by nature and the other over slaves; also, household management is a monarchy (since every house-

20 hold is ruled by one person), while political rule is over people who are free and equal. Now someone is not called a master on account of knowledge, but for being of a certain sort, and similarly with slave and free, but there could be a knowledge pertaining to both mastery and slavery. That pertaining to slavery would be just the sort of thing the person in Syracuse used to teach, for someone there used to take a fee and give slave boys training in their daily chores; there could also be a kind of learning that went further into such things, such as refined cooking and other such items of domestic service. For there are jobs of one kind and jobs of another, some held in higher honor, some of greater neces-sity; as the proverb says, "slave above slave, master above

30 master." So all these sorts of knowledge apply to the slave, but knowledge for a master is for the use of slaves. For one is a master not in acquiring slaves but in using slaves. This

---

56   This conclusion is often overlooked. By the very argument that justi-fies slavery as natural, any slavery not based on the defect of intellec-tual capacity described at 1254b 22-23 is disadvantageous to the mas-ter as well as to the slave, and a source of mutual hostility or hatred.

sort of knowledge has nothing great or profound about it, since this person needs to know how to be in charge of the things a slave needs to know how to do. Hence, for all those who have the opportunity to avoid being bothered with it themselves, a manager takes on that office, while they devote themselves to political or philosophic activity. Skill at acquiring slaves is different from both of these—acquiring them justly, for instance, being a certain skill at war or hunting. So let the distinctions that pertain to slave and master be made in this way. **40**

Chapter 8

Let us take an overall view of property and provision- **1256A** ing that follows the usual course,[57] seeing as how the slave was also a particular part of property. And first of all, one might be hard put to say whether provisioning is the same as household management, or part of it, or subordinate to it, and if subordinate, whether in the way making shuttles is to weaving or the way working bronze is to sculpture. (For these are not subordinate in the same way: the one provides instruments and the other material, and by material I mean the underlying something out of which a work is brought to final form, such as wool for a weaver and bronze for a **10** sculptor.) It is evident, then, that household management is not the same as provisioning, since the role of one is providing and of the other it is using. For what else apart from household management will be the skill at using things for the household? But whether provisioning is some part of it or different in form is highly disputable. For if it is the role of someone skilled at provisioning to see where money and property are going to come from, property at any rate takes in many parts, and wealth as well, so that first of all there is the question, is skill at farming, and the whole responsibil-

---

57   As at 1252a 17-18 (see note), this phrase (*ho huphêgêmenos tropos* this time) indicates that Aristotle will be adopting a starting point from popular or received opinion, and the conclusions he draws here will all reflect the assumptions contained within that usual way of thinking. At the end of the *Nicomachean Ethics*, where Aristotle describes the need for a study of politics, he says that unwritten laws, national character, and a heritage of opinions and habits inevitably have strength in public life and are always already present in the human beings lawmaking has to work with (1180a 34-b 7).

20 ity for food and property, a part of provisioning or a different kind of thing? But in fact there are many forms of food, which is why there are also many ways of life that belong to animals as well as human beings. For it is not possible to live without food, so that the differences among foods have produced differences among animals. For some of the beasts are in herds and others scattered, whichever way gives an advantage for their food, since some of them are carnivorous, some herbivorous, and others omnivorous. So it is for convenience and selectivity that nature has made their ways of life distinct, and since the same things are not pleasing to each, but different things to different kinds, ways of life among carnivorous and herbivorous animals themselves are divergent from one another.

30 And it is similar with human beings as well, for the ways of life belonging to them are much different. The laziest are nomads (since their food comes to them without labor while they are at leisure, from tame animals, though when it is necessary for their flocks to change their place for the sake of pastures, they too are compelled to to follow along, as if they were farming a living farm). Others live off hunting, and different groups off different kinds of hunting; some, for example, live off piracy, and others, who dwell near lakes, marshes, rivers, or the right parts of the sea, off fishing, still others off birds or wild beasts. But the largest class of hu-
40 man beings live off the earth and cultivated crops. So there are just about that many ways of life, those at any rate that have a productive activity of their own and do not provide
1256B their food by exchange or commerce: nomadic, piratical, fishing, hunting, and farming. Some also live pleasantly by making a mixture of these, making up for a deficient way of life in any respect in which it comes up short of being self-sufficient; some, for instance, are nomadic and piratical at the same time, while others combine farming and hunting, and similarly with the rest. As their need contributes its pressures, they pass their lives in such a manner. So property of this sort is obviously given to all by nature itself, just as it is right from the first moment of birth, so too when they
10 are full-grown. For at birth, from the beginning some of the animals also bring forth enough food to be sufficient up to the time when the offspring itself has the power to provide for itself, as with those that produce larvae or lay eggs; those

that are live-bearing have food for their offspring in themselves up to a certain time, in the nature of what is called
milk. So similarly for those that have come into being, it is
clear that it is appropriate to assume that plants are for the
sake of animals and the other animals for the sake of human
beings,[58] the tame ones both for use and for food, and if not
all the wild ones, at least most, for the sake of food and other assistance, so that clothes and other kinds of gear might   20
come from them. So if nature makes nothing incomplete and
nothing useless, it is necessary that nature has made them all
for the sake of human beings. Hence even skill at war will
in a certain sense be a natural acquisitive skill (since skill at
hunting is part of it), which ought to be used both against
animals and against those human beings who are of such a
nature as to be ruled, but are unwilling, on the grounds that
this sort of warfare is naturally just.

So one form of natural skill at acquisition is a part of
household management, because it either needs to have
available or to provide a means to make available a supply
of possessions necessary for life and useful for association   30
in a city or household. And it seems that true wealth, at any
rate, is made up of these things. For self-sufficiency in this
sort of property for a good life is not unlimited the way
Solon claims in the verse "no upper limit of wealth is laid
down in the sight of men." It is laid down, in the same way
as for the rest of the arts; for nothing that is instrumental to
any art is unlimited in either multitude or magnitude, and
wealth is the multitude of instruments belonging to a household manager or political ruler. It is clear, then, that there is

58   It is a central claim of Aristotle's theoretical works that living things
      are for their own sake. He invented the word *entelecheia* as a fusion
      of the notions of completeness and activity, or being-at-an-end and
      being-at-work. That word is the heart of the definition of the source
      of life in *On the Soul* (412b 4-6), of the discovery of the primary in-
      stances of being in the world of experience in the *Metaphysics* (1028b
      9-10, 1050b 2-3, 1050a 21-23), and of the intelligibility of motion in the
      Physics (201a 9-11). The question whether living things also have ends
      external to themselves is raised in *On the Soul* in relation to their off-
      spring (415a 26-b 3), and in the *Metaphysics* in relation to the organiza-
      tion of the cosmos as a whole (1072b 1-4). The positive statement here
      that living things exist for our sake follows the beaten path of popular
      opinion of which Aristotle reminds us at the beginning of this chapter.
      In the *Physics* (194a 34-35), he says instead: "we treat everything there
      is as though it is for our sake."

a certain art of acquisition in accord with nature for household managers and political rulers, and for what reason.

Chapter 9

40   But there is another kind of skill at acquisition which people refer to especially as provisioning—and it is just to re-
1257A fer to it that way—on account of which there seems to be no limit for wealth and property. Many people regard it as one and the same as the skill described, because they are close together, but it is neither the same as the one mentioned nor far removed from it. But one of them is natural and the other is not natural, but comes about instead through a certain kind of experience and art.

Let us take our beginning about it from this point: the use of every possession is twofold, both ways in virtue of itself but not in virtue of itself in the same manner, but one particular to the thing and the other not particular to it. With a shoe, for instance, there is wearing on the feet and also
10   exchange, and both are uses of shoes. For a person who exchanges a shoe with someone who needs one, in return for currency or food, does use the shoe as a shoe but not in its particular use, since it did not come into being for the sake of exchange, and it is the same way with the other possessions as well. For there is a skill at exchanging all things that has its first origin from something that is in accord with nature, the fact that human beings have more of some things and less of others than is sufficient. (And it is clear from this that commercial trade is not a natural part of skill at provisioning, since it would have been necessary then for the traders to make an exchange for just the amount that was sufficient
20   for them.) So in the first association (that is, the household), it is obvious that there is no work for exchange to do, but it belongs to an association from the point at which it consists of more than one household. For those who belonged to the same one shared all things in common, while those in separate ones, on the contrary, had many things that differed, of which it was necessary to make exchanges according to their needs, just as many of the barbarian nations still do, by barter. For they exchange useful items themselves for themselves, and nothing more, wine for grain for instance, giving one and taking the other, and each of the other things of

that sort. Skill at this sort of exchange, then, is not contrary to nature and is not any form of provisioning (since it was 30 aimed at filling out a self-sufficiency in accord with nature). The other sort of exchange, however, came along out of this one in a reasonable way. For when the assistance of those from more foreign places came along to import things that were needed and export those they had in excess, the use of a currency was supplied out of necessity. For each of the natural necessities was not easily transported, and so for their exchanges they agreed to give and take some sort of thing that was comparable to those things themselves, which, being itself one of the useful things, had a use for living that was easy to handle, such as iron or silver or any other such thing there might be, determined at first simply by size and weight, but ultimately people also stamped a mark on it in 40 order to spare themselves from measuring, for the mark was placed as a sign of the amount.

So from the point at which a currency was provided 1257B out of necessary exchange, another form of provisioning came into being, the commercial sort, at first probably in a simple way, then through experience already more a matter of art, about what items exchanged in what way will make the most profit. This is why it seems that provisioning is especially concerned with the currency, and that its job is to be able to see where a greater amount of money will come from, since it is productive of wealth and money.[59] For people often even assume that wealth is a large quantity of currency, because provisioning and commercial skill are concerned 10 with that. Sometimes, though, on the contrary, the currency seems to be nonsense, a matter of convention through-and-through and nothing natural, because it is worth nothing when its users alter it and is not useful for any of the necessities; in fact, someone who is wealthy in currency will often go without necessary sustenance. And yet it would be absurd for wealth to be the sort of thing that one could have in abundance and die of starvation, like that Midas people tell the story about, that because of the insatiable greed of

---

59   In effect this sentence traces a transformation in the meaning of money (*chrêmata*), from the easy-to-handle usable things of the preceding paragraph to the agreed upon and stamped quantitative measures of wealth embodied in the currency.

his prayer, everything set in front of him turned into gold. Hence people look for some other sort of wealth and provisioning, and they are right to look for it. For there is a differ-
20   ent sort of provisioning and wealth which is in accord with nature, and this is household management; but commercial skill makes money not in every way but only by exchange of useful goods, and this seems to be concerned with currency, since the currency is the element and limiting factor of the exchange. And this sort of wealth, the sort that comes from this sort of provisioning, is in fact unlimited. For just as the medical art is for being healthy to an unlimited extent, and each of the arts is for its end to an unlimited extent (since they want to produce that to the greatest possible extent), but as far as the things leading to the end are concerned, an art is not of unlimited extent (since the end is a limit on them all), so too with this sort of provisioning there is no limit for
30   its end, and the end is wealth of this sort and property consisting of money.

But with the sort of provisioning involved in household management, on the other hand, there is a limit, since this is not the job of household management. This is why in one sense it appears necessary for there to be a limit to all wealth, but in what happens we see things turning out the opposite way. For all those who engage in provisioning increase their supply of currency to an unlimited extent. The reason is the close proximity of the two sorts of provisioning, since each, involving the same thing, crosses over into the other in its use. For their use is of the same property, though not in the same respect, but the end of the one is different, while of the other the end is increase. So it seems to some people that this is the job of household management, and they conduct themselves throughout in the belief that
40   they have to preserve or increase to an unlimited extent an estate consisting of currency. What is responsible for this
1258A   attitude is being zealous about living but not about living well. So since that desire is of unlimited extent, they also desire what produces an unlimited supply of things. And even those who devote themselves to living well seek what leads to bodily enjoyments, so since this too appears to be available through property, all the time they spend is connected with money, and this is where the other form of provisioning comes from. For since there is enjoyment in extravagance,

they seek what produces the extravagance that leads to enjoyment, and if they are incapable of providing this through provisioning, they attempt it through other sources, using each of their capacities in a way not in accord with its nature. For the nature of courage is not to make money but to produce confidence, and the natures of military and medical skill are not to make money but in the one case victory, in the other health. But some people turn all these into provisioning, as though this were their end and everything had to press ahead to the end.

About the non-necessary sort of provisioning, then, what it is and what causes us to be in need of it have been stated, and about the necessary sort, that it is different from that, a natural skill of household management that has to do with food, not unbounded like that other sort but having a limit.

Chapter 10

And the original difficulty, whether provisioning belongs to the household manager or political ruler, or does not but this needs to be available, is clear. For just as political skill does not produce human beings, but takes them from nature and uses them, so too it is necessary for nature to provide the earth or sea or something else for food, while it belongs to the household manager to get the things that come from these into the condition they need to be in. For it does not belong to skill at weaving to produce wool but to use it, and to recognize the sort that is usable and appropriate or useless and inappropriate. For one could also raise the question why provisioning is part of household management but doctoring is not part of it, even though the people in the household need to be healthy, just as they need to live or do any of the other necessary things. But since there is a sense in which seeing about health belongs to a household manager and to a ruler, and a sense in which it does not, but belongs to a doctor, so too is there a sense in which seeing about possessions belongs to a household manager and a sense in which it does not, but to a subordinate skill. And this one especially needs to be present by nature, as was said before. For it is the job of nature to supply food to something that has been born, since for all of these, the remainder

of that out of which they are born is food. Hence, skill at
acquiring possessions from crops and animals is in accord
with nature for everyone. But since it is of two forms, as we
said, one belonging to commerce and the other to household
40 1258B management, and one of these is necessary and praised,
while the one involving skill at exchange is justly criticized
(since it is not in accord with nature but taken by one person
from another), usury is very reasonably hated because what
is acquired comes from the currency itself and not from the
thing for which it was provided. For currency came into
being for the sake of exchange, but the interest makes it be
more. (And this is where the name[60] is taken from, since offspring are like those who gave birth to them, and interest is
currency that comes into being out of currency.) So this is the
most contrary to nature of the forms of provisioning.

Chapter 11

    Since we have made enough distinctions having to do
10 with knowledge, it is necessary to go over what has to do
with practical usage. All such matters have a free-ranging
study but also a necessary experience. And the useful parts
of provisioning involve being experienced with property,
and where and how different sorts are most profitable, for
instance what sort of property in horses, cattle, or sheep, and
similarly with the rest of the animals. (For it is necessary to
be experienced as to which of these are most profitable in
comparison with one another, and also which ones in which
places, since different ones thrive in different regions.) Next,
they involve farming, and within this, both simple crops and
vine-cultivation, as well as keeping bees and other winged
20 and aquatic animals, all the sorts from which it is possible to
get support. These, then, are the parts of provisioning in its
most proper and primary sense, while trade is the greatest
part of commercial provisioning. (And this has three parts:
shipping, carrying, and retail marketing. Among these, some
differ from the others by being more safe, others by providing a greater profit.) A second part is money-lending and a
third is wage labor, one sort of which involves the menial
crafts, while the other involves unskilled but useful labor
with the body alone. And there is a third form of provision-

---

60   Interest on money was called *tokos*, "offspring."

ing between this sort and the primary one, since it has some part in both the natural and the commercial sorts, namely for those things that are from the earth and derived from things from the earth, and are barren but useful, such as timber-cutting and all sorts of mining. And this includes many kinds, since there are many forms of things mined from the earth. Each of these has now been spoken of in general, and while giving a precise discussion of the subject part by part would be useful with a view to the various kinds of work, dwelling on them would be tedious. The most artful of the kinds of work are those where chance is present the least, the most mechanical those in which people's bodies get the most wear and tear, the most slavish those where there is the greatest use of the body, and the most debased those where there is the least need of virtue in addition.   30

And since there are things written about these matters by some people, for example Chares the Parian and Apollodorus the Lemnian on farming, about both simple crops and vine-cultivation, and similarly by others on other topics, let these things be studied from these writings by anyone who cares to. Also, the scattered writings on the means by which some have been successful at acquiring provisions need to be collected. For all these things, such as the means used by Thales the Milesian, are of benefit to those who hold provisioning in honor. For this is an idea that pertains to provisioning, but people attribute it to him on account of his wisdom, and it happens to be something of universal utility. For when people reproached him for his poverty on the grounds that philosophy was useless, they say that having noticed from his astronomical study that there was going to be an abundance of olives, he found the means, while it was still winter, to put down a little money as a deposit on all the olive presses in Miletus and Chios, which were rented out at a small fee because no one was taking an interest in them. But when the opportune moment came and all of a sudden many of them were sought out at the same time, he rented them out on whatever terms he wanted and amassed a lot of money, to show that it is an easy thing for philosophers to get rich if they want to, though that is not what they are serious about. So Thales is said to have made a display of his wisdom in this way, though as we said, this sort of provisioning technique is a universal one, if anyone is able to   40 1259A 10 20

arrange a monopoly for himself. And hence some cities too resort to this device when they are in need of money, for they create a monopoly in items for sale. In Sicily, someone who had cash that had been deposited with him bought up all the iron from the iron-works, and afterward, when merchants came from their markets, he alone was selling it, and without making much of an increase in price he still took in a hundred talents on an outlay of fifty.[61] Now when Dionysius became aware of this, he ordered him to get his money out
30   of Syracuse, and by no means to stay there any longer, since he had discovered a technique detrimental to Dionysius's own affairs. But the thing Thales had seen is the same as this case, since both men had contrived to bring about monopolies for themselves. And it is useful for political rulers too to recognize these things, since there is a need of provisions and for techniques of this sort in many cities, just as in a household, only more so. Consequently, some of those who engage in political administration do so in these ways only.

Chapter 12

And since there were three parts of household management, one pertaining to mastery of slaves, which has been discussed earlier, one paternal, and a third pertaining to marriage, [the latter two remain to be discussed.][62] And
40   one rules a wife and children as free people in both cases,
1259B but not with the same manner of rule, but in a political manner[63] in the case of a wife and a kingly manner in the case of children. For the male is by nature more suited to leadership than the female, unless something in his make-up runs contrary to nature, and so is the elder and full-grown in comparison to the younger and immature. Now in most instances of political rule there is an interchange among those who rule and are ruled, since they tend by nature to be on

---

61   One talent was a vast sum, set in Athens as equivalent to 57.75 pounds of silver, or to 6000 drachmas. One drachma was considered a good day's wage for a skilled craftsman or a sailor. Two tyrants of Syracuse, the major city of Sicily, a father and son, had the name Dionysius.

62   Something is missing in the manuscripts.

63   This is described first at 1255b 20 as rule over free and equal subjects, so the natural superiority Aristotle attributes to the male must leave room for an equality of a kind other than merely natural.

an equality and have no difference; nevertheless, whenever one rules and another is ruled, the former wants there to be a difference in formalities, words, and tokens of respect, as Amasis said in the story about the footpan.[64] The male is always related to the female in this manner. But rule over children is kingly, for the progenitor is a ruler on the basis of love as well as of greater age, which is precisely the form of kingly rule. This is why Homer spoke beautifully when he addressed Zeus, the king of them all, as "father of men and gods." For the king ought to have distinction, and yet be the same in kind, the very thing which characterizes the older in relation to the younger and the progenitor in relation to the offspring.

Chapter 13

It is clear, then, that the serious concern of household management is greater for human beings than for the acquisition of things without souls, for their virtue rather than for the property of theirs which we call wealth, and for the free people rather than the slaves. And as far as slaves are concerned, one might first raise the question whether there is any virtue befitting a slave other than what belongs to implements and servants, any virtue more deserving of respect than those things, such as moderation, courage, justice, and the other active conditions of that sort, or whether there is none apart from their bodily services. For there is an impasse either way, since, if there are virtues, in what respect do they differ from free people? And if there are not, that would be strange, since they are human beings and have a share in reason. And pretty much the same point of inquiry also concerns a woman and a child, whether they too have virtues, and a woman ought to be moderate, courageous, and just, and a child can be dissipated or moderate, or not. So this is something that needs to be examined about one who is ruled by nature and one who rules: whether virtue is the same or different. For if both ought to participate in

---

64 See Herodotus, *History*, II, 172. Amasis was a commoner of low family who became king of Egypt, and was at first held in low esteem. He had a golden footpan turned into an image of a god, and then told the people that they were worshipping something into which they used to vomit and urinate.

complete goodness,[65] why should the one rule and the other be ruled once and for all? For it is not possible for them to differ by greater and less since being ruled and ruling differ in form and in no respect as greater and less. But it would be amazing if one needed it and the other did not. For if the ruler is not going to be moderate and just, how will he do a beautiful job of ruling? And if the one ruled is not, how will he do a beautiful job of being ruled? For if he is dissipated and cowardly, he will do none of the things that are his duties. It is clear, then, that it is necessary for both to participate in virtue, but for there to be differences in this, just as there are in those who naturally rule. And this leads straight to a consideration of the soul, for there is in it by nature something ruling and something ruled, of which we claim there are different virtues, as of the part having reason and the irrational part. It is evident, then, that things are the same way in the other cases as well, so that most things are ruling or ruled by nature. For it is in different ways that the free rules the slave, the male the female, and the man the child, and while the parts of the soul are present in them all, they are present in differing ways. For the slave wholly lacks the deliberative capacity, while the female has it, but without authority,[66] and the child has it, but incomplete. It must likewise be assumed that this necessarily holds for the virtues of character as well, that everyone needs to participate in them but not in the same way, but each to the extent that concerns his own work. Hence the one who rules ought to have complete virtue of character (for work is the responsibility of the master-craftsman in an unqualified way, and reason[67] is a

40
1260A

10

---

65   *Kalokagathia*, the word the high-born classes applied to themselves to connote a combination of beauty of manners and goodness of character.

66   The word *akuron* was commonly applied to laws that were either invalid or unenforced. Aristotle could mean that the deliberative capacity in a woman is without force either because it is by nature weaker in her than feelings or because it is conventionally unrecognized and unrespected.

67   Aristotle's argument here is elliptical, and depends on the account he gives in the *Nicomachean Ethics*. Although the intellectual virtues belong to the part of the soul with reason, the virtues of character which govern the irrational part necessarily involve reason in the act of choice. It is presumably in the form of the deliberative capacity that

master-craftsman), but each of the others as much as falls to his lot. So it is clear that ethical virtue belongs to all of those mentioned, and that moderation is not the same in a woman and a man, and neither are courage and justice, in the way that Socrates supposed,[68] but there is a courage appropriate to ruling and another to being a subordinate, and it is similar with the other virtues.

And this is clear also to those who examine the matter part-by-part instead. For those who speak in general terms are fooling themselves, saying that virtue is the good condition of the soul, or acting rightly, or anything of that sort. Those who count up the virtues, as Gorgias does, speak much better than those who define it that way. Hence one ought to consider that the way it is for everyone is the way the poet[69] has spoken about woman, saying "silence brings adornment to a woman," while this is no longer the case for a man. And since a child is incomplete, it is clear that virtue does not belong to its present self in relation to itself but in relation to its end and the one guiding it there; and it is similar with a slave in relation to a master. We set it down that the slave is useful for matters of necessity, so it is clear that he too needs a little virtue, enough that he not fall short in his tasks on account of dissipation or cowardice. But if what is now being said is true, one might raise the question whether craftsmen too will need to have virtue, since they often fall short in their tasks on account of dissipation. Or does this differ in the greatest manner? For the slave is a partner in life, while the other is more remote from it, and exactly as much virtue falls to his lot as slavery does. For the mechanical craftsman has a certain restricted slavery, and while the slave is what he is by nature, no leatherworker is, nor any of the other craftsmen. It is clear then that the master

---

reason acts as the master craftsman of practical life, and excellence of practical judgment would thus be what makes virtue of character complete.

68   In Plato's *Meno*, Meno speaks as though the virtues of various kinds of people had nothing in common, and Socrates speaks as though they had no differences. In the dialogues, Socrates typically leaves it to his listeners to find the middle ground where truth might lie, and in references to the dialogues, Aristotle typically takes the written arguments at face value.

69   Sophocles (*Ajax*, 293) has a character quote this line from her husband.

needs to be responsible for this sort of virtue in a slave, and not the person who has a skill at teaching his tasks. Hence people are not speaking beautifully who deprive slaves of reason and claim one should make use of command only.[70] For gentle admonishment needs to be used with slaves more than with children.

So let the distinctions about these matters be made in this way. As for a husband and wife and a child and father, and the virtue that pertains to each of them as well as what is done beautifully or otherwise in their relations with one another, and how one ought to pursue what is done well and avoid what is done badly, it is necessary to go over all this in treatments of the different forms of government.[71] For since every household is part of a city, and these things are parts of a household, and one ought to look at the virtue of the part in relation to that of the whole, then it is neces- sary to educate both children and women with a view to the form of government, if indeed it makes any difference to the city's being of good moral stature whether its children and women are of good moral stature. But it necessarily does make a difference, since women are a one-half portion of the free people and associates in the government come from the children. So since distinctions have been made about these things and the rest must be spoken of in other places, leaving off the present discussions as being complete, let us make another beginning for our discussion, and let us first consider the opinions that have been put forward about the best form of government.

10

20

---

70   This applies to the Athenian Stranger in Plato's *Laws*, 777E-778A.

71   If Aristotle is referring to his own treatments of this topic later in the *Politics*, he appears not to have kept this promise.

BOOK II

Chapter 1 1260B

Since, in regard to political associations, we propose to look into which is the most effective of them all for those capable of living to greatest possible extent as one would wish, we ought to examine other forms of government as well, both those used by certain cities that are said to be under good laws and any others that might happen to be spoken of by certain people that also seem to be beautifully set up, so that one might see what is rightly done and useful and also so that looking for something different from them might not seem to be entirely the act of people who want to engage in sophistry, but we might be held to be embarking on this course for this reason: because those forms of government now present are *not* beautifully set up. The beginning that needs to be made first is the one that is the natural beginning for this investigation. For it is necessary that all citizens share either everything, or nothing, or some things and not others. Now to share nothing is obviously impos- sible, since a form of government is some sort of association, and in the first place necessarily has a shared location; there is one location for one city, and the citizens are associates 1261A in one city. But of all those things that are capable of being shared, is it better for a city that is going to be beautifully run to have them all shared, or better to have some shared and not others? For it is possible for the citizens to share children and women and property with one another, as in Plato's *Republic*, since Socrates claims there that children and women ought to be held in common, and property as well. So is it better for things to be the way they now are in this regard, or to go by the law set down in the *Republic*?

27

Chapter 2

10   There are many other inconveniences to having women be common to all, but the reason for which Socrates claims that things ought to be legislated in this way manifestly does not even follow from his arguments. Further still, the end which he claims the city ought to have is, as was just said, impossible, and no qualifications are made about how one ought to interpret it. I am speaking of the claim that it is best for the city to be entirely one to the greatest possible degree, for Socrates adopts that hypothesis.[72] And yet it is evident that by advancing and becoming more of a *one* it will not *be* a city. For a city is by nature a certain kind of multiplicity; by becoming more of a one it would turn from a city into a
20   household and from a household into a human being. For we would claim that a household is more of a one than a city is, and a single person than a household; so even if someone were capable of doing this, it ought not to be done, since it would abolish the city.

And a city is made up not only of a multiplicity of human beings, but also of human beings differing in form, for no city comes about from people all alike. For a city and an alliance are different. For the latter is useful in virtue of its size, even if it is homogeneous in form (since an alliance is by nature for the sake of back-up), as if more weight were pressing down a scale. And a city will also be different from a nation in this sort of way, whenever the multitude is not separated into villages but is like the Arcadians.[73] But those
30   out of whom it needs to become one are different in form, which is why reciprocal equality preserves cities, as was

---

72   It is worth pointing out that Socrates deliberately adopts this assumption in the *Republic* as a way of making a magnified image of the human soul, which Aristotle agrees has a structure of ruling and ruled parts (1254b 2-9 above). But Aristotle is right in saying that Socrates does not explicitly tell his hearers how to interpret the city he constructs to reflect the soul, and it is natural for readers to regard it as a practical political program. By addressing it in those terms, Aristotle is following the lead of Socrates and Plato to uncover the nature of the city as disclosed by the limits of their analogy.

73   Arcadia was the inland, infertile region of the Peloponnese, inhabited by a primitive nation of hunters and herders. During Aristotle's lifetime the Arcadians had built a central fortified city called Megalopolis, which drew in people from its various scattered villages.

said earlier in the *Ethics*,[74] since this is necessarily present even among those who are free and equal; for it is not possible for them all to rule at the same time, but either for a year or according to some other arrangement of time. So it turns out in this way that they all rule, just as if by an interchange of leather-workers and wood-workers the same people were not always shoemakers and carpenters. And since it is also better for it to be that way in matters that pertain to the political association, it is clear that, if possible, it is better for the same people to rule all the time, but in cases where this is not possible because they are all equal by nature, it is **1261B** better for them all to have a share in ruling, and it is at the same time a just thing, whether ruling is something good or something lowly; this at least reflects their being like equals during their terms as well as being alike when out of office. For some rule and others are ruled in turn as if they had become other people, and in the same way among those ruling, different people hold different ruling offices.

It is clear from these things, then, that it is not the nature of the city to be one in the way some people say, and that what is alleged to be the greatest good in cities abolishes cities, despite the fact that the good of each thing in fact preserves it. And it is clear in another way as well that **10** seeking to unify the city too much is not the better course. For a household is more self-sufficient than one person, and a city than a household, and what it means to *be* a city is to be at that point at which the association of a multiplicity of people turns out to be self-sufficient. So if what is more self-sufficient is more worthy of choice, then what is less of a *one* is more worthy of choice.

Chapter 3

But even if that is best, for the association to be one to the greatest possible degree, that does not appear to be demonstrated by the argument if all people say "mine" and "not mine" at the same time; for Socrates supposes that to be a sign of the city's being wholly one. But "all people" has **20**

---

74 The reference is to 1132b 31-34 of the *Nicomachean Ethics*, understood as the inquiry immediately prior to the *Politics*. The point there is that it is not strict equality but a proportional balance of reciprocal contributions that holds cities together.

two senses. If it is meant in the sense of "each," it might be more what Socrates wants to produce. For each will call the same boy "son" and the same woman "wife," and similarly with his property and with each thing that comes his way. But people who have women and children in common do not actually speak that way, but *all* and not each of them are speaking, and likewise all and not each about their property. It is clear, then, that there is a certain error in reasoning in speaking of them all. (For because of the double sense,

30   "all" and "both" and also "odd" and "even" produce syllogisms of the sort debaters use in arguments.[75]) Hence for all people to say the same thing is in one sense beautiful but not possible, but in another sense not even indicative of like-mindedness. And aside from these things, there is a different way saying it is harmful. For what is common to the most people gets the least attention. People are concerned most about the things that are particularly theirs, and less so about things held in common, or as much as belongs to each one. For aside from other things, they slight them more on the assumption that someone else is taking care of them, just as in domestic service many attendants sometimes give worse service than fewer. A thousand sons end up belonging to each of the citizens, and these not as each one's own, but

40   any random son belonging alike to any random citizen, so that everyone will slight them alike.

1262A   Also, each one means "mine" in relation to one of the citizens who is doing well or badly in proportion to the number there happen to be, meaning "mine" or "so-and-so's," for instance, as a particular one of the thousand, or of however many the city consists of, and dubiously at that, since it is unclear who happened to have a child born, and one that survived once it was born. So which way is more important, for each one of two thousand or ten thousand to say "mine" as referring to the same person, or instead, the way people say "mine" in cities now? For one refers to as his

10   son the same person whom another refers to as his brother, still another as his cousin, or by some other relationship of

---

75   The classic discussion of this topic is in Plato's *Hippias Major* (300E-302B). What belongs to all together may not belong to each at all, and certainly not with the intensity of a personal attachment. An example of the same fallacy is given below at 1264b 19-22.

blood, or through an extended relationship by marriage, his own first of all or of people related to him, and in addition to these connections, another person refers to him as a member of the same fraternal organization or tribe. For it is more important to be someone's own particular cousin than his son in *that* sense. And it is not even possible to prevent people from assuming that certain others are their own brothers and children and fathers and mothers, since they will necessarily take grounds for belief about one another from the likenesses to their parents that turn up in children. And some of those who write accounts of world travels claim that this very thing happens, for they say that among some people in upper Libya who hold women in common, the children who are born are still distinguished by their likenesses. And there are some women, and some other animals as well, such as horses and cows, who have a strong natural tendency to produce offspring resembling their fathers, like the Pharsalian mare named Honest.

Chapter 4

Also, it is not easy for those who set up this sort of association to ward off such inconveniences as assaults and involuntary manslaughter, as well the voluntary kind, and fights and insults, none of which are pious things when done to fathers and mothers and people not far off in kinship, as if they were being done to outsiders. There will necessarily turn out to be more of these among those who are unaware than among those who are aware of their relations, and while it is possible, when they do happen among those who are aware, for amends to be made according to custom, it is not possible at all among those who are not. And it is strange that even though he makes sons common, he deprives lovers only of the act of intercourse, but does not hinder them from being in love, or from other displays of feeling that are most inappropriate between a father and son or a brother and brother, since even for them to be in love at all is inappropriate. It is strange too that he prohibits the act of intercourse for no other reason than that the pleasure becomes too strong, and supposes that it makes no difference that it is a father and son or a pair of brothers.

20

30

40

And having women and children in common seems
1262B more likely to be useful for the farmers than for the guardians. For there will be less affection where children and
women are held in common, but it is those who are ruled
who ought to be in that condition with a view to their being
obedient and not rebellious. And in all respects, the results
that follow from such a law are necessarily the opposite of
those that it is appropriate for laws rightly set down to be responsible for, which were the reason Socrates supposed one
ought to arrange matters concerning children and women
his way. For our supposition is that affection is the greatest
good for cities (since people feeling that way would be the
least likely to divide into factions), and Socrates gives the
10   highest praise to the city's being one, which seems to be the
work of affection, and he himself claims it is. It is in this very
way, as we know, that Aristophanes in the speeches on love[76]
talks about lovers who, because of their strong feeling of affection, both desire to grow into each other and become one
out of the two that they are. In this case, then, it is necessary
for both, or one of them, to pass out of being, but in the city
affection would necessarily be watered down by this sort of
association, and least of all would a son say "mine" about
a father or a father about a son. Just as a little sweetening
mixed into a lot of water makes the blending imperceptible,
the same thing also results for the mutual kinship one ex-
20   pects from these words, since there is the least necessity in
such a form of government for a father to care about anyone
as a son, or a son as a father, or brothers about each other.
For there are two things which most of all make human beings feel care and affection, something that is one's own and
something that is one's favorite, neither of which can be
present for people governed in this way.

Now as for the shifting of the children that are born,
from the farmers and craftsmen to the guardians or from
the latter to the former, there is great confusion about the
way this will be done. It is necessary for those doing the giving and shifting to know whom they are giving to whom.
30   Also, the things mentioned long ago will result with even
greater necessity in these cases, that is, assaults, love affairs,
and killings. For those who are given to the other citizens

76   That is, in Plato's *Symposium*.

will no longer refer to the guardians as brothers, children, fathers, and mothers, nor will those going the other way to the guardians speak that way of the other citizens, so as to ward off doing any such things because of their kinship. So let the matter of holding children and women in common be settled in this way.

Chapter 5

Looking into the matter of property is next after these things, to see in what way one ought to make arrangements for those who are going to be governed under the best form of government, and whether property ought to be held in common or not. And one might examine this even separately from the laws set down about children and women. I mean that, on matters pertaining to property, even if those other things are held separately in the way they now are by everyone, one might examine whether it is better for items of property, or the use of them, to be common. For example, farmland could be separate while people bring the yield from it into a common stock to consume it (which is exactly what some of the nations do), or on the contrary, the land could be held in common and people could farm it in common while they divide up the yield from it into private stocks for use (and people say that some of the barbarians also engage in this form of communal activity), or both the farmland and its yield could be common. Another and easier way would be to have different people be the ones who work the land; if people performed the labor for themselves, more headaches would present themselves about property. For if they turn out not to be equal but unequal in their rewards and their work, complaints will necessarily be made against those who enjoy or take a lot while laboring little by those who take less while laboring more. Living together and sharing things is difficult in all human circumstances, and especially in matters of this sort. People who share in travels make this clear, for the majority of them, just about, fall into differences, taking offence at one another over trivial and petty things. Also, we take the most offence at those servants we use the most for routine chores.

So having property held in common has these inconveniences as well as others of the sort, while the way things

40

1263A

10

20

are now, if it is given the crowning touch with customs and an arrangement of correct laws, is no small improvement over it. For it would have something good from both sides, and by both sides I mean from having property in common and from having it private. For it ought to be common in a certain way, but private in general. Responsibilities will not produce mutual complaints when they are separated; they will produce an increased yield instead, since each person will watch over it as his own, while as for the use of it, the
30   things of friends will be common, as the proverb has it, as a result of virtue. Even now this approach is present in a sketchy way in some cities, and thus it is not impossible, and especially in those that are beautifully run some of these things are present and others could come to be. For even though each person has private property, he makes some of it useful to his friends and uses other things in common. In Sparta, for instance, people use each other's slaves as their own, one might say, and horses and dogs as well, and any supplies they need from the fields in their countryside. It is clear, then, that it is better for property to be private, but to make the use of it common; how it might come to be that
40   way—that is the special job of the lawmaker.

And in addition, regarding something as one's own makes an indescribable difference as far as pleasure is con-
1263B   cerned. For it is not for nothing that each person has a love for himself; this is something natural. Selfishness is justly blamed, but this is not loving oneself, but loving more than one ought, as with the love of money, for one might say that everybody loves everything of that sort. And surely it is extremely pleasant to do favors and help out friends and guests and associates, which happens when property is private. And these things do not result when people make the city too much of a one, and beyond that, they clearly do away with deeds that result from a pair of virtues, namely
10   from moderation where women are concerned (since staying away from someone else's wife out of moderation is a beautiful thing to do), and from generosity with possessions. For obviously no one will be generous or perform any generous act, since a deed of generosity is involved in the use of possessions.

There is a superficial appeal to this sort of legislation,

and it may seem to be compassionate. Someone who hears about it responds with delight, believing there will be some wonderful loving feeling in everyone for everyone, especially when someone charges that the evils now existing in governments arise because wealth is not held in common. I   20
mean lawsuits with one another over contracts, judgments based on false testimony, and obsequiousness toward rich people. None of these things come from a lack of communal property, though, but from badness of character, since we see people who have common possessions and are partners falling into disputes far more than people who have wealth separately. This is in spite of the fact that the people we observe in disputes arising out of partnerships are few in comparison with the large number who enter into contracts about the possessions they have acquired privately. And it is also just to speak not only of those evils people will be spared by holding things in common, but also of the good things, and it appears that life would be utterly impossible.

And we ought to acknowledge that the reason Socrates   30
was knocked off course was that his hypothesis was not correct. Both a household and a city ought to be one in a certain way, but not in every way. There is a point at which a city proceeding in that direction will not be a city, and a point at which, though it will be a city, the fact that it is close to not being one will make it a worse city. It is just as if one were to turn a harmony into unison or a rhythm into a single metric foot. But while the city is a multiplicity, as was said before, one ought to make it communal and one through education. And it is bizarre that the very person who proposed to introduce an education, and believed that the city would be of high stature by that means, would suppose it could be set right by these sorts of arrangements, rather than by   40
customs, philosophy, and laws, the way the lawgiver made things pertaining to property communal in Sparta or Crete   1264A
by means of shared meals.

And one must not ignore this point, that one should pay particular attention to the long time and many years during which it could not have gone unnoticed if this was a beautiful way to do things. For practically everything has been discovered, though some things have not been understood, and others that people are aware of are not put to

use. The matter would become clear most of all if one could
see such a government being set up in fact, since it would
not be possible to produce the city without partitioning
and dividing it, into meal-sharing groups or into fraternal
organizations and clans. So if the law is adopted, nothing
10   else will result except that the guardians will not engage
in farming, the very thing the Spartans try to bring about
even now. But what form the government as a whole will
take for those associated with them, Socrates has not said,
and it is not easy to say. And yet the great mass of the city
comes pretty much from the mass of other citizens, about
whom nothing is determined as to whether property ought
to be held in common by the farmers or be held in private
by each one, or whether women and children ought to be
private or common. If everything is common to everyone in
the same way, what difference will there be between these
people and those guardians? What extra benefit will there be
for those who submit to their rule, or what reason will they
20   have for submitting to that rule, unless they come up with
some clever strategy such as the Cretans use? For the latter allow their slaves to have all the same things otherwise,
and only bar them from athletic exercise and bearing arms.
But if, as in other cities, they are going to have things like
that too, what form of association is there going to be? For
within one city there will necessarily be two cities, and these
opposed to each other. For he makes the guardians a sort of
corps on guard duty, while the farmers, craftsmen, and the
rest are the citizens, and the accusations and lawsuits and
all the other evils he says are present in cities will be present
among them too.

30   And yet Socrates speaks as though, as a result of education, they will have no need for a lot of regulations, such as
those governing policing and commercial transactions and
other such matters, even though he assigns an education
only to the guardians. Also, he puts the farmers in control of
their property as long as they pay a rent, but they are much
more likely to be fractious and full of opinions than the helots, serfs, and slaves some cities have. But as it is, nothing is
determined about whether it is necessary for these arrangements to be alike or not, or about matters connected with
these—what form of government, education, and laws these
citizens will have. And it is not easy to find out what sort of

people these are going to be, but it makes no small differ- 40
ence to the preservation of their association with the guardians. But if he is going to make women common while prop- 1264B
erty is private, who is going to manage the household the
way the men manage their fields? And this applies also if the
farmers' property *and* wives are common. And it is absurd to
draw an analogy from the animals to the effect that women
ought to have the same occupations as men, when they have
nothing to do with household management.

And it is risky to appoint the rulers the way Socrates
does, since he makes the same people rule permanently. This
becomes a cause of faction even among those who have no
prominence, and emphatically so, of course, with spirited 10
and warlike men. But it is obvious that he had to make the
same people rule, since it is not sometimes in some people
and other times in others that gold from the god is mixed in
their souls, but in the same people permanently. He claims
the god mixed gold in some right when they were born, silver in others, and bronze and iron in those who are meant to
be craftsmen and farmers. And even though he does away
with happiness in the case of the guardians,[77] he claims the
lawgiver ought to make the city as a whole happy; but it is
impossible for it to be happy as a whole when all its parts, or
most of them, or some of them have no happiness. For being
happy is not in the same class of things as evenness; for this 20
is capable of belonging to a whole but to neither of its parts,
while this is impossible with being happy. But if the guardians are not happy, who else is? Certainly not the craftsmen
and the mass of lowly workers. So the form of government
Socrates spoke about has these difficulties, as well as others
no less serious than they are.

Chapter 6

Things are pretty much along the same lines with the

---

77   It is Adeimantus who makes this claim in the *Republic* (419A), while
     Socrates cautions against believing it (420B), before granting it to
     make a more complex argument. Aristotle's opinion that happiness
     depends on virtue, and virtue on a harmony of divergent parts of the
     soul (*Nicomachean Ethics* 1098a 16-18, 1102b 27-28) is in fact closer to
     the argument Socrates gives, though he criticizes it here in the way
     he does throughout these chapters, from the standpoint of a practical
     political program.

Laws, but since it was written later, it would be better to take a little look at the form of government there as well. For Socrates has determined quite a small number of things in
30   the *Republic*, about the communal arrangement with women and children, how that ought to be done, and about property and the way the constitution is ordered. For he divides the mass of the population into two parts, one group consisting of farmers and the other the part that defends the city, and out of the latter comes the part that deliberates and has authority over it. As for whether the farmers and craftsmen should take part in no ruling functions at all or in some, and whether they too should bear arms and have a share in fighting wars or not, Socrates has determined nothing on these matters, although he does suppose the women ought to have a share in fighting wars and take part in the same education as the guardians. As far as the rest is con-
40   cerned, he has filled his discussion with extraneous matters,
1265A   and with detail about what sort of education the guardians ought to get. But in the *Laws* the greatest part deals precisely with laws, while it says few things about the form of government, and despite wanting to make this have more in common with cities, it little by little brings it back around toward the other government. For outside of the communal arrangement of women and property, he gives both forms of government the same provisions in other respects. They are the same as far as education is concerned, and in living a life free of necessary tasks, and likewise with common meals, except that this dialogue says there ought to be common
10   meals for women too. Also the one has a thousand people bearing arms and the other five thousand.[78]

Now while all Socrates' discourses have something extraordinary about them, something elegant that breaks fresh ground, and all in a spirit of inquiry, it is perhaps difficult to handle all subjects beautifully, since even in the case of

---

78   In the *Republic* (423A-C), Socrates says that even with only 1000 fighters, a city that is unified can be stronger than any other. In the *Laws* (737E), the Athenian Stranger picks 5040 as a likely number of heads of household prepared to go to war, in a territory of appropriate size for a city. Aristotle rounds off the Athenian Stranger's number, which is seven factorial, a number chosen to allow for exact division into parts in any way needed for purposes of military duties, taxes, or distributions.

the number just mentioned, one ought not to let pass unnoticed the fact that it would require a territory as big as that of
Babylon or some other place of boundless extent from which
they would feed five thousand men who do no work, as well
as another throng just as big of women and attendants surrounding them. And one ought to make hypothetical proposals however one wishes, but surely none that are impossible. It is said that the lawgiver ought to set down laws with
an eye on two things, the territory and the people. But it   20
would also be a beautiful thing to add a consideration of
the neighboring regions, first of all if the city has to live like
a city and not in isolation, since for war it will have to use
not only such arms as are useful in its own territory but in
the places outside it as well; but if one does not adopt such
a way of living, either as a private person or in the common
life of the city, it is still no less necessary to inspire fear in
enemies, and not just in those who invade their territory but
also when they go outside it.

And one ought to look at the amount of property as
well, whether it might be better to determine this differently
in some clearer manner. For he says it ought to be enough   30
to live moderately, as if one were to say enough to live well,
since that is more general. Yet it is possible to live moderately but wretchedly, and a better limit would be "with moderation and generosity" (for apart from the one, luxuriousness would result, and drudgery apart from the other), since
these are the only states of character worthy of choice that
have to do with the use of wealth; there is no such thing as
using wealth gently or courageously for example, but there
is such a thing as using it moderately and generously, so it is
necessary for these states of character to apply to it as well.

And it is also absurd for something that makes property equal to make no provision regarding the multitude
of citizens but to leave the production of children alone as   40
something that would be sufficiently balanced out at the
same amount, no matter how many are born, by cases of
childlessness, since it seems also to turn out that way now   1265B
with cities. But the degree of precision this matter needs is
not the same in this case as in those, for as things are, no one
does without because of the dividing up of estates among
whatever number there are, but in this case, where estates

are indivisible, excess children would necessarily get nothing, whatever greater or lesser number of them there may be. One might suppose that one ought to limit the production of children rather than wealth, so that no more than a certain number are born, setting this number with an eye on the chances that some of those born would turn out to
10   die, and on childlessness on the part of others. But leaving it alone, as is done in most cities, would necessarily become responsible for poverty among the citizens, and poverty brings in faction and crime. Pheidon of Corinth, who was one of the most ancient lawgivers, thought that even if all the portions of land had originally been unequal in size, the households ought to remain constant and equal to the number of citizens, but things are opposite in these *Laws*. But the way we believe things could be done better in these matters needs to be spoken of later.[79]

And concerning the rulers, how they are going to be different from those who are ruled is also left incomplete
20   in these *Laws*. It says it ought to be the same way the warp comes from different wool than the woof does, so that is the relation the rulers ought to have to those who are ruled.[80] Also, since it permits someone's entire wealth to become up to five times greater, why should this not be permitted up to some limit in the case of land? And one ought to consider whether the division of homesteads might not be advantageous to household management, for it allots two homesteads to each property owner, broken up in separate places, but it is difficult to maintain two households.

The way the whole is organized is meant to be neither a democracy nor an oligarchy but a middle ground between them, which people call constitutional rule,[81] for the govern-

---

79   In Book VII, Chapters 5, 10, and 16.

80   The warp is the set of stiff parallel threads around which the more flexible threads of the woof are woven. At 734E-735A of the *Laws*, the Athenian Stranger makes the obvious comparison to steadfastness and softness of human character; in Plato's *Statesman*, beginning at 305E, the Eleatic Stranger extends the analogy to the characteristics of different human virtues.

81   This is the general term for any form of government (*politeia*), but it is commonly applied to democracies that are not pure but limited by constitutionally prescribed qualifications for holding ruling offices. See 1279a 37-b 4 below.

ment consists of those who bear arms. Now if it sets this
up as having the most in common with cities compared to   30
the rest of the forms of government, perhaps it has spoken
beautifully, but not so beautifully if it sets it up as the next
best form of government after the first-ranked one. For one
would probably give higher praise to that of the Spartans, or
even to one more aristocratic than that. Accordingly, some
people say that the best form of government is made up of a
mixture of all the forms, and they praise that of the Spartans
for that reason (for some claim it is made up of oligarchy,
monarchy, and democracy, calling the office of king monarchy and that of the elders oligarchy, while saying it is democratically ruled by virtue of the office of the ephors, since the
ephors come from the general populace, but others say the   40
office of the ephors is a tyranny, but the city is democratically ruled by virtue of the common meals and the rest of their
everyday life.)[82] But in these *Laws* it is said that the best form   1266A
of government ought to be put together out of democracy
and tyranny, which one ought not to take as forms of government at all, or else take as the worst of all. Those who mix
in more forms speak better, since the resulting form of government will be better when it is compounded out of more
elements. And in the next place, it obviously has nothing
monarchical at all about it, but is oligarchic and democratic,
though it tends to lean more toward oligarchy. This is clear
from the way those who rule are appointed. The practice of
drawing lots from among a chosen group is common to both
forms, but the fact that the wealthier people are required   10
to be in the assembly, appoint the rulers by their votes, and
do anything else that is the job of citizens, while the others
are relieved of those duties—that is oligarchic, and amounts
to an effort to have more of the rulers come from among
the wealthy and the highest rulers from the highest prop-

---

82   There were two kings in office at any time, with limited powers; their
     chief prerogative was to lead any military advance and trail any re-
     treat. Twenty-eight elders were chosen from among the hereditary
     landowners by shouts of the whole assembled population, and along
     with the two kings they formed a senate. The ephors (literally "su-
     pervisors"), five men chosen from among the common people, were
     introduced some time after the government was instituted, to hold the
     ultimate power; calling this office a tyranny is to regard it literally as a
     usurpation of the kingship, even though it was introduced by peaceful
     means.

erty classes. It also makes the choosing of the council oligarchic. For everyone is required to take part in the choice, but
to choose from among the first property class, and then an
equal number again from the second class; then they choose
from the third, except that not everyone from the third or
fourth class was required to vote, and only those from the
first and second class were required to choose from among
those in the fourth class. Then from among these it says they
20   need to bring out an equal number from each class. So it
will be the case that more candidates, and better ones, will
be chosen by those from the highest property classes, since
some of those in the general populace will not be voting because it is not required.[83]

That such a form of government ought not to be organized out of democracy and monarchy is also clear from
these considerations, as well as from others that will be spoken of later, whenever the investigation applies to that sort
of government.[84] And on the matter of choosing rulers, having them chosen from among a chosen group also has a danger. For if some people want to join together, even if there
is only a moderate number, choices will always be made as
they wish. So this is the way things are in regard to the form
30   of government in the *Laws*.

Chapter 7

There are also certain other forms of government,
some described by private persons and others by philosophers and people engaged in politics, all of which are closer
than those two to established forms under which people are
governed. For no one else has introduced novel ideas about
having children and women in common or about common
meals for women; instead, they start from matters of necessity. To some the matter of landed estates seems to be the
most important thing to get beautifully arranged, since they
claim that all factional divisions are produced over these.

---

83   The entire process was to extend over several days, so those needing
to earn a living would not be likely to be present at its later stages,
when the richer citizens would be choosing the nominees for the council positions reserved for the poorer classes.

84   The most directly relevant passage is perhaps 1284a 3-b25, on the in-
compatibility of democracy and monarchy.

Phaleas the Chalcedonian was the first to make a proposal
about this; he declared that citizens ought to have equal   40
properties. He supposed this would not be difficult to do   1266B
right off while cities were being founded, but more troublesome for those already established, but that they could still
be quickly equalized by having the rich give dowries but not
get them and the poor get them but not give them. Plato, in
writing the *Laws*, supposed one ought to allow estates up to
a certain size, but that none of the citizens should be entitled to possess more than five times as much as the smallest
estate, as was mentioned above. But those who make laws
of this sort ought not to overlook this point, which they do
overlook now, that it is the duty of those who set limits to   10
the size of an estate to set limits also to the quantity of children. For if the number of children gets beyond the capacity
of the estate, it is necessary for the law to be nullified, and
apart from the nullification, it is bad policy to have a lot of
people go from being rich to being poor, since it is hard work
to keep such people from being rebellious.

   That a uniformity of wealth has some power over a
political association is something that some of the ancients
were obviously aware of; Solon, for instance, made laws
about it, and there is a law among others that prevents one
from acquiring as much land as one wants, and similarly,
laws that prevent the selling of one's estate. Along these lines
is the law among the Locrians that one may not sell an es-   20
tate unless one can demonstrate a clear misfortune that has
befallen him, and also laws to maintain intact the original
allotments of land. It was also the rescinding of this law in
Leucas that made their form of government too democratic,
since the result was that people no longer entered into ruling
offices from the designated property classes. But it is possible where an equality of wealth is present for the amount to
be either too great, and lead to luxuriousness, or too small,
and lead people to live shabby lives. It is clear, then, that it is
not enough for the lawgiver to make wealth equal; he needs
to aim at a mean. And even if one were to ordain moderate
wealth for everyone, it would not do any good; one would
need to make desires equal rather than estates, but this is   30
not possible where people are not adequately educated by
their laws. But perhaps Phaleas would say that this is exactly what he was talking about, since he believed equality

needed to be present in cities in these two things together, property and education. But one needs to say what the education is going to be, and it would do no good for it to be one and the same, since it is possible to have it be the same and one and still be of such a kind that people will come out of it with an inclination to choose to outdo other people in money or honor or both.

Also, people engage in factional conflict because of inequality not only in property but also in honors, though for
40 an opposite reason in each case; for the majority of people
1267A do so over property because it is unequal, but those who feel a cut above the rest do so over honors if they are equal, whence the line "in single honor whether bad or worthy."[85] And human beings are not unjust only because of necessities, for which he regards equality of wealth as a remedy, so that people will not steal because they are cold or hungry, but also in order to feel pleasures and not desires. For if they have a desire for more than what is necessary, curing it will make them be unjust, and that is not the only reason, but even without desires, they may be unjust in order to enjoy pleasures without pains. So what is the remedy for
10 these three sorts of people? For one sort, modest wealth and employment, for the other moderation, and in the third case, if some might want to enjoy pleasures depending on themselves they should not look for a remedy other than from philosophy, since the other pleasures need people. In fact, people commit the greatest injustices on account of excesses and not on account of necessities; they do not become tyrants, for instance, so they will not be cold. And this is why the honors are great not when someone kills a thief but when he kills a tyrant. So the technique of Phaleas's form of government is helpful only with regard to minor injustices.

Also, for the most part he wants to make arrangements by which people will be beautifully governed among themselves, but it is necessary also to have regard to their neigh-
20 bors and all those outside the city. Therefore, it is necessary for the government to be organized with a view to strength in warfare, about which he has said nothing. And likewise in the matter of property, there needs to be a sufficient amount available not only for uses related to the city but also to meet

85   Achilles' complaint at *Iliad* IX, 319.

external dangers. And for just this reason the amount available ought not to be so large that those nearby and more powerful will desire it, while they who have it will not be able to ward off the attackers, or so small that they will not be able to sustain a war even with those like them and equal in strength. So while he has determined nothing about it, one must not overlook this matter of what amount of wealth is advantageous. And perhaps the best limit is an amount   30
such that the excess will give those who are more powerful no profit-motive to go to war, so it would be the same as if they did not even have that much wealth. For example, when Autophradates was about to besiege Atarneus, Euboulus urged him to consider how much time he would spend taking the place and reckon up the expense of that time; he himself, if he got a smaller sum than that, was willing to surrender Atarneus immediately. And by saying these things, he made Autophradates reconsider and give up the siege.

So having estates be equal is one of the things that contributes to preventing the citizens from forming factions against one another, but it is by no means what one could call any big thing. For those who feel a cut above the rest   40
would even be annoyed at the idea that they deserved to be equal, which is obviously why they are so often aggressive and rebellious. And what is more, the corruption of human   1267B
beings is insatiable; at first a two obol subsidy[86] is enough by itself, but once this becomes a traditional practice, people constantly need more until they go beyond all bounds. For the nature of desire is infinite, and that is what most people devote their lives to satisfying. A more effective start on such matters than equalizing wealth would be to arrange things so that, while naturally decent sorts of people do not want to have more than others, the inferior sort do not have the power to, and this is the case if they are weaker but are not treated unjustly.

But he has not spoken beautifully even about the equality of wealth. For he equalizes property only in land,   10
but there are also riches in the form of slaves and cattle, and

---

86 An obol was 1/6 of a drachma (see note to 1259a 28). Members of the Athenian lower classes were given two obols to attend dramatic performances, and there is speculation that they also received subsidies in that amount at certain times as welfare payments.

currency as well, and a large stock of it in those items called equipment. So equality, or some moderate regulation, needs to be sought in all these things, or all of it needs to be left alone. And it is obvious from his lawgiving that he is setting up a small city, at least if all the skilled craftsmen are going to be public slaves and not make up any portion filling out the city. But if there ought to be public slaves at all, it ought to be in this way: as people engaged in public works, as at Epidamnus and as Diophantus once set up in Athens. As far as Phaleas's form of government is concerned, then, one can pretty much see from these remarks whether he has succeeded in saying anything beautifully or not.

Chapter 8

Hippodamus the Milesian, son of Euryphon, who devised a way of dividing cities and laid out the grid of the Peiraeus, became rather eccentric in other details of his life on account of a love of distinction—so much so that he seemed to some to be living too affectedly, long of hair, lavish of ornament, and yet in cheap but warm clothes not only in winter but around summertime as well, while professing to be an expert on the whole of nature. He was the first of those who had not run a city to try his hand at saying something about the best form of government. He designed a city of ten thousand men in size, divided into three parts, for he made one part skilled craftsmen, one farmers, and a third part to defend the city and bear arms. And he divided the territory into three parts: sacred, public, and private—a sacred part from which people would carry out the customary worship of the gods, a common part which the city's defenders would live off, and private land belonging to the farmers. And he believed that there are only three forms of laws as well, since the things over which cases at law arise are these three in number: outrage,[87] damage, and death. He also made a law that there would be one supreme court to which all lawsuits that were thought not to have been beautifully decided had to be referred, and he set this up to con-

---

87 The Greek word is *hubris*. Its legal meaning is defined by Aristotle in Bk. II, Chap. 2, of the *Rhetoric* as injury or insult committed out of cruelty in order to cause humiliation as well as harm. Athenian law treated it as a much more serious crime than offenses committed for the sake of gain or revenge, and it could even bring the death penalty.

sist of certain selected elders. And he believed judgments   1268A
in the lawcourts ought not to be arrived at by casting votes,
but each member should carry a tablet on which to write his
verdict, if he found the defendant guilty simply, but leave
it blank if he acquitted simply, and if it was not one way or
the other, he was to indicate this by making distinctions. For
he believed the way laws are now applied is not beautifully
done, since it forces people to commit perjury by judging
either this way or that. He also set down a law about those
who discover anything advantageous to the city, that they
should get an honor, and one that support for the children
of those killed in war should come from the public treasury,
in the belief that this had not yet been enacted into law by   10
anyone else (though this law is now in force in both Athens and other cities). All the rulers were to be chosen by the
populace, and the three parts of the city made up the populace; those selected were to look after common concerns and
matters pertaining to foreigners and orphans.

These, then, are most of the particulars of Hippodamus's scheme, and those most worthy of comment. One
might first raise a difficulty about his division of the multitude of citizens. For the craftsmen, farmers, and arms bear-
ers all share in the government, though the farmers have
no weapons and the craftsmen neither land nor weapons,   20
so they would practically become slaves of those who possessed the weapons. So for them to share all the offices would
be impossible, since the generals, the guardians of the citizens, and what one might call the offices of highest authority
would necessarily be appointed from among those bearing
arms. But how is it possible for people who have no share
in the government to be amicably disposed toward the government? "Well then, those who possess arms will just have
to be stronger than the other two parts together." But that is
not easy unless there are a lot of them, and if that is going to
be the case, why should the others share in the government
and have authority in the appointment of the rulers? And
how are the farmers of use to the city? Craftsmen would be   30
necessary, since every city has need of craftsmen, and they
would be able to survive the way they do in other cities, by
their skill. If the farmers were to provide sustenance to those
bearing arms they would reasonably have been made a part
of the city, but as it is designed, they have private property

and they will farm it for private use. And as for the common property from which the city's defenders will get their sustenance, if they are going to farm it themselves, there would be no difference between the fighting and farming parts, but the lawgiver intends there to be one; and if there are going to be some people who are different from both the private farmers and the fighters, this will be yet a fourth part
40   of the city, sharing in nothing, estranged from their form of government. But if one prescribes that the same people should farm both the private and the common property, the
1268B quantity of the crops from the land each one will farm will be inadequate for two households. Otherwise, why would they not just take their sustenance and supply the fighters too, straight from their own allotments of land? So all these matters have a lot of confusion in them.

And in regard to judging, the law that considers it right to decide cases by making distinctions, even when the charge is made simply, is not beautifully designed either, and the juror becomes an arbitrator. This is admissible in an arbitration, even by a number of people, since they confer with one another about the decision, but it is not possible in lawcourts; most lawmakers even make a provision opposed
10   to this that the jurors should not confer with one another. And then how will the decision not be confused, when a juror supposes the defended owes something, but not the amount the testimony claimed? It claims twenty minae, but the juror decides on ten (or it claims more and he decides on less), while another juror says five and still another four— and it is clear they will divide up in just that way—and some pass sentence for all of it but others for none. What is going to be the method for totaling up the votes? Anyway, nothing forces someone who simply acquits or condemns to commit perjury if the charge is drawn up simply, and justly so, since
20   the one who acquits is not judging that the accused owes nothing, but that he does not owe the twenty minae; but that person who condemns him without believing he owes the twenty minae is at that point committing perjury.

To make a law that those who discover something advantageous to the city ought to get an honor, though it seems attractive to hear, is not safe; for it has in it the seeds of misrepresentations and, it may so happen, changes in the form of government. But this runs into another problem and a different inquiry, for some people raise the difficulty whether it is harmful or advantageous to cities to change their hereditary laws, if something else is better. This is why it is not easy to go along without further ado with the law that is being spoken of, in case it is not advantageous to   30 change, and it is possible that some people would propose doing away with the laws or the constitution as a matter of common good. And since we have made mention of this, it would be better to go into a little more detail about it. For it has difficulty, as we said, and changing might seem to be better. In the other kinds of knowledge, at any rate, this has been beneficial, for instance for medicine to have changed from its hereditary practices, and gymnastic training as well, and all the arts and skills in general. So since politics too must be counted as one of these, it is clear that there must necessarily be something similar about it as well. And one might claim that a sign of this is right there in the facts themselves, for the ancient laws were overly simplistic   40 and barbaric. For the Greeks used to wear armor, and buy women from one another, and whatever is left anywhere of the ancient regulations is absolutely silly; in Cyme, for ex-   1269A ample, there is a law about homicide cases, that if someone bringing an accusation of murder produces a certain number of witnesses out of his own family, the person accused is guilty of murder. And in general, everyone is seeking not what is hereditary but what is good, and it is likely that the first people, whether they were sprung from the earth or survived some disaster, were like run-of-the-mill, unintelligent people, as is, in fact, said about those sprung from the earth, so that it would be absurd to stick to their opinions.

In addition to these things, it is not better to leave written laws unchanged either, for just as in the other arts, in a   10 political arrangement too it is impossible to write everything down with precision. For writing is necessarily universal, while actions are concerned with particulars. So it is obvious from these things that some laws ought to be changed at some times, but to those who look at it in another way, this would seem to be a matter for much caution. For when the better thing is something small, since it is bad to get people in the habit of undoing their laws lightly, it is obvious that some errors of the lawgivers and rulers ought to be left

alone. For one will not be benefitted as much by the changes as harmed by being habituated to disobey the rulers. And
20   the precedent from the arts is a false one, for changing an art is not like changing a law; for the law has no strength to be obeyed apart from habit, and this does not come about except through length of time. So to change easily from the existing laws to other, new laws is to make the power of the law weak. And further, even if they ought to be changed, ought all of them to be, and in every form of government, or not? And by any random person, or by which ones? For that makes a big difference. So let us let this inquiry go for now, since it is for other occasions.

Chapter 9

About the Spartans' form of government and the Cre-
30   tan form, and just about all the other forms of government as well, there are two things to examine. One is whether anything is set down beautifully or not in the laws with a view to the best way of arranging things, and the other is whether anything is at cross purposes with the underlying principle and way of going about things of the form of government they have proposed for themselves. It is agreed that leisure from necessities has to be present in a city that is going to be beautifully governed, but in what manner it is to be present is no easy thing to get hold of. For the Thessalians' serf class used to attack the Thessalians often, and the helots do the same to the Spartans (for it is as if they bide their time
40   lying in wait for their misfortunes), while with the Cretans no such thing has yet happened. The reason, perhaps, is that
1269B the neighboring cities, even though they make war on one another, are in no case allied with those who revolt, because it would not be to their advantage since they have surrounding dependent populations of their own. But all the Spartans' neighbors, the Argives, Messenians, and Arcadians, were hostile to them, and from the beginning there were revolts against the Thessalians because of their ongoing wars with the peoples living nearby, the Achaeans, Perrhaebeans, and Magnesians. And even if there were no other issues, the matter of their supervision, and what kind of dealings one ought to have with them, is likely to be troublesome; for if they are treated permissively they become insolent and re-

gard themselves as worthy of equality with those in author-   10
ity, but if they live lives of misery they form plots and feel
hatred. It is clear, then, that people whom this happens to
are not figuring out the best way to deal with serfdom.

Also, their permissiveness toward their women is
harmful both to the intention of their form of government
and to the happiness of the city. For just as a man and a
woman are part of a household, it is clear that one ought to
regard a city too as being divided nearly in two in its multitude of men and women; consequently, in those governments in which matters involving women are in a sorry state,
one ought to regard half the city as being unprovided for by
the laws. This is just what has happened there, for while the
lawgiver wanted the whole city to be capable of endurance,   20
and it is obviously that way as far as the men are concerned,
he has been utterly careless about the women. For they live
lives of luxury that are unrestrained in every way a life can
be unrestrained. So it is necessary that people will honor
wealth in such a form of government, especially when they
are in subjection to their women, as many of the military
and warlike races are (apart from the Celts and any others
there may be that openly hold sexual relations among men
in honor). For it seems that whoever first told the story was
not unreasonable in coupling Ares with Aphrodite, since all
such people are obviously obsessed with intercourse with   30
either males or females. So this was prevalent among the
Spartans, and when they were the dominant power, many
matters were managed by their women. And if the rulers
are ruled by their women, how is that different from having
women rule? It ends up being the same thing. Audacity is
useful in none of the ordinary routine of life, but if at all, in
war, but the Spartans' women were highly detrimental even
to that. They made this evident in the Theban invasion, for
they were not at all useful the way women in other cities
are, but caused more disturbance than the enemy. Now the
permissiveness toward their women seems to have turned   40
up among the Spartans from the beginning, understandably   1270A
so. For they were away for long times on campaigns outside
their own land, when they were waging war on the Argives
and then again on the Arcadians and Messenians. When
they were at leisure they submitted themselves to the lawgiver highly trained by the military life (for it involves many

parts of virtue), but where the women were concerned, they say that while Lycurgus tried to bring them under the laws, he gave up again because they were recalcitrant. So these are the causes of what happened, and consequently, obviously,
10   of what went wrong, but that is not what we are examining—whom one ought or ought not to make excuses for—but what is rightly or wrongly done.

And it seems likely, as was said before, that the fact that matters were not in a beautiful condition regarding the women not only produced a certain impropriety in their form of government in its own right but contributed in some degree to their greed for money. For following on the things just mentioned, one might criticize them for the disparity in their property. For some of them ended up owning too large an estate, and others a miniscule one, on account of which the land came into few hands. And this too has been badly
20   arranged by the laws, for he made it a dishonorable thing to buy or sell an existing estate, and did so rightly, but he gave anyone who wanted to give one away or bequeath it the license to do so, even though it necessarily ended up the same one way as the other. And in fact just about two-fifths of all the land belongs to women, since many have become heiresses and because of the giving of large dowries. And yet it would have been better to have arranged for none at all, or small or even moderate ones. But as things are, one is permitted to give an heiress in marriage to whomever one wants, and if he dies having made no such dispositions, whomever he leaves as his heir can give her to anyone he wishes. Consequently, though the land was capable of sup-
30   porting fifteen hundred cavalry and thirty thousand heavy infantry, they came to be not even a thousand in number. It has been made clear by the facts themselves that the provisions of this arrangement left them in bad shape, for the city did not hold up under a single blow, but was destroyed as a result of being undermanned. But they say that under their earlier kings they brought others into the government, and consequently did not become undermanned at that time, even when they were at war for a long time; they claim that at one time there were in fact ten thousand in the Spartiate class. Whether these things are true or not, the better way is nevertheless for the city to increase the number of men by
40   having property evened out. But the law about having chil-

dren is also an obstacle to getting this right. For the lawgiver, out of a desire for the Spartiate class to be as large as possible, encourages the citizens to produce as many children as
possible, for they have a law that anyone who has fathered
three sons is exempt from guard duty, and anyone who has
fathered four is exempt from all taxes. Yet it is obvious that
when many are born and the land is divided accordingly, it
is necessary that many become poor.

But matters pertaining to the institution of ephors are
badly arranged too. For this office is in charge on its own
of the greatest concerns among them, but it comes from the
whole populace, so that ordinary people of great poverty
often turn up on the board, people who because of their   10
hardship have been susceptible to bribery. They showed
this often, both in earlier times and recently among the
Andrians;[88] for some, who had been corrupted by money,
ruined the whole city as much they could. And because the
office was too great, equal in fact to a tyranny, even the kings
were forced to seek popularity with them, so that collateral
damage was done by this to their form of government, and
it ended up turning from an aristocracy into a democracy.
Now this board does hold the government together, since
the populace stays calm as a result of sharing in the highest office; so whether it is due to the lawgiver or to chance   20
that it has turned out this way, it has been conducive to their
interests. For if a form of government is going to survive, all
the parts of the city have to want it to exist and to continue
along the same lines. Now the kings are so inclined because
of the honor they have, the aristocracy[89] because of the court
of elders (for this office is a prize for virtue), and the populace because of the ephorate (for it is appointed from among
them all). And it was indeed right for the latter office to be

---

88   What Aristotle is referring to is not known, but there is speculation
that some ephors may have made a deal with Persian representatives
on the island of Andros, shortly before a major victory over the Persians by Alexander the Great. Spartan power had decisively diminished after an earlier defeat by the Thebans, and remained in continual
decline during Alexander's ascendancy.

89   Literally "the beautiful and good," a common way Greek aristocracies referred to themselves, used here for the hereditary ruling class
called Spartiates. At 1271a 23 below it is used literally, as was the corresponding noun at 1259b 34-35 above.

chosen from among all the people, but not in the way it actually is chosen, which is too childish.[90] What is more, though
they are random people, they are sovereign in major judg-
30   ments, which is exactly why it would have been better to
have them judge not at their own discretion but in accord
with written regulations and laws. And the way the ephors
live is not in agreement with the tendency of the city, since
it is itself too permissive, while among the rest of the people
the tendency is to go too far in the direction of severity instead, so much so that they are not able to endure it but se-
cretly evade the law in order to enjoy bodily pleasures.

And what pertains to their office of the elders is not
beautifully arranged either. For assuming that they are decent people and adequately educated in manly virtue, one
would probably say the office is advantageous to the city,
though having them be in authority throughout life in ma-
40   jor decisions is a debatable point (for there is old age in the
1271A thinking power too, just as there is in the body). But when
the way they have been educated makes the lawgiver himself
doubtful about whether they are good men, it is not safe. It
is obvious that those who have shared this office have taken
bribes and shown favoritism in many matters involving the
common interest. This is exactly why it is better that they not
be exempt from review, as they are now. And it might seem
good to have the office of the ephors review all the offices,
but this is too great a grant of power to the ephorate, and it
is not in this way that we are saying one ought to assign the
powers of review. And furthermore, the choice which they
10   make for the elders is childish in the way it is decided,[91] and
it is not right for anyone who would be considered worthy
of the office to beg for it himself, for the person worthy of the
office ought to hold office whether he wants to or not. But
actually the lawgiver is obviously doing the very thing he
also does with the rest of the constitution; for he makes the
citizens ambitious for honor and uses this for the choice of

90   In Plato's *Laws* (692A) the Athenian Stranger says the ephorate
amounted to an office chosen by lot. At 1317b 17-21 below, Aristotle
says that choosing rulers by lot is characteristic of democracy. Elections, which permit the voters to take merit into account, imply that
people are not all equal.

91   By the loudest shouts of the whole assembled populace.

elders, since no one who was not ambitious for honor would beg to hold office. And yet, of the deliberate acts of injustice committed by human beings, just about the greatest number result from ambition for honor and greed for money.

As for kingship, and whether it is better for it to be present in cities or not, let that be another discussion, but it is certainly better that it not be present in the way it is now, but for each of the kings to be determined on the basis of his own life. It is clear that even the lawgiver does not think it is possible to make them beautiful and good; he lacks trust in them at any rate, as if they would not be sufficiently good men. That is why they sent out their adversaries as fellow ambassadors, and considered having kings engaged in factional conflict something that preserved the city.[92]

The laws about the common meals, the so-called "phiditia,"[93] were not made beautifully either by the one who first established them. The gathering ought to have been at common expense instead, the way it is in Crete; with the Spartans, each person has to bring something, even though some of them are exceedingly poor and not able to pay the cost, so that the lawgiver gets the opposite of the result he intended. For he wants the set-up of the common meals to be democratic, but the way the law is designed it becomes the least democratic it can be. For it is not easy for the very poor to participate, but the traditional limit on the government among them is this: someone who is unable to bear this expense cannot take part in it.

Some others have objected to the law about naval commanders, and objected to it rightly, since it becomes a cause of faction. For on top of the kings, who are permanent generals, the naval command has practically established another kingship.

One might also object to this underlying principle the lawgiver adopted (the very objection Plato has made in the *Laws*), namely that the whole organization of the laws is di-

20

30

40

1271B

---

92 The first part of the sentence probably refers to the practice of sending some ephors along on military campaigns to participate in negotiations with the enemy, the second to rivalries between the two kings and their adherents.

93 There are two opinions about the meaning of this name, making them either "friendly" or "frugal" meals.

rected at a part of virtue, the military part, since this is useful
for conquering. Consequently, they were preserved as long
as they were fighting wars, but they were destroyed once
they were ruling, because they did not know how to live
at leisure and had not had any other training directed at a
higher end than the military sort. And it is an error no lesser
than this that, while they hold the good things people fight
over as coming from virtue rather than from vice, and this is
a beautifully held, they assume these things are more impor-
10   tant *than* virtue, which is not beautiful thinking.

Also, things are in bad shape for the Spartiates in the
matter of common funds. For there is nothing in a common
treasury for the city even when they are forced to fight great
wars, and they are bad about paying taxes. For since most
of the land belongs to the Spartiates, they do not look too
closely into the taxes paid by one another. The upshot of this
for the lawgiver has been the opposite of beneficial, because
he has produced a city devoid of funds and private citizens
greedy for money. So let the discussion of the Spartans' form
of government go this far, since these are the things one
might most object to about it.

Chapter 10

20   The Cretan form of government is pretty close to this
one, and while it has a few features that are no worse, for the
most part it is less polished. It seems likely and is in fact said
that the Spartans' form of government is in most respects an
imitation of the Cretan one, and in most cases ancient things
are less fully worked out than newer ones. People say that
Lycurgus, when he left off the trusteeship of King Charillus
and went abroad, spent most of his time on Crete because of
his family connection. For the Lyctians were Spartan colonists, and those who went to the colony took up the array
30   of laws already present among the people living there at
the time. This is why the subject population follows them in
the same way even today, in the belief that Minos first established their array of laws.

The island seems both naturally suited and beautifully
situated for rule over the Greek world; for it sits across the
whole sea, and just about all the Greeks are settled around
the sea. It is a little way from the Peloponnese in one di-

rection, and in another from the region of Asia around the Triopian promontory and Rhodes. Hence Minos established an empire over the sea, subduing some islands and settling others, and in the end he attacked Sicily and ended his life there near Camicus.   **40**

The Cretan arrangement is analogous to the Spartan one. The helots do the farming for the latter and the subject population for the Cretans, and there are common meals in both places, which in ancient times the Spartans called not "phiditia" but men's clubs, exactly as the Cretans do, which also makes it clear that they came from there. And the arrangement of their form of government did as well, for the ephors have the same power as the so-called cosmoi[94] in Crete, except that in number the ephors are five while the cosmoi are ten. The elders are equivalent to the Cretans' elders, whom they call the council. There was previously a kingship, but the Cretans later abolished it, and the cosmoi hold the leadership in war. Everyone takes part in an assembly, but it has no authority other than to ratify the enactments of the elders and cosmoi.   **1272A**   **10**

Arrangements for the common meals are better designed among the Cretans than among the Spartans. For in Sparta, each contributes the prescribed amount per person or else the law prohibits him from taking part in the government, as was said above, but in Crete things are done in a more communal way. From all the crops and livestock yielded by the public lands, and from the levies paid by the subject peoples, part is assigned to the gods and communal public service and part to the common meals, so that all of them—women, children, and men—are supported from the common supply. The lawgiver designed many measures with the philosophic view that moderation in eating is beneficial, and also for the segregation of women so they would not have many children, bringing about sexual relations among men; on that matter, there will be another occasion to examine whether his thinking was shoddy or not.[95]   **20**

So it is clear that matters pertaining to the common

---

94   This might perhaps be translated "bastions of order."

95   This is not a reference to a later passage but a dismissal of the subject with a hint of Aristotle's opinion.

meals are better arranged among the Cretans than among the Spartans, but matters pertaining to the cosmoi are even worse than with the ephors. For the bad feature the board
30   of ephors has belongs to them as well (since random people become cosmoi), but the thing that is advantageous there is absent here. There, because the choice is from among them all, the populace shares in the highest office and wants the form of government to remain as it is; but here they do not choose the cosmoi from among them all but from certain families, and the elders from those who have been cosmoi. And one might state the same arguments about them as about those who become elders in Sparta: for them to be exempt from review and serve throughout life is a privilege beyond what they deserve, and for them to rule not by written laws but at their own discretion is unsafe. The fact
40   that the populace stays calm even though they do not share in the office is no sign that things are beautifully arranged. There is no monetary profit to be had by the cosmoi as there
1272B is with the ephors, since they live on an island, far away from potential corruptors.

What they do as a remedy for this fault is absurd and characteristic not of constitutional but dictatorial[96] rule. For often some people, either some of their fellow-rulers themselves or private persons, conspire and oust the cosmoi, and it is also open to the cosmoi to abdicate their office in mid-term. It would be better for all these things to take place in accord with law rather than at the will of human beings, which is not a safe standard. The worst of them all is the practice of the suspension of the cosmoi[97] by the powerful, which they often put in place when they do not want to abide by a legal
10   judgment; from this it is clear that while their arrangement has some semblance of a constitution it is not constitutional government but rather a confederacy of the powerful. They are in the habit of introducing divisions between the populace and their friends in order to bring about anarchy, fo-

---

96   *Dunasteutikê*, characteristic of a *dunasteia*, or small group of arbitrary rulers (see Bk. IV, Chaps. 5-6 below). Not a dynasty but a shared tyranny. It is absurd in that, as a remedy for arbitrariness among lawfully chosen rulers, it substitutes arbitrary rule by a few powerful usurpers.

97   "Suspension of the cosmoi" (*akosmia*) is also the word for disorder. So a few powerful citizens can dissolve the government by declaring it ineffective.

ment factions, and fight among themselves. Yet what difference is there between this sort of thing and having the city no longer be a city for a certain length of time, which means doing away with the political association?

A city in this condition is in danger from those who want to attack it and have the power to do so. But as was said, it is kept safe by its location, since its remoteness has had the effect of a ban on foreigners. This is also the reason the subject population remains under the Cretans while the helots frequently rebel. For the Cretans take no part in external imperial rule, and only recently has a foreign war crossed over to the island, which has made the weakness of the laws there evident. So let this much be said by us about this form of government.

Chapter 11

The Carthaginians are also thought to be beautifully governed in many ways that are exceptional in comparison to those of other people, and especially in some ways that approximate those of the Spartans. For these three forms of government are in some way close to one another and much different from the rest: the Cretan, the Spartan, and third among them that of the Carthaginians. Many of the arrangements work beautifully among them, and it is a sign of an orderly form of government that the populace remain within the order the constitution prescribes and that no factional division that is even worth mentioning has come about, and no tyrant. The resemblances it has to the Spartan form of government include the common meals of their clubs, like the phiditia, the office of the hundred and four, like the ephors (but not worse, for the latter are taken from among random people but they choose this office on basis of excellence), and the kings and council of elders, analogous to the kings and elders there, but also better in that the kings are not a family of their own, and that a random one, but chosen from among those that happen to excel in any manner, rather than by age. For they are put in authority over great matters, and if they are mediocre people they can do great damage, and such people have already damaged the city of the Spartans.

Now most of the objections that may be made to it for

deviations happen to be common to all the forms of government mentioned. Of things that deviate from the underlying principle of aristocracy and constitutional government, some incline it more in the direction of the populace, others toward oligarchy. Over the question of what to refer or not refer to the people, the kings along with the elders are in charge, if they are all in agreement, but if they are not, the populace is in charge of those things. And on whatever

10   measures they do bring to the people, they allow them not just to hear things enacted by the rulers, but the people are in charge of deciding on them, and it is open to anyone who wishes to speak against the things proposed, which is precisely what cannot happen in the other governments. On the other hand, the fact that committees of five, which are in charge of many great matters, are self-appointed, while they choose the greatest office, that of the hundred, and also rule for a longer time than the rest (both after those have left office and before they enter it) is oligarchic. But the fact that they are unpaid and not chosen by lot must be set down as aristocratic, along with anything else there might be of that sort, as well as the fact that all lawsuits are judged by

20   the rulers (and not different kinds by different persons as in Sparta). The arrangement the Carthaginians have that deviates most from aristocracy toward oligarchy follows a certain line of thought which seems good to many people, for they believe one ought to choose rulers not only on the basis of excellence but also on the basis of wealth, because it is impossible for someone without resources to do a beautiful job of ruling and have the leisure for it. So if choosing on the basis of wealth is oligarchic and according to virtue is aristocratic, a third arrangement would be this one by which things pertaining to the government are organized by the Carthaginians, since they make the choice with an eye on

30   these two things, especially for the highest offices, the kings and generals.

But one ought to consider this deviation from aristocracy an error on the part of the lawgiver. For this is one of the most necessary things to see to from the beginning, how the best people will be enabled to be at leisure and not do anything demeaning, not only while they are ruling but even in private life. But if one does have to look also to abundance of resources for the sake of leisure, it is a bad thing for the highest of offices, kingship and military command, to be for sale. For this law causes wealth to be held in honor more than virtue, and turns the whole city into a money-loving place. Whatever the authoritative part of the city assumes is valu- **40** able, the opinion of the rest of the citizens will necessarily follow theirs. And wherever virtue is not honored most of all, it is impossible for that place to have a stable aristocratic **1273B** government. It stands to reason that those who lay money out will get used to making a profit, when they rule as a result of buying the position. For if someone who is poor but honest will want to get a profit, it would be strange if someone who is worse would not want to after he has spent money. Hence those capable of ruling excellently[98] ought to be the ones to rule. And even if the lawgiver has neglected the resources of decent people, it would still be better to take care for their leisure, at least while they rule.

And it would also seem to be a bad thing for the same person to rule in more than one office, yet that very thing is prestigious among the Carthaginians. For one job is car- **10** ried out best by one person. The lawgiver ought to see that this happens, and not assign the same person to play the flute and be a shoemaker. So where the city is not tiny, it is more suited to political life, as well as more democratic, for more people to share in ruling; for it is both more commu- nal, as we said, and each person carries out his own tasks more beautifully and quickly. This is clear among members of armies and navies, for in both of these, ruling and being ruled spread out to virtually everyone.

And while the government is oligarchic, they avoid faction in a most effective way because some part of the populace is always getting rich when they send people out to the cities, since by this means they cure the problem and **20** make the government stable. But this is the work of chance, while they ought to be free of faction on account of the law- giver. As things are, if some misfortune were to arise and a large number of those who are ruled revolted, there is no remedy through the laws to restore calm.

So this is the way it is with the Spartans' form of gov-

---

98   The translation follows the manuscripts; Ross emends to "those ca- pable of using idle time best."

ernment, the Cretan one, and that of the Carthaginians, which are indeed justly highly regarded.

Chapter 12

Among those who have declared themselves in any way about government, some took no part in any political actions whatever, but lived out their lives as private persons.

30   As far as there is anything worth saying about them, it has already been said about pretty much all of them. But some became lawgivers, either for their own cities or for certain foreign ones as well, entering the political realm themselves. Some of these became craftsmen of laws only, but others, such as Lycurgus and Solon, of governments as well, for they established laws and governments too. That of the Spartans has been spoken of. In the case of Solon, some believe him to have been a lawgiver of great stature, since he abolished an oligarchy that was too unmixed, stopped the populace from being enslaved, and established a democracy bound by tradition, producing a beautifully mixed form of government—

40   for the council of the Areopagus is oligarchic, the election of rulers is aristocratic, and the lawcourts are democratic. And

1274A   it seems that Solon refrained from abolishing those elements that were present beforehand, the council and the election of rulers, but established the populace in power by making the lawcourts come from all the people. And some people criticize him for this, on the grounds that he destroyed the other institutions by making the lawcourt, which was selected by lot, sovereign over everything. For when this became strong, by gratifying the populace as though it were a tyrant, they transformed the government into the present democracy. Ephialtes curtailed the power of the council of the Areopagus and so did Pericles, and Pericles instituted payments for

10   jury duty; and in this way each of the popular leaders made an advance in growing the city into the present democracy.

But it appears that this did not happen in accord with Solon's intention but instead just fell out that way. For when the populace had been responsible for naval supremacy in the Persian Wars, it became arrogant and took up inferior men as popular leaders when decent men had policies opposed to its wishes. Solon though, at any rate, seems to have granted the populace only the most necessary power, that of electing and reviewing their rulers, for a populace that was not in authority even over this would be a slave and an enemy. But he set things up for all the rulers to come from among distinguished and well-off people, from owners of extensive lands, owners of teams of oxen, and from a third   20 class called horsemen; but the fourth class, the menials, had no share in office.[99]

Zaleucus became a lawgiver for the Italian Locrians, and Charondas of Catana for his own fellow-citizens and for the other Chalcidian cities in Italy and Sicily. Some people try to connect them, on the grounds that Onomacritus, a Locrian living abroad in pursuit of his art of soothsaying, first became proficient at lawgiving by being trained in Crete, that Thales became a companion of his, and that Lyc- urgus and Zaleucus were students of his and Charondas of   30 Zaleucus; but they say these things with too little attention to the dates. Philolaus the Corinthian became a lawgiver for the Thebans. Philolaus was of the family of the Bacchiads and was a lover of Diocles who had been victorious in the Olympic games. When Diocles, in abhorrence of his moth- er Alcyone's lust, left the city and went to Thebes, he and Philolaus both lived out their lives there. Even now people point out their tombs, each easily visible from the other, but one with and the other without a view toward the land of the Corinthians, and story they tell is that the men them- selves arranged the burial that way, Diocles, out of hatred   40 of the passion, so that Corinth would not be visible from his mound and Philolaus so it would be visible from his. So   1274B they came to live among the Thebans for this sort of reason, and Philolaus became a lawgiver for them both on certain other matters and on the procreation of children, framing what they call the laws on adoption; this is legislation de- signed in a way peculiar to him so that the number of inher- ited estates would be kept constant.

There is nothing peculiar to Charondas except lawsuits for perjury, for he was the first to make this a legal charge,

---

99   Solon's laws formalized four classes of citizens. The first owned suf- ficient land to yield 500 measures of agricultural produce per year; the second (Aristotle reverses the order of the middle two classes) owned enough land to maintain horses and serve as cavalry; the third farmed some land of their own; the fourth, the general populace, had to work for others.

but in the precision of his laws he is more polished than even the lawgivers of the present day. Peculiar to Phaleas is the equalization of properties; to Plato, the community of women, children, and property, common meals for women, and also the law about drunkenness, that sober people should be in charge of drinking parties, as well as one about training for military service in such a way as to make people become ambidextrous by practice, since one of a pair of hands ought not to be useful while the other is useless. And there are Draco's laws, but he framed his laws for an existing constitution; there is nothing in his laws at all worthy of mention apart from the harshness due to the size of the penalty.[100] Pittacus also became a craftsman of laws but not of a constitution; a law peculiar to him is one that requires people who are drunk to pay a greater penalty if they transgress than those who are sober. For since more people commit violent outrages when drunk than when sober he did not look kindly on the excuse that one ought to be more forgiving of those who are drunk, but looked to what would do some good. And Androdamas of Rhegium became a lawgiver for the Chalcidians in Thrace; their laws about homicides and heiresses are his, but there is nothing peculiar to him in them that one could name. So on matters concerning forms of government, both those holding sway and those described by some people, let them have been held up to view in this way.

---

100 Draco was considered Athens' first lawgiver, a generation before Solon. The penalty in the Draconian laws is referred to in the singular because it was death for all crimes. Legend has it that when asked why he assigned this penalty to all offenses, he said, "Because I had none greater."

Book III

Chapter 1

For someone examining what each form of government is and what its character is, nearly the first question to look into concerns the city, and what a city is. For as things stand, people have disputes, with some claiming the city carried out an action while others claim it was not the city but the oligarchy or the tyrant. We see all the activity of the politician or lawgiver being concerned with the city, and a form of government is a particular arrangement of those who live in the city. But since a city is in the class of composite things, and like any of the other composite wholes **40** is made up of many parts, it is clear that a prior topic of inquiry is the citizen, since a city is a multitude of citizens. **1275A** Consequently, whom one should call a citizen and what a citizen is need to be examined. For the citizen too is often a matter of dispute, because not everyone agrees that the same person is a citizen. There are many instances in which someone who is a citizen in a democracy is not a citizen in an oligarchy. Now those who receive this title in any qualified sense, such as adopted citizens, need to be left aside, and the citizen is not a citizen by living in a place (for resident aliens and slaves also share the living area). Also, citizens are not those who share in legal rights to the extent that they can be sued and bring lawsuits (for this belongs also to those par- **10** ticipate as a result of treaties, and in many places even resident aliens do not share these rights fully, but need to have a sponsor, and so they participate in this form of association in an incomplete manner). It is the same as with children who have not yet been put on citizenship rolls on account of age and old people who have been relieved of obligations; they need to be called citizens in a sense, though not just simply but with a qualification added—"immature" or "retired" or anything else of the sort (it makes no difference since the meaning is clear).

We are looking for the citizen in an unqualified sense

20 and not one who has any blemish on his title of a sort that needs to be explained away, since even with people who have been deprived of civic rights or exiled it is possible to raise and resolve questions of that kind. And a citizen in an unqualified sense is defined by no other single thing more than by taking part in judging and ruling. And while some ruling offices are divided up according to time in such a way that the same person is not permitted to hold certain ones twice, or within certain specified times, other offices, such as those of juror or assembly member, are unlimited. Perhaps someone might claim that such people are not rulers and do not take part in any ruling office on account of these positions, yet it would be ridiculous to deprive those with the highest authority of rulership. But let it make no difference,

30 since the argument is about a name. For there is no common name for a juror and an assembly member by which one ought to refer to them both; so for the sake of a definition let the name be unlimited office. And so we set it down that citizens are those who take part in office in this manner.

So the definition that best fits all those called citizens is pretty much like that, but one ought not to overlook the fact that in things whose underlying principles differ in kind, with one of them primary, another secondary, and another following that, a common element, insofar as they are of that sort, is present in them either not at all or hardly at all. And we do see that forms of government differ from one

1275B another in kind, with some being less primary and others more, since the ones that are faulty and deviant are necessarily less primary than the ones that are without fault. (It will be clear later in what sense we mean "deviant.") So it is necessary that a citizen would also be something different in each form of government. Hence the person described is a citizen in a democracy most of all, and may be, but is not necessarily a citizen in other governments. The populace has no role in some constitutions; they do not customarily hold an assembly except those that are specially called, and they partition the judging of lawsuits. In Sparta for instance, different ephors judge different cases involving contracts, the elders judge cases of homicide, and some other office may judge other cases. It is the same way in Carthage as well, for all the offices have certain lawsuits that they judge. But the definition of a citizen has a way of being revised, since in the other forms of government it is not a ruler with an unlimited term who is an assembly member or juror, but one who is limited in office. For either all or some of these are assigned the task of deliberating and judging on either all matters or certain ones. So it is clear from these things who a citizen is, for we say that one who has a right to share in deliberative and judicial rule is for that reason a citizen of that city, and a city, to put it simply, is a multitude of such people adequate for self-sufficiency in life.

Chapter 2

But by usage, people define a citizen as someone born of citizens on both sides and not just one, whether father or mother, while some trace this even farther back, to two or three or more generations of grandparents. But when the definition is made in this way, for political purposes and roughly, some people raise the question of how that third or fourth ancestor is going to be a citizen. So Gorgias of Leontini, perhaps in some respects recognizing the force of the question while in other respects being ironic, said that just as mortars are what are made by mortar-makers, so too Larissaeans are what are made by craftsmen, since some of them are Larissa-makers.[101] It is, however, a simple matter; if the ancestors took part in the government in accord with the stated definition, they were citizens. It is not possible to make "born of a citizen father" or "born of a citizen mother" fit the first inhabitants or founders.

But perhaps that question involves more difficulty for those who began their participation when a revolution took place, such as those whom Cleisthenes made Athenians af-

---

101 The ordinary word for craftsman is *demiourgos*, a public workman as opposed to a household slave or servant, but some cities used the same word for their officials, with a meaning similar to our own phrase "public servant." Hence Gorgias was making the point that citizens are any people the current office holders say they are.

ter the expulsion of the tyrants, for he adopted many foreigners and immigrant slaves into the tribes. The point of dispute about them is not who is a citizen but whether they are citizens unjustly or justly. And yet one might still

1276A raise that original question as well, whether someone who is not justly a citizen is a citizen at all, on the grounds that "unjust" has the same force as "fake." But since we also see some people ruling unjustly, whom we claim do rule, but not justly, and the citizen is defined by a certain sort of rule (for someone who has a share in that particular kind of rule is a citizen, as we assert), it is clear that one must call those people citizens too.

Chapter 3

The matter of "justly or not justly" is connected with a point of dispute mentioned above. For some people raise the question of when the city performed an action and when it was not the city, for instance after a democracy comes into

10 being from an oligarchy or tyranny. For at such a time, some people do not want to fulfill agreements, on the grounds that they were undertaken not by the city but by the tyrant, or to do many other such things, on the grounds that some forms of government exist by force but not for the common advantage. But then if some cities are ruled democratically in that same manner, one must say that the acts of this government and those stemming from the oligarchy and the tyranny are all alike acts of the city. But the argument seems to be akin in some respects to that difficulty about when one should say the city is the same, or not the same but different.

20 And the most superficial way of inquiring into the question is concerned with the place and the people, since the place and people are capable of being split up, with some living in one area and others in another. So this is too glib a way for the question to be settled (for since a "city" is spoken of in more than one sense, inquiring in that way has an easy time of it). And similarly in the case of human beings occupying the same place: when ought one to regard them as being one city? For that is certainly not determined by the walls, since it would be possible to put up one wall around the Peloponnese. And perhaps Babylon is an instance of this sort, and every place that has the compass of a nation rather

than a city; people claim that on the third day after it was   **30**
conquered, a certain part of the city was unaware of the fact.

But an examination into this question will be useful on
another occasion (for someone skilled at politics ought not
to overlook the matter of the size of the city, both the number
of people and whether it is advantageous for them to be of
one or more nationalities). But when the same people occupy the same place, should they be said to be the same city
as long as the occupants are of the same stock, despite the
fact that some are always perishing and others being born,
on the same basis that we are accustomed to speak of rivers
and streams as the same even though water is always flowing in and flowing out? Or should it be said for that sort of   **40**
reason that the people are the same but the city is different?   **1276B**
For if the city is in fact a certain type of association, and this
is an association of citizens within a form of government,
when this comes to be of another kind and is a different form
of government, it would seem that the city too is necessarily
not the same, just as we claim that a chorus is different when
it is comic on one occasion and tragic on another, though it
is often made up of the same people. And it is similar with
every other kind of association and every other composite
thing if the form of the composite is different; we say, for
instance that a musical scale made up of the same tones is
different if it is Dorian in one case and Phrygian in the oth-
er.[102] So if this is how it is, it is clear that a city is to be called   **10**
the same with a view to its form of government most of all; it
is possible to call it by a different name even when it has the
same occupants, and by the same one even when it consists
of entirely different human beings. But whether it is *just* to
fulfill or not fulfill agreements when the city changes to a
different form of government is different story.

Chapter 4

Connected with the things now being spoken of is an
examination of whether the virtue of a good man and that

---

102 A Greek scale consisted of interlocking perfect fourths divided into
     sub-intervals. Even when all the tones used are the same, the choice of
     different fundamental tones could produce music in different modes.
     Aristotle describes some differences among the modes at 1340a 40-b 5
     below.

of an excellent citizen should be held to be the same or not the same. But surely if this topic needs to get an inquiry, the virtue of a citizen needs to be grasped first in some sort of
20   outline. And just as a sailor is one in a group of associated people, so too do we claim a citizen is. And despite the fact that sailors are dissimilar in capacity (since one is a rower, another a helmsman, another a lookout man, and another has some other such title), it is clear that while the most precise description of their virtue will be particular to each capacity, a common account will still fit them all similarly. For the safety of the voyage is the work of them all, since this is what each of the sailors is aiming at. Similarly, then, even though citizens are dissimilar, the safety of the association is their work, and their form of government is the associa-
30   tion they share. Hence the virtue of a citizen is necessarily related to the form of government. So if there is in fact more than one form of government, it is clear that there cannot be one complete virtue of an excellent citizen. But we claim someone is a good man as a result of one complete virtue.

It is clear, then, that it is possible for someone who is an excellent citizen not to possess the virtue by which he would be an excellent man. But it is possible to get to the same proposition in still another way by raising a question about the best form of government. For if it is impossible for a city to be made up entirely of people who are excellent, each one still needs to do the work that belongs to him well,
40   and that means doing so out of virtue. But since it is impos-
1277A   sible for all the citizens to be alike, it could not be a single virtue that belongs to a citizen and to a good man. For the virtue of the excellent citizen has to belong to them all (since that is necessarily the way the city is best), but it is impossible that the virtue of the good man would, unless it were necessary for all the citizens in an excellent city to be good men. Further, seeing as how a city is made up of dissimilar people, just as an animal is made up to begin with of a soul and a body and a soul of reason and desire, and a household of a man and a woman, and a property of master and slave, in the same way a city too is organized out of all these and
10   various other kinds of people in addition to them. So it is necessary that there is no single virtue belonging to all the citizens, just as there is no single one belonging to the leader of a choral troop and his right-hand man.

Why, then, it is not simply the same is evident from these things. But will there be any person for whom the virtue of an excellent citizen and an excellent man will be the same? We claim that an excellent ruler is someone of good character and good judgment, but that an excellent citizen is not necessarily someone of good judgment. And some people say that the education of a ruler is different right from the start, just as the sons of kings obviously get educated for horsemanship and war; and Euripides says "nothing fancy for me...just the things required for a city,"[103] as though there is a particular education for a ruler. And if the same virtue belongs to a good ruler and a good man, and one who is ruled is also a citizen, the same virtue could not belong to a citizen and a man simply, though it could for a certain kind of citizen. For the virtue of a ruler is not the same as that of a citizen, and perhaps this is why Jason said he was hungry when he could not be a tyrant, because he did not know how to be a private man.

But surely being able to rule *and* be ruled is praised, and the virtue of an admirable citizen is held to be the ability to do a beautiful job of both ruling and being ruled. So if we set it down that the virtue of a good man pertains to ruling, while that of a citizen is of both sorts, they would not both be deserving of praise on the same grounds. So since it sometimes seems that they are different, and that the things someone who rules needs to learn are not the same as for someone who is ruled, while the citizen needs to know both sides and have a share in both, one can see where to go from here. For there is such a thing as rule of a master over slaves, and we say that this is the sort that has to do with necessities, things the one who rules has no need to know how to do but only how to use; in fact that other capability is slavish—I mean being able also to do service in actions of a servile kind. But we speak of more than one kind of slave, since their jobs are of more than one kind. One portion of these are the jobs manual laborers hold down; these are, as the name itself implies, people who live by their hands, and someone skilled in a mechanical craft is one of these. This is why among some people in the old days, before democracy in an extreme form came along, craftsmen had no share

20

30

1277B

103   A fragment from the lost play *Aeolus*.

in ruling offices. So the tasks of those who are ruled in this fashion are things a good political ruler or good citizen does not need to learn, except from time to time for use by himself for his own sake, since that does not have the further result that one person becomes a master and another a slave.

But there is a certain kind of rule by which one rules those who are similar in kind and free. For this is what we 10 say political rule is, which the ruler has to learn by being ruled; one learns to lead cavalry by being led, to be a general or squadron leader or company commander by being commanded. Hence it is said, and beautifully at that, that it is not possible for anyone to rule well except someone who has been ruled. And while virtue in these roles is different, a good citizen needs to have the knowledge and capacity both to be ruled and to rule. This is the virtue of a citizen: knowing the rule of free people from both sides. So both of these belong to the good man as well, and if there are different forms of moderation and justice that pertain to ruling, they do too. For it is clear that a virtue of a good person who is ruled but free, such as justice, could not be single, 20 but has forms by which one rules and is ruled, in the same way that moderation and courage are different in a man and a woman. (For a man would seem to be a coward if he were as courageous as a courageous woman, and a woman would seem overly talkative if she were as well-behaved as a good man, since even household management is different in a man and a woman; for the job of the former is to acquire and of the latter to maintain.) Practical judgment is the only virtue peculiar to a ruler. The rest necessarily seem common to those who are ruled and those who rule, but it is not practical judgment that is a virtue in one who is ruled but rather true opinion. The one ruled is like a flute maker while the 30 ruler is like the flute player who uses it.

So whether the same virtue or a different one belongs to a good man and an excellent citizen, and in what way they are the same and different, are clear from these things.

Chapter 5

One of the difficulties having to do with a citizen still remains. Is the only person who is a citizen in the true sense someone who has the right to share in a ruling office, or should one hold that people in the mechanical crafts are also citizens? Now if it is to be held that those who take no part in ruling are citizens, it is not possible for that sort of virtue to belong to every citizen (since this sort of person is a citizen); but if no such person is a citizen, in what class should each of them be held to belong? For they are not resident aliens or foreigners. Or shall we claim that nothing out of the way 1278A results from this argument? For the slaves and freed slaves are not in any of the classes mentioned either. For this is true, that one should not hold all those without whom there could not be a city to be citizens, seeing as how children are not citizens either in the same sense as men; the latter are citizens simply, but the former presumptively, since they are citizens but incomplete ones. So in ancient times among some people the mechanical craftsman was a slave or foreigner, which is why many are of that sort even now. And the best city will not make a mechanical craftsman a citizen. If, however, he too is a citizen, then the virtue which we were speaking of should not be said to belong to every citizen, not even just 10 to every free citizen; instead, only those who are relieved of jobs involving necessities should be said to be capable of it. In the case of necessities, those who perform such services for one person are slaves, and those perform them in common are mechanical craftsmen and menials.

How it stands with them will be evident to those who examine the matter a little further from here, since what has been said makes it clear. For since there is more than one form of government, there is necessarily more than one form of citizen, especially in the case of citizens who are ruled. So in one form of government the mechanical craftsman and menial laborer are necessarily citizens, but in others this is impossible, for instance in any there might be that people call aristocratic, in which honors are given in accordance 20 with virtue and merit; for it is not possible to pursue the things involved in virtue while living the life of a mechanical craftsman or menial laborer. In oligarchies, though, while being a citizen is not open to a menial laborer (since participation in offices is based on large property assessments), it is open to a mechanical craftsman, for many of those in the skilled crafts are in fact rich. There was a law in Thebes that someone could not take part in an office unless he had been out of his trade for ten years. But in many governments the law draws in even certain foreigners, since anyone born of a citizen mother is a citizen in some democracies, and among many peoples the same approach applies even in cases of

30   illegitimate births. However, since they make such people citizens due to a shortage of legitimate citizens (because they use the laws in this way as a result of underpopulation), once they have adequate numbers of people they little by little eliminate first those born of a slave father or mother, then those with descent on the female side, and finally they make citizens only of those born of native townspeople on both sides.

It is clear from these things, then, that there is more than one form of citizen, and that a citizen means most of all someone who shares in honors, in the spirit in which Homer wrote "as if I were some tramp bereft of honor."[104] For someone who has no share in honors is like a resident alien. But wherever this sort of thing is covered over, that is for the purpose of misleading their fellow inhabitants. And on the

1278B matter of whether one should hold that by which a man is good to be different from or the same as that by which a citizen is excellent, it is clear from what has been said that in one city they are the same person and in another they are different; and the person in the former case is not every citizen but one involved in political affairs and having authority, or capable of having authority, either on his own or along with others, over the management of common concerns.

Chapter 6

Since these things have been determined, the next thing that needs to be examined after them is whether one should hold that there is one form of government or more than one, and if more than one, what and how many they are and what the differences are among them. But a form of government is an arrangement of the ruling offices of a city,

10   both the others and especially the one with authority over them all. For what is in authority everywhere is the administration of the city, and the administration is the government. I mean, for instance, that in democracies the populace is in authority, while in oligarchies, on the contrary, it is the few,

---

104   *Iliad* IX, 648 and XVI, 59.

and we also claim that the form of government in them is different; and we would make the same statement about the others as well.

So what needs to be set down first as a basis for the argument is that for the sake of which a city is organized and how many forms of rule pertain to a human being and an association in life. Now it was said in our first discussions, in which distinctions were made about household management and mastery of slaves, that a human being is by nature an animal meant for a city. For this reason, even when they have no need of assistance from one another, people are no less desirous of living together. But their common advantage brings them together too, in proportion as it falls to the lot of each to have a part in living beautifully.[105] This, then, is the highest end for them all, both in common and separately. But they also come together and hold the political association together for the sake of life itself. For there is perhaps some portion of the beautiful present in and resulting from the mere and sole activity of living, as long as the hardships that come along with life are not too great a burden. It is obvious that most human beings will endure great suffering while clinging to life, as if there is in it a certain joyfulness and natural sweetness.

And the types of rule that people speak of are easy to distinguish, for even in popular writings we often make distinctions about them. As for mastery of slaves, even though in truth the same thing is advantageous to the natural slave as to the natural master, it is still nonetheless rule with a view

---

105 In the *Nicomachean Ethics* (1115b 12-13, 1122b 6-7), Aristotle says that the end at which all virtues of character aim is the beautiful (*to kalon*). He characterizes it as the highest form of good, distinct from all instrumental goods because it is chosen for its own sake, and distinct from pleasure because of its seriousness. A beautiful action is one that gets everything right. From the beginning of the *Politics* (1252b 29-30) Aristotle has been saying that a city is not merely for the sake of living but for the sake of living well (*to eu zên*). Here his notion of living well is made more definite; he does not have in mind a "high standard of living" in the material sense but the full development of the human potential that produces a complete and happy life. (See 1280b 40-1281a 2 below.) Twice earlier in the *Politics* he has linked the beautiful with virtue (1260b 8-11, 1263b 10-11). To single out the beautiful as the aim of the city is equivalent to recognizing the political association as the medium in which human virtue can come into being.

to the advantage of the master, and incidentally to that of the slave (since it is impossible for mastery to be preserved if the slave is destroyed). But rule of children, a wife, and a whole household, which we call household management, is either for the sake of those who are ruled or for the sake of some-

40   thing common to both ruler and ruled; in its own right it is for the sake of those who are ruled, just as we see with the

1279A   other arts, such as those of the doctor or gymnastic trainer, though they could incidentally be for their sake. For there is no reason why the trainer himself could not sometimes be one of those being trained, the same way the helmsman is always one of the sailors. So while the trainer or helmsman looks to the good of those who are ruled, whenever he himself becomes one of these, he incidentally shares the benefit, since the latter is a sailor and the former becomes one of those being trained, even though he is the trainer. Hence in the case of political offices too, whenever they are organized

10   on a basis of equality and similarity among the citizens, they expect to take turns ruling. In former times, in a way that was natural, they expected to take turns doing public service, while having someone look after *their* good in return, just as, when that person was ruling before, someone had looked after *his* advantage. But nowadays, because of the profits to be made from common funds and from holding office, people want to be in office continuously, as though people who were sick ended up being healthy by ruling perpetually. They would probably seek offices in the same way too.

It is clear, then, that it is precisely those forms of government that look to the common advantage that are right according to simple justice, while all those that look only

20   to the rulers' own advantage are misguided and deviations from the right forms of government. The latter are forms of mastery, but a city is an association of free people.

Chapter 7

Now that these distinctions have been made, the next thing is to examine the forms of government, how many they are in number and what they are, and first among them the right forms. For once these have been distinguished the deviations will also be clear. And since a form of government and an administration refer to the same thing, and an administration is what is in authority in cities, and it is necessary that there be either one person, or few, or many in authority, whenever that one or those few or those many rule with a view to the common advantage, these forms of government are necessarily right, while those that look to   **30** the private advantage of either the one or the few or the multitude are deviations. For either those who do not take part in them must not be called citizens or they must share in the advantage.

Now we are accustomed to call a form of government that looks to the common advantage kingship, in the case of monarchies, and in the case of rule by more than one person, but by few, aristocracy (either because the best people rule or because they rule with a view to what is best for the city and those who share in it), but when it is the multitude that governs with a view to the common advantage, it is called by the name common to all forms of government, constitutional rule. And this happens reasonably, since it is possible for one person or a few people to be outstanding in virtue,   **40** but it is difficult for any more than that to be rigorous about   **1279B** the whole of virtue, though it is possible most of all with military virtue, since that comes about in a large number of people. This is why the war-fighting part is the highest authority in this form of government and those who bear arms take part in it. And the deviations from the forms mentioned are tyranny from kingship, oligarchy from aristocracy, and democracy from constitutional rule. For tyranny is monarchy with a view to the advantage of the sole ruler, oligarchy rule with a view to that of those who are well off, and democracy to the advantage of the poor. None of them looks to what is profitable to them in common.   **10**

Chapter 8

But it is necessary to say what each of these forms of government is at a little greater length. For the subject has some difficulties about it, and it is the proper business of someone who is treating any pursuit philosophically, and not just looking ahead to the practice of it, not to overlook or leave out any difficulty, but to bring to light the truth about each one. As was said, tyranny is monarchy that rules the political association like a master of slaves, and government is oligarchy when those who have wealth are authoritative in it and democracy in the opposite case, when those in authority are the ones who do not have an abundance of wealth but

20   are poor. The first difficulty is concerned with the definition. If the majority were well off and were in charge of the city, and it is a democracy when the multitude is in authority— or similarly in turn if the poor happened to be fewer somewhere than the rich, but were stronger and were in authority in the government, but wherever the number of people in authority is small people say it is an oligarchy—it would seem that not so beautiful a job of defining the forms of government has been done. And even if one were to combine fewness with being well off and manyness with being poor and name the forms of government on that basis, oligarchy as that in which those who are well off and few in number

30   hold the offices, and democracy as that in which those who are poor and many in number hold them, there is another difficulty. For what are we going to say about the governments just mentioned, in which the rich are the majority or the poor are the minority and in each of the two cases they are in authority in their governments, if there are no other forms of government besides the ones mentioned?

The argument seems to make it clear, then, that the fact that few are in authority in oligarchies and many in democracies is incidental, because the rich are few and the poor many everywhere (and hence the alleged causes turn out not to be the reasons for their differences). That on account

40
1280A of which democracy and oligarchy differ from each other is poverty and wealth, and necessarily, wherever people rule on account of wealth, whether there is a lesser or greater number of them, this is oligarchy, and wherever it is the poor, this is democracy, and it is incidental, as we said, that the former are few and the latter many. For few are well off but all share in freedom, which are the reasons the two sides are in dispute over the form of government.

Chapter 9

What needs to be taken up first is what people say the defining marks of oligarchy and democracy are, and what justice is in an oligarchic and a democratic sense. For everyone gets hold of some aspect of justice, but they only go up to a certain point and do not speak of justice as a whole in an authoritative sense. For what is just seems, in a way, to be something equal, and it is, but not for all people but for those who are equal. And the unequal also seems to be just, because it is too, but not for all people but for those who are unequal. But people leave out this "for whom" and judge badly. The reason is that the judgment involves themselves, and it is generally true that most people are bad judges in their own cases. So since what is just is just for certain persons, and is divided among them in the same way as with the things, as was said previously in the *Ethics*,[106] people agree about the equality of the thing but dispute that which applies to the persons; this is primarily because of what was just mentioned, the fact that they judge matters related to themselves badly, but also because each side holds that by speaking of something that is just up to a certain point it is speaking of what is just simply. For one group, if it is unequal in any respect, such as money, believes it is unequal in every respect, while the other group, if it is equal in any respect, such as freedom, believes it is equal in every respect.

But they do not state the thing that is most authoritative. If people came together and entered into association for the sake of possessions, they would have a share in the city exactly as much as they had a share in property, and the argument of the oligarchs would consequently seem to be strong. For it would not be just for someone who gave one mina to have an equal share in one hundred minae with the person who contributed all the rest, and not in what it

10

20

30

---

106 In Bk. V, Chap. 3 of the *Nicomachean Ethics* Aristotle discusses distributive justice, using the word for distribution (*nomê* or *dianomê*) instead of the verb *diairein* that he uses here for the dividing up of communal resources, and especially of honors, and especially among them of ruling offices, according to some notion of who deserves them. In the *Ethics* he argues that justice in such matters consists not in any simple equality of things distributed but in an equality of ratios, such that the things granted are to one another in a relation that matches the relative merits of the persons receiving them. He calls this sort of equality geometrical, as opposed to the simple arithmetic equality governing the corrective justice of court decisions, which seek to restore what a victim has lost or make the punishment of an offender fit the crime.

brings in any more than in the original amount. But[107] they do so not just for the sake of living but instead for the sake of living well. Otherwise there could even be a city made up of slaves, or of the other animals, but as it is there is none, because they do not share in happiness or in living in accordance with choice. Nor do they do so for the sake of an alliance to keep injustice from being done to them by anyone, or for exchange and mutual utility. Otherwise even the Etruscans and Carthaginians, and all those who have agreements with one another, would be like citizens of one city, since they do, at any rate, have treaties about imports, agreements

40 not to commit injustice, and documents of alliance. But no
1280B offices common to them all are set up, but different ones among the different peoples, and those in one group pay no attention to what sort of character those in the other groups ought to have in order that none of the people covered by the agreements would *be* unjust or have any vice, but only to assure that they *do* no injustice to one another.

But those who pay attention to good order give careful consideration to political virtue and vice. And this makes it clear that there needs to be a concern about virtue in a city that bears that name truly and not just for the sake of argument. Otherwise the association becomes an alliance

10 that differs from other, long-distance, alliances only by its location, and law becomes a contract and "a mutual pledge of just dealings" as the sophist Lycophron said, and not the sort of thing that could make citizens good and just. It is obvious that this is the way it is. For even if one were to pull the locations together into one, so that the city of the Megarians and that of the Corinthians were joined by walls, it would still not be one city, not even if they introduced the right of intermarriage with one another, even though that is one of the communal practices peculiar to cities. And by the same token, even if there were some people living separately, but not so far apart that they could not associate, and there were laws among them not to commit injustice among

20 themselves in their transactions, and one was, say, a carpenter, one a farmer, one a shoemaker, and another something else like that, and their number was ten thousand, but they

---

107 Aristotle begins this sentence with an "if" but never gets to a "then" clause.

were not associated in anything other than matters such as exchange and alliance, not even so would it reach the point of being a city.

What is the reason? It is not from a lack of proximity within the association; for even if they were to meet together to associate in this manner, while each one still treated his own household as if it were a city, and themselves as if they were a defensive alliance assisting each other only against those who commit injustice, not even so would it seem to be a city to those who study the matter with precision, if they were interacting the same way when they came together as when apart. It is obvious, then, that a city is not   30
an association in a place for the sake of not doing injustice among themselves and doing business. These things necessarily have to be present if it is going to be a city, but when they are all present it is not on that account a city; a city is instead an association of households and families in living well, for the sake of a complete and self-sufficient life. This will not be possible, however, unless they occupy one and the same place and practice intermarriage. This is why marriages came within the purview of cities, along with fraternal organizations, religious rites, and shared forms of recreation. And this sort of thing is the work of friendship, because friendship is a choice to live life in common. The end aimed at by a city is living well, and these things are for   40
the sake of that end. And a city is an association of families   1281A
and villages in a complete and self-sufficient life. And we claim that this is living happily and beautifully. It must be set down, therefore, that the political association is for the sake of beautiful actions and not for the sake of living together. For this reason, those who contribute most to such an association play a greater part in the city than those who are equal to them in freedom or superior to them in birth but are unequal in political virtue, or those who surpass them in wealth but are surpassed in virtue.

So it is clear from the things that have been said that all those who dispute about the forms of government are talking   10
about some partial aspect of what is just.

Chapter 10

What the authority in a city ought to be is a matter of

difficulty. For it is either the multitude, or the rich, or the decent people, or the best person of all, or a tyrant. But all these involve something hard to swallow. For what if the poor, because they are the majority, divide up the things that belong to the rich? Is that not unjust? "Well by Zeus, it was enacted justly by the authority!" Then what should one say the utmost injustice is? If, after everything has been taken, a majority once again divides up the things that belong to the minority, it is obvious that they will destroy the city. But it

20   is certainly not virtue that destroys the thing that possesses it, and justice is not something that can destroy a city, so it is clear that this law cannot be just. It would also mean that whatever actions a tyrant undertook would necessarily all be just; he is stronger and uses force, just as the multitude does with the rich. But is it a just thing, then, for the minority and the rich to rule? If they do the same things, then, and seize and take possession of the property of the multitude, that is just; therefore the other is too. So it is obvious that all these things are bad and *not* just. So should the decent people rule and be in authority over everyone? Then it is

30   necessary that the others all be deprived of honor, since they are not honored with political offices; for we speak of offices as honors, and when the same people are always ruling the rest are necessarily deprived of honor. So is it better for one person of the highest excellence to rule? But that goes still further in the oligarchic direction, since more people are deprived of honor. But perhaps one might claim that it is a bad thing for the authority to be a human being at all and not the law, since he is bound to have the passions attendant upon the soul. But if law can be oligarchic or democratic, what difference will that make to the difficulties that have been raised? For the things already said will follow just the same.

Chapter 11

Now on the other points, let there be a discussion some
40   other time. But the claim that the multitude ought to be in authority, rather than those who are best but are few in number, would seem to be maintained and to have a certain difficulty but also, perhaps a certain truth. For the many, none of
1281B whom is a man of excellent stature, are nonetheless capable when they come together of being better than those who

are of such stature, not each in particular but all combined, just as dinners made up of contributions can be better than those furnished at one person's expense. For when there are many people, each can have a portion of virtue and good judgment, and when they come together the multitude can become like a single human being with many feet and hands and having many senses, and similarly with their characters and their thinking. This is why the many also do a better job of judging works of music and of the poets; for different people respond to different parts, and all of them to all the parts. But the excellent ones among men differ from each of the many in this way: just as people claim that the beautiful differ from those who are not beautiful, and things painted by art differ from actual things, by bringing things scattered apart together into one. For when they are separated, the eye of this particular person, and some other part of someone else, may be more beautiful than the painted one. Now it is unclear whether it is possible for this superiority of the many to the few people of excellent stature to be present in every populace and every multitude. Perhaps one should say, "by Zeus, it *is* clear that in some of them it is *im*possible!" (For the same argument could be applied to beasts, yet what difference is there, in a word, between some of them and beasts?) But nothing prevents the thing stated from being true for a certain kind of multitude.

And hence by these means one might resolve both the difficulty mentioned above and one connected with it, namely what things the multitude of those who are free and citizens ought to have authority over. These are the sort of people who are not rich and have no claim to any single virtue. For them to take part in the highest ruling offices would not be safe, since they would be bound to commit some injustices and make some mistakes due to a lack of justice or good judgment. But to give them no share and have them not take part at all is dangerous, for when many people are in it who are dishonored and poor, that city is necessarily filled with enemies. What is left is for them to share in deliberating and judging. This is the reason Solon and certain other lawgivers assign them the election and review of those who rule, but do not allow them to rule on their own. For when they are all joined together they have sufficient perception, and when they are mixed with their betters they benefit their cities, just as food that is not pure, when mixed with a little pure food, makes the whole more nourishing; separately, each group is imperfect at judging.

But this arrangement of the government does have a 40 difficulty, because, in the first place, judging who has been correctly cured would seem to belong to the same person whose job it was to cure the disease when it was present and make the sick person healthy, and that is the doctor. And it 1282A is similar with the other kinds of experience and art. So just as a doctor ought to hold himself accountable to doctors, the others too should be reviewed by their peers. But a doctor is either a practitioner or a master of the art, or thirdly someone educated on the subject, for there are some people of this sort with just about all the arts, and we turn over the act of judging to those who are educated in the subject no less than to those who know it. So then it might seem to be the same way with electing as well. For making a right choice is a job for those with knowledge; it belongs, for example, to 10 geometers to choose a geometer and to helmsmen to choose a helmsman. For some laymen might also participate in the choice for certain jobs and arts, but they do not take a greater part in it than those with knowledge. So by this argument, it would not be appropriate to give the multitude authority for either electing or reviewing officials. But perhaps these things are not all beautifully argued, because of the previous argument that if the multitude is not too slavish, even though each member of it will be a worse judge than those with knowledge, all of them combined will be either better or no worse, and also because with some arts the maker would not be the only one or the best one to judge. These are those arts in which even those who do not have the art have a familiarity with its products. Being familiar with a house, 20 for instance, is not something that belongs only to the one who makes it; the one who uses it is even better at judging it, and it is the household manager who uses it. A helmsman is a better judge of a rudder than a carpenter is, and the guest, not the cook, is a better judge of a meal.

So it would probably seem that one could resolve this difficulty adequately in this way, but there is another difficulty connected with this one. For it seems absurd that people of inferior character should be in authority over greater

matters than decent people, but the greatest matter is the reviewing and electing of those who rule. And as was said, this is turned over to the populace in some constitutions, since the assembly is in authority over all such things. Yet those who take part in the assembly and do the deliberating   30
and judging come from the low property classes and are of any random age, while those who control the treasury and serve as generals and rule in the highest offices come from the high classes. But one could resolve this difficulty too in a similar way. For perhaps these things too are done rightly, since it is not the person who judges or deliberates or serves in the assembly who is ruling, but the court or deliberative council or populace, and each of the persons mentioned—I mean the councilor, assemblyman, or judge—is part of these bodies. So the multitude is justly in authority over greater matters, since the populace and deliberative council and lawcourt are made up of many people, and the property as-   40
sessment of them all is greater than that of each one, or the few, who hold the high ruling offices. So let these things be determined in this way.   1282B

And the first difficulty stated makes nothing else so clear as that laws rightly laid down ought to be in author- ity, while the ruler, whether this is one person or more than one, ought to be in authority over those things that laws are utterly incapable of speaking precisely about, since it is not easy to make universal determinations about everything. Nothing is yet clear, however, about what particular sort of laws ought to *be* rightly laid down, and the difficulty raised some time ago still remains. For the laws will be bad or ex- cellent and just or unjust together with and in a similar fash- ion to the forms of government. This much is clear, though,   10
that the laws ought to be laid down with a view to the form of government. And surely if that is the case, it is evident that those that accord with the right forms of government will necessarily be just and those that accord with the devi- ant ones will not be just.

Chapter 12

And since in all kinds of knowledge and art the end is something good, and is the highest and greatest good in the most authoritative kind, and this is the political capacity, and the political good is justice, and this is the common advantage, and justice seems to everyone to be some kind of equality, and up to a certain point they are in agreement with

20   the writings on philosophy in which matters pertaining to ethics are determined (since they say that justice is a certain thing for certain people and ought to be equal for equal people), one ought not to overlook the matter of what sorts of things the equality and inequality consists in.[108] For this has difficulty, and involves political philosophy. Perhaps someone might claim that superiority in any good thing requires offices to be distributed unequally, if people happened to be alike in all other respects and had no differences, since what is just and in accord with merit is different for people who differ. But if this were true, any advantage, even in coloring or height or any other good thing whatever would be an advantage in just political rewards for those who had the

30   superiority. Is this not false on the face of it? And it is obvious in the case of other kinds of knowledge and capacities. Among fluteplayers who are alike in art, an advantage in flutes would not be given to those who are better born, since they would not play the flutes better; one ought to give the superiority in instruments to someone who is superior in the work. And if what is being said is not clear yet, it will be still more obvious to those who draw out the point. For if there were someone superior at fluteplaying, but with great shortcomings in birth and looks, then even if each of these things—I mean good birth and beauty—is a greater good

40   than fluteplaying, and is superior *to* fluteplaying in a greater proportion than he is superior *in* fluteplaying, he should

1283A   nevertheless be given the exceptional flutes. For the superiority has to contribute to the work, and wealth and good birth contribute nothing.

Also, by that argument every good thing would be comparable with every other. For if some particular height were a criterion, height in general would be a criterion in comparison with both wealth and freedom; so if this person excels in height more than that person does in virtue, then even if virtue in general is more excellent than height, everything would be comparable. For if a certain amount is great-

---

108   This long conditional sentence seems to take its beginning from Bk. I, Chap. 2 above, and link it with Bk. V, Chap. 3, of the *Nicomachean Ethics*.

er than a certain other amount, then clearly some amount is
equal to it. And since that is impossible, it is evident that in   10
the case of political offices too, it is reasonable that people do
not dispute them on the basis of every inequality. For if some
are slow and others fast, there is no need on that account
for one sort to hold more offices and the other sort fewer;
it is rather in gymnastic contests that a superiority in these
things takes the honors. It is necessary to make the dispute
on the basis of those things out of which a city is organized.
Hence it is reasonable for those who are well born or free or
rich to lay claim to honor. For there have to be free people
and also people who pay taxes, since there could not be a
city consisting entirely of the poor, just as there could not
be one consisting entirely of slaves. And surely if there is a
need for these things, it is clear that there is also a need for   20
justice and political virtue. For without these it would not
even be possible for a city to be managed. Or rather, without
the former it is impossible for there to be a city and without
the latter it is impossible for one to be managed beautifully.

Chapter 13

In connection with the being of the city, all or at least
some of these inequalities might seem right to dispute
about, but in connection with a good life, education and
virtue would be argued for most justly, as was said above.
And since those who are equal in only one respect ought not
to have equality in all respects, and those unequal in one
respect ought not to have inequality in all, then all forms
of government of those sorts are necessarily deviant. And it
was also said above that everyone has a just argument in a   30
certain way, but not everyone has an argument that is simply just. The rich argue justly that they have a larger share
of the land, and the land is something common, and what
is more, they are for the most part more trustworthy about
agreements. But the free and well born argue justly in the
sense that they are close to one another, for the better born
are citizens to a greater degree than the base born, and good
birth is honored by each local group, and also because those
descended from better people are likely to be better people,
since good birth is virtue of a family. And similarly, we will
claim that virtue has a just argument, since we claim that

40   justice is communal virtue, and from it all the rest necessarily follow.[109] And certainly the majority also has a just argument against the minority, since the greater number, taken together, are also stronger, richer, and better than the smaller number.

1283B   Well then, if they were all present in one city—I mean the good, the rich, and the well born, and a citizen multitude as still another thing—will there or will there not be a dispute as to who ought to rule? In each form of government among those mentioned, the decision as to who ought to rule is indisputable, since they differ from one another by those in authority; one, for instance, is distinguished by being ruled by the rich, another by the excellent men, and the same way with each of the others. All the same, though, let us consider how this ought to be determined when these

10   are all present at the same time. And if those having virtue were utterly few in number, in what way ought one to make the decision? Should their fewness not be considered as it bears on their job, and whether they are capable of managing the city, or else so many in multitude that a city could be made up of them? But there is a certain difficulty related to all disputes over political honors. For it might seem that those who consider themselves worthy of ruling on account of wealth, or similarly on account of family, have no just argument at all, for it is clear that if in turn there is some one person richer than all of them, then obviously by this same justice that one person will have to rule them all, and likewise with the those who make their argument on the basis of

20   freedom when one person surpasses them all in good birth. And perhaps this same thing will happen even in aristocracies in the case of virtue; for if some one person were a better man than the rest of those in the administration, even though they were excellent, then by the same justice that one person would have to be in authority. And by the same token, if the multitude ought to be in authority because they are stronger than the few, and one person, or more than one but fewer than the many, were stronger than the rest, then *they* ought to be in authority instead of the multitude.

---

109 In the *Nicomachean Ethics*, Aristotle distinguishes a sense in which justice is obedience to law (1129b 11-12), which commands all the external acts of the other virtues (1129b 19-25).

So all these things seem to make it evident than none of these criteria is right, according to which people consider themselves worthy of ruling while everyone else deserves to be ruled by them. For even against those who consider themselves worthy to be in authority over the administration on grounds of virtue, and similarly against those who base their argument on wealth, the masses would have an argument of some justice to make; for nothing prevents a multitude from sometimes being better than the few or the wealthier, not one-by-one but as a whole. Hence it is also possible in this way to meet the difficulty which some people inquire about and propose. For some people raise the question whether, if a lawgiver wants to lay down laws that are right in the highest degree, he ought to make those laws for the advantage of the better people or of the greater number, when things turn out the way that was stated. Perhaps what is right needs to be grasped, and what is right is perhaps what is for the advantage of the whole city and for the citizens in common. Now a citizen, in the sense common to all forms of government, is someone who shares in ruling and being ruled, but is someone different in each form; in the best form of government, it is someone who has the capacity for and chooses to be ruled and to rule for a life in accord with virtue.

30

40

1284A

If there is some one person who so greatly surpasses the rest by a superiority in virtue—or more than one but not enough to be able to make up a full city—so much so that the virtue and political capacity of all the rest are not comparable to theirs (if there is more than one) or to his alone (if there is one), they can no longer be held to be part of a city. For they would suffer injustice by being held to deserve equal shares when they are so unequal in virtue and political capacity. Such a person would likely be like a god among human beings. It is clear from this that lawgiving too is necessarily for those who are equal in kind and capacity, and that for people of that sort there is no law, for they are a law in themselves. It would be ridiculous for anyone even to try to give laws for them. For they might perhaps reply the way Antisthenes says the lions did when the hares made rabble-rousing speeches claiming that all deserve to have equal shares. And it is for this sort of reason that democratically run cities impose ostracism. For they seem to pursue equality as the

10

20   highest of all things, and so they used to ostracize, to banish from the city for a definite period of time, those who seemed to be superior in power on account of wealth or abundance of friends or any other kind of political strength. A story is also told that the Argonauts left Heracles behind for such a reason, for the *Argo* was not willing to carry him with the other sailors since he so greatly outweighed them.[110] Hence, too, those who criticize tyranny ought not to be considered simply right in blaming the advice Periander gave Thrasybulus. They say Periander said nothing to the messenger who was sent to him for advice, but removed the ears of corn that

30   stood out, to make the field level; when the messenger, who was ignorant of the reason, reported what had happened, Thrasybulus got the point from it that he ought to get rid of the outstanding men. This is advantageous not just to tyrants, and it is not just tyrants who do it, but it is similar with oligarchies and democracies as well. For ostracism has, in a certain manner, the same force as cutting down and exiling those who are superior. Those who wield authority in power do the same thing to cities and nations, as the Athenians did

40   with the people of Samos, Chios, and Lesbos, for as soon as they had their empire under firm control they brought

1284B   them into submission in violation of their treaties; and the king of the Persians often used to cut down the Medes and Babylonians and others who got big ideas because they had once been in power.

The problem is one that concerns all forms of government in general, even the right forms. For while the deviant ones act this way in looking out for their private good, the same way of acting applies to those looking toward the common good. And this is clear in the case of the other arts and kinds of knowledge as well; for no painter would allow an

10   animal to have a foot that exceeded its proportion, even if if it were surpassing in beauty, nor would a shipbuilder do so with a stern or any other part of a ship, and the conductor of a chorus would not let someone with a stronger and more beautiful voice than the whole chorus be a member of it. So there is no reason why, on this account, monarchs would not

---

110   The ship had in its timbers a piece of the speaking oak of Dodona. The Periander/Thrasybulus story is told, with the roles reversed, in Herodotus's *History* (V, 92).

be in concord with their cities if they do this, provided that their own rule is beneficial to their cities. Hence, in cases where superiority is acknowledged, the argument in favor of ostracism has some political justice. And while it is better for the lawgiver to organize the government from the beginning in such a way that it has no need for this sort of remedy, the second best course,[111] if the occasion should arise, is to try to set things right by some such corrective measure. This is exactly what did *not* happen with the cities that used to make use of ostracisms, since they were not looking to what was advantageous to their own governments, but using it for factional purposes.

So in the deviant forms of government, it is obvious that this is advantageous and just from a private point of view, but perhaps it is also obvious that it is not simply just. But in the best form of government this is a great impasse; if the superiority is not in other goods such as strength and wealth and abundance of friends, but someone comes along who is outstanding in virtue, what is the right thing to do? For no one would claim people ought to throw out and exile someone like that, but neither would they rule over such a person. That would be about the same as if they considered themselves worthy of ruling over Zeus by dividing up his ruling functions. What is left, therefore, is exactly what seems to be the natural thing: for everyone to obey such a person gladly, with the result that such people would be perpetual kings in their cities.

Chapter 14

And perhaps what would go beautifully after the arguments that have been discussed is to change course and examine kingship, since we claim this is one of the right forms of government. What needs to be examined is whether it is advantageous for a city and a land that is going to be run beautifully to be ruled by a king or not, but to have some other form of government instead, or whether it is advantageous in some cases but not in others. And first it is necessary to distinguish whether kingship is of some one kind, or

20

30

40

1285A

---

111   Literally, "the second way of sailing," (*deuteros plous*), a phrase used by Socrates in a famous passage in Plato's *Phaedo* (99D). It was commonly used to mean that when the wind fails, you get out your oars.

whether it has more than one variety. And it is easy to determine this much, at least, that it includes more kinds than one and that there is not one single manner of ruling in them all. For in the Spartan form of government there seems to be a preeminent instance of kingship under law. The king is not in authority over all things, but whenever he goes outside the land he is the leader in matters pertaining to war; also, matters pertaining to the gods are assigned to the kings. So this kingship is sort of a permanent generalship of supreme commanders. The king has no authority to put people to death except for cowardice on military expeditions, in actual combat, as was the case in ancient times. Homer makes this clear, since Agamemnon put up with hearing himself abused in assemblies, but when they went out he had authority to put people to death. He says, anyway, "Anyone I [see] far away from battle...will have no chance of escaping the dogs and birds, for death is in my power."[112] So this is one form of kingship, generalship for life, and some of these are by family descent, others elective.

Another form of monarchy besides this one is present in the sorts of kingships there are among some of the barbarians. These all have about the same power as in tyrannies, but they are in accord with law and traditional. For since their characters are more slavish by nature—barbarians than Greeks, and those in Asia than those in Europe—they put up with rule like that of a master over slaves without discontent. So they are on this account tyrannical, but are secure on account of being traditional and in accord with law. Their guards are kingly rather than tyrannical for the same reason. For citizens serve as armed guards for their kings, while tyrants have a foreign guard, since the one sort rule according to law over willing subjects, the others over unwilling ones, so while the former have a guard from among the citizens, the latter have a guard over the citizens.

So these are two forms of monarchy, and another is one there used to be among the Greeks of early times, under those people call caretakers.[113] This is, simply put, elective tyranny, and differs from the barbarian form not in not being

112   *Iliad* II, 391-3, with part omitted and the last clause added.

113   The word is *aisumnêtai*. Its derivation is not known, but the parts of it may bear some such sense as "those mindful of what is due."

lawful but only in not being traditional. Some were rulers for life in this office, others for definite periods of time or for certain actions; the Mytilenians, for instance, once elected Pittacus against the exiles that Antimenides and the poet Alcaeus led. Alcaeus makes clear in one of his round-songs that they chose Pittacus as a tyrant, for he complains that "the assembled throng with great acclamation set up the 1285B low-born Pittacus as tyrant of a gutless and ill-fated city." These are and were tyrannical on account of being like rule of a master over slaves, but kingly on account of being elected by willing subjects. And there was a fourth form of kingly monarchy in the heroic age, when there were willingly accepted hereditary kings in accord with law. Since the first ones to come along were benefactors of the multitude as a result of arts or war or by bringing them together or providing them with land, they became kings over willing subjects, and their descendants became hereditary kings. They were in authority for leadership in war and over those sacrifices 10 that were not conducted by priests, and in addition to those things, they judged lawsuits. Some did this without swearing an oath, others under oath, and the seal of the oath was the lifting of a scepter. Those in ancient times ruled perpetually over city, regional, and foreign affairs, but later the kings gave up some of these functions and the masses took away others, and in other cities the sacrifices were the only things left to the kings; where there was anything worth calling kingship, they had only leadership over military matters beyond their borders.

So these are the forms of kingship, four in number. 20 One is that of the heroic age, and this was over willing subjects for certain limited functions; the king was a general and a judge, and in authority over things pertaining to the gods. A second is the barbarian form, and this is rule of a master, by family descent, according to law. A third is what people refer to as caretaker rule, and this is elective tyranny. And fourth among them is the Spartan form, and this, to put it simply, is perpetual generalship by family descent. These are different from one another, then, in this way. But there is a fifth form of kingship, when there is one person who is in 30 authority over everything in the same way each people and each city is sovereign over common concerns, and this is arranged along the lines of household management. For just

as household management is a sort of kingship of a household, kingship conducted in this manner is household management of a city and a people—one or more.

Chapter 15

So two forms of kingship, one might say, are about all
that need to be examined, this last one and the Spartan form,
since most of the others are between these. For they are in
authority over fewer things than full-scale kingship and
more than the Spartan kind. So the matter to be examined
just about comes down to two things. One is whether it is
advantageous or not for cities to have a permanent general,
1286A whether this is by family descent or by turns, and the other
one is whether it is advantageous or not for one person to
be in authority over all things. Now the one about this sort
of generalship has the look of examining laws rather than a
form of government, since it is possible for this to come up
in all forms of government, so let the first one be set aside.
But the mode of kingship that is left is a form of government,
and so one must look into this and run over the difficulties
inherent in it. The beginning of the inquiry is this: whether
it is more advantageous to be ruled by the best man or the
best laws.

10   Now to those who consider it advantageous to be
ruled by a king, it seems that laws speak only of what is universal and give no directions for particular circumstances.
Consequently, in any art whatever, it is foolish to govern
things by written rules. In Egypt, doctors are rightly permitted to change a treatment after the fourth day, but if they do
so before that it is at their own risk. So for the same reason it
is obvious that the best form of government is not one under
written rules and laws. But surely that sort of universal account ought to be present to those who rule. And that which
has no passionate ingredient in it at all is superior to that in
which it is innate, and while this is not present in the law, ev-
20   ery human soul necessarily contains it. Perhaps in response
to this one might claim, though, that one person would do
a more beautiful job of deliberating about particular things.
So it is clear that he must necessarily be a lawgiver and laws
must be laid down, but they must not be in authority in any
matter in which they go beyond their scope, although they

need to be authoritative in other respects. But on those matters which the law is not able to decide at all, or decide well, should the one best person rule, or all the people? Even now, people come together and judge and deliberate and make decisions, and these decisions are all about particular things. What is contributed by any of them one-by-one is perhaps inferior, but a city is made up of many people, and for this reason, in the same way a feast consisting of contributions is more beautifully made than a simple single one, a crowd judges better on many matters than any one person.

30

Also, a large quantity is more incorruptible; like a larger amount of water, so too the multitude is harder to corrupt than a few people. And when one person is overcome by anger or any other such passion, his judgment is necessarily corrupted, but it takes some doing for everybody to get angry and go astray at the same time and in the same direction. But let it be assumed that the multitude are free persons, not acting in any way outside the law other than on matters it necessarily leaves out. And if this is not easy in a large group, still if there were a number who were both good men and good citizens, which would be more incorruptible, the one ruler, or rather those who are more than one in number and and all good? Is it not obvious that it is the greater number? "But they would have factions, while a single person is immune to faction." But to counter this, perhaps it should be posited that they are excellent in soul, as it was with that one person. So if rule by more people than one, who are all good men, is to be set down as aristocracy, while that of one person is kingship, aristocracy would be more choiceworthy for cities than kingship, whether its rule is with or without force of arms, as long as it is possible to get a number of people alike in virtue.

40

1286B

And perhaps it was for this reason that people were ruled by kings in earlier times, because it was a rare thing to find men who far surpassed the rest in virtue, both for other reasons and because the cities they lived in at that time were small. Also, they made people kings as a result of their public services, which is precisely the work of good men. But when there came to be many people alike in virtue, they no longer put up with a king but sought something communal and set up a constitution. And when people became worse

10

and enriched themselves from public funds, it was reasonable at that point from that cause for oligarchies to arise,
since they took wealth to be a mark of honor. And from these
they changed first into tyrannies and from tyrannies into democracy, for by constantly drawing things into fewer hands
on account of greed, they made the multitude stronger, so
20   much so that they attacked them and democracies came into
being. And now that cities have gotten to be larger, it would
probably not be easy any more for any other form of government to come into being except democracy.

But if someone were to hold that it is best for cities to
be ruled by kings, how will matters stand in regard to their
children? Should the family have the kingship as well? But
if they turn out to be the sort of people some have happened
to be, that would be harmful. "Then since he is in charge, he
will not pass it on to his children." But this is no longer easy
to believe, for it is a difficult thing, and requires a greater
degree of virtue than what is in keeping with human nature.
And there is also a difficulty about power, namely whether
someone who is going to be king needs to have some force
30   around him by which he will be able to compel those who
are not willing to obey. How else would it be possible to administer his ruling office? For even if by law he was in authority, and he acted in no way at his own will contrary to
law, it would still be necessary for him to have available a
power by which he could defend the laws. Now it is probably not difficult to determine these things in the case of a
king of this sort. For he ought to have a force, and that force
ought to be made so great as to be stronger than any one
person or any group of several together, but weaker than
the multitude. This is the manner in which the ancients gave
bodyguards when they set up someone whom they called a
caretaker or tyrant of the city, and when Dionysius asked for
40   bodyguards, someone advised the Syracusans to give him
that many.

Chapter 16

1287A   The argument has now gotten to the sort of king who
acts in all matters according to his own will, and an examination must be made of this topic. The so-called king according to law is not a form of government, as we have said

(since a permanent generalship is capable of being present in all forms, in democracy and aristocracy for instance, and many governments put one person in charge of the administration—there is an office of that sort at Epidamnus, and to a somewhat lesser extent at Opus). But as for what is called full-scale kingship, this being that in which the king rules   10 everything by his own will, it seems to some that it is not natural for one person to be in authority over all citizens, where the city is organized out of people who are alike. For it is natural that the same thing would be just for those who are alike by nature, and that they would have the same worth. So if having equal food or clothing is harmful for those who are unequal in their bodies, it is the same way with things that have to do with honors, and likewise harmful for people who are equal to have what is unequal. For this reason it is no more just for them to rule than be ruled, and therefore it is just for them to do the same things by turns. And this already is law, since an orderly arrangement is a law. Therefore having the law rule is more choiceworthy than having any one of the citizens do so, and by the same argument, even if   20 it is better for some of them to rule, they should be set up as protectors and servants of the laws. For it is necessary that there be some rulers, but they claim it is not just for that to be one person so long as all the people are alike. And as for those things the law does not seem capable of determining, a human being would not be capable of knowing them either. But the law educates people for this very purpose, and sets up rulers to judge and administer what it leaves out as justly as their judgment permits. Furthermore, the laws allow themselves to be corrected by whatever seems to those with experience to be better than what they lay down. So it seems that one who bids law to rule is bidding a god and reason to rule by themselves, while one who bids a human being   30 to rule is adding a beast. For that is the sort of thing desire is, and spirited passion warps even the best men when they rule. That is why the law is intellect without appetite.

And the example from the arts seems to be a false one, when it is claimed that doctoring by written rules is bad, and that it is preferable to rely on the people who have the arts. For such people do not do anything contrary to reason out of friendship, but earn their fees by healing the sick, while those in political offices habitually act in many matters for

spite or as favors. Even with doctors, if people ever suspect
40   they had been persuaded by someone's enemies to destroy
him for profit, they would rather seek a treatment in that
case by written rules. And when doctors are sick, they bring
1287B   in other doctors for themselves, and gymnastic trainers do
the same when they are in training, since they are unable
to judge the truth when the judging concerns their own affairs and they are under stress. So it is clear that in seeking
what is just, people are seeking the mean, since law is the
mean. Also, laws based on customs are more authoritative
and deal with more authoritative matters than written laws,
so if it is safer for a human being to rule than to go by written
rules, this is still not safer than going by custom.

And surely it is not easy for one person to watch over
many things; therefore there will have to be a number of
10   people appointed by him as rulers. So what is the difference between having that in place right from the start and
having one person make the appointments that way? And
there is also what was mentioned before, that if it is just for
the excellent man to rule because he is better, then surely
two good men would be better than one. This is the point of
"when two go together" and Agamemnon's prayer "that I
might have ten such counselors."[114] Even now, there are rulers empowered to decide, like a judge, certain matters which
the law is incapable of determining; but no one disputes that
the law would be the best ruler and judge on those matters
it is capable of determining. But since, while some matters
20   are capable of being encompassed by the laws, there are others for which this is impossible, these latter are the things
that make people raise the question and inquire whether it
is more choiceworthy for the best law or the best man to
rule. For making laws on matters people deliberate about
is something impossible. And people do not argue against
this, claiming that it is not necessary for the one who decides such matters to be a human being, but only claim that
it should not be just one person but many. For everyone who
rules does a beautiful job of making decisions if he has been
educated by the law, and it would perhaps seem to be absurd if someone could see better with two eyes, judge better
with two ears, and act better with two feet and hands than

---

114   *Iliad* X, 224 and II, 372.

many people with many. For even now, monarchs make
many eyes and ears and hands and feet for themselves,   30
since they make their friends collaborators in their rule. If
they were not friends they would not act in accord with the
monarch's intention, but if they are friends of his and of his
rule, a friend is someone equal and alike, so he is assuming that those who are equal and alike ought to rule alike.
So this is pretty much what people say who dispute against
kingship.

Chapter 17

But perhaps things are this way in some cases but not
in others. For there is a certain situation that naturally calls
for mastery as both just and advantageous, another for kingship, and another for constitutional government. But there is
none that calls for tyranny by nature, or for any of the other   40
forms of government that are deviations, since these arise in
violation of nature. But from what has been said, it is clear   1288A
at any rate that among people who are alike and equal there
is nothing advantageous or just about having one person be
in authority over everything, whether there are no laws and
he is like a law himself, or even if there are laws, no matter whether he and his subjects are good, or neither he nor
they are good, or even if he is superior in virtue, except in
one case. What this case is needs to be stated, though it has
already been mentioned in a certain way before.

But first, distinctions must be made as to what it is that
calls for kingship, what for aristocracy, and what for constitutional government. And what calls for kingship is the sort
of multitude that naturally produces a family line excelling
in virtue that fits it for political leadership. What calls for   10
aristocracy is a multitude that naturally produces a stock of
people capable of being ruled as free persons by those fitted by virtue for leadership in political rule. And what calls
for constitutional government is a multitude in which there
naturally arises a military stock capable of being ruled and
ruling under a law that distributes offices according to merit
among those who are well off.[115] So whenever a whole fam-

---

115 The translation departs from Ross's text in preferring those manu-
     scripts that call the appropriate stock of people military. This is jus-
     tified by reference to 1279a 37-b 4. Military virtue is the only kind,

ily, or even one particular person among the rest, turns out to be surpassing in virtue to such an extent that his virtue exceeds that of everyone else, it is in that case just for that family or that one person to be king and have kingly author-
20   ity over all things. For as was said before, this is how it is, not only based on the sort of justice people customarily put forward when they set up aristocratic, oligarchic, and even democratic governments (since they all make claims of mer-it based on superiority, though not the same superiority), but also based on what was argued above. For it is surely not appropriate to kill or exile or ostracize such a person, or to claim he deserves to be ruled in his turn. For while it is not the natural thing for the part to exceed to the whole, this is what has happened with someone who has such a great superiority. So the only thing left is for such a person to be obeyed and for him to be in authority not by turns but sim-
30   ply. So about kingship, what different kinds it has, whether it is or is not advantageous for cities, and which ones, and how, let things be determined in this way.

Chapter 18

And since we claim there are three right forms of gov-ernment, the best of these would necessarily be the one man-aged by the best people, and this is the sort of government in which one person, or a whole family or multitude, would turn out to be surpassing in virtue compared to all the rest together, the latter capable of being ruled while the former are capable of ruling with a view to the life most worthy of choice, and since it was shown in our first discussions that in the best city the virtue of a man and that of a citizen are nec-
40   essarily the same, it is clear that one would organize a city under an aristocracy or kingship in the same manner and by the same means that a man becomes excellent. Hence the
1288B   education and states of character that make a man excellent will be just about the same as those that fit a man for politi-cal or kingly rule.

Now that these things have been determined, one needs to try to speak about the best form of government,

according to Aristotle, that can be present throughout a large popula-tion, and it gives higher responsibilities to those who can afford to equip and train themselves with heavy arms.

and say in what manner it may naturally arise and how it may be established.[116]

---

116 The transition anticipated here is picked up at the beginning of Bk. VII, and some modern scholars and translators have presumed to rearrange the order of the books. But it is characteristic of Aristotle's works to ascend dialectically, interweaving independent strands of argument, and it makes sense to back up and review existing governments and institutions before completing the more theoretical treatment of the inherent nature of all political association.

Book IV

Chapter 1

In all arts and all kinds of knowledge that have not come about piecemeal but are fully developed with regard to some one class of things, it is the business of a single kind to study what is suitable within each class—for instance, what sorts of training are advantageous for what sort of body as well as what the best training is (since the best kind is necessarily suited to a body that is most beautifully formed by nature and best furnished with resources), and also what single kind is best for the greatest number among them all (since this too is the task of the trainer's art), and further, if someone has a desire for fitness or knowledge not reaching the level involved in competition, it is no less the business of the coach or trainer to provide that capacity. And we see this likewise in doctoring and shipbuilding and clothing and every other art.

So it is clear that with the best form of government as well, it belongs to the same kind of knowledge to study what it is and of what sort it would be if it were most in accord with one's wishes and had no external impediments, and also what form is suited to what people (since it is perhaps impossible that many would achieve the best one, and consequently a good lawgiver and anyone who is a student of politics in the true sense ought not to overlook either the form that is most effective simply or the best form that can come from the underlying conditions). Also, thirdly, there is a government based on an assumption (for one ought to be able to study what is given, both how it might have come into being from the beginning and in what manner, once it has come into being, it might be preserved for the lon-

gest time; I am speaking of the sort of case in which some
city has ended up not governed by the best form of government, being unprovided with the necessary conditions for
it, or even by the best possible in the circumstances, but by
some inferior form). And besides all these things, one ought
to recognize the form of government that best suits *all* cities.

And so most people who have made pronouncements
about forms of government, even when they have spoken
beautifully in other respects, go astray when it comes to
what is useful. For one ought to study not only the best but
also the possible, and likewise the form that is easier to bring
about and more common to all people. At present, some seek
40   only the ultimate form, which requires a lot of equipment,
while those who speak of something more common just
1289A   praise the Spartan form of government, or some other one,
throwing out the existing array of forms. But they ought to
put forward an arrangement of a sort that would be easy
for people to be persuaded about and to introduce out of
their existing circumstances, since it is no less work to reor-
ganize a government than to put one together from the start,
just as unlearning something is no less work than learning
it from the start. Hence in addition to the things mentioned,
someone with the political art also ought to be able to help
existing governments, as was also said before. But this is impossible for someone who does not know how many forms
of government there are. As it is, some people think there is
one kind of democracy and one kind of oligarchy, but this
10   is not true. So one must not leave out of consideration the
varieties within the forms of government, how many there
are, and how many ways there are to combine them.

And it is also the business of this same sort of judgment to look into laws, both those that are best and those
that suit each form of government. For laws ought to be
adapted to forms of government, and not governments to
laws, and that is how people set them up. For a form of government is an arrangement for cities about the manner in
which ruling offices are distributed, what the authority in
the government is, and what the end sought by a particular community is, while the laws by which rulers ought to
rule and guard against those who violate them are separate
20   from the declarations that set forth the form of government.

So it is clear that it is necessary to have an understanding of the varieties and definition of each form of government for the purpose of setting up laws, since it is not possible for the same laws to be advantageous to all oligarchies and democracies, if in fact there is not one kind of democracy or oligarchy but more than one.

Chapter 2

And since in our first inquiry we distinguished three right forms of government, kingship, aristocracy, and constitutional rule, and three deviations from them, tyranny from kingship, oligarchy from aristocracy, and democracy from constitutional rule, and aristocracy and kingship have been spoken about (for studying what has to do with the best form of government is the same thing as speaking about these terms, since each of the two is meant to be organized on the basis of virtue furnished with resources), and it was also determined earlier what differences aristocracy and kingship have from each other, what remains is to go over constitutional rule, which is referred to by their common name, as well as the other forms of government, oligarchy, democracy, and tyranny.

And it is obvious which is the worst of these deviant forms and which second worst. For necessarily the deviant form of the one that is first and most divine would be the worst, and kingship necessarily either has the name alone without being kingship, or is kingship in virtue of a great superiority in the person ruling as king. So necessarily tyranny, being the worst, is the farthest removed from a constitution, and oligarchy is the second worst (since aristocracy is very far from this form of government), while democracy is the most tolerable. And one of the earlier thinkers has already pointed this out, but not by looking to the same criterion we are. For he judged that, when all the forms of government are decent, such as an honest oligarchy and so on, democracy is the worst, but when they are all bad it is best.[117] But we claim that these forms are completely misguided, and that it is not beautifully put to say one oligarchy

30

40

1289B

10

---

117 In Plato's *Statesman* (302E-303B), the Eleatic Stranger argues that the weakness of democracy makes it worse than any decent government that has power in fewer hands, but safer than any corrupt one.

is better than another, but only less bad. But let the verdict on this sort of thing be dismissed for now.

What needs to be determined first by us is how many varieties there are within the forms of government, if indeed there are a number of forms of democracy and oligarchy; next, which is most common and which most choiceworthy after the best form of government, and if any other form turns out to be aristocratic in character and beautifully organized, and at the same time suitable for most cities, what it is; next, which of the others is to be chosen for which cities (for it may be that for some, democracy is necessary rather than oligarchy, and for others, the latter rather than the former); 20 and after that, in what manner one who wants these forms of government—I mean democracy in each of its forms and oligarchy in its—ought to set them up; and finally, when we have made mention of all these things with the brevity they admit, an attempt needs to be made to go over what kinds of destruction and preservation belong to governments, both in common and to each kind separately, and by what causes it is especially in the nature of these things to happen.

Chapter 3

What is responsible for there being more than one form of government is that the number of parts of every city is more than one. For we see that all cities are composed first of 30 all of households, and then too that within this group, some are necessarily well off, others poor, and others in between, and of the well off and the poor, one group is armed and the other unarmed. And we see that the general populace is engaged in either farming, the business of the marketplace, or mechanical trades. And among the eminent people there are differences based on wealth and the extent of landed property, with respect to raising horses, for example, since this is not easy to do without being rich. This is why, in ancient times, there were oligarchies in all those cities whose power depended on their horses; people such as the Eretrians, the Chaldeans, the Magnesians on the Maeander, and many oth- 40 ers in Asia used horses for their wars against neighboring cities. Also, in addition to the differences based on wealth, 1290A there are differences based on either family or virtue, or anything other such thing that may have been mentioned as being part of a city in our remarks about aristocracy, for there we specified how many necessary parts every city consists of. Sometimes all of these parts take part in the government, sometimes a lesser or greater number of them. So it is obvious that there would necessarily be a number of governments differing from one another in form, since these parts differ among themselves in form. For a form of government is an arrangement of ruling offices, and these are all distributed in accord either with the power of the constituent parts or with some sort of equality they share among   10 them—I mean either among the poor, among the well off, or in some respect common to both. Therefore, there are necessarily exactly as many forms of government as there are arrangements reflecting superiorities and differences among the parts.

But there are thought to be two most of all; just as in the case of winds some are called north and others south while the rest are deviations from these, so too among forms of government there are two: the general populace and oligarchy. For people categorize aristocracy as a form of oligarchy, since it is a certain kind of rule by few, and the so-called constitutional rule as a form of democracy, just as, among the winds, they take an east wind as northerly and a west wind as southerly. And the way some people speak of the musical   20 modes is similar; there too they set down two forms, Dorian and Phrygian, and call the other scales Doric or Phrygic. So this is the assumption people are mostly in the habit of making about forms of government, but the way we distinguish them is truer and better: that while one or two forms are beautifully organized, the rest are deviations, in one sense from well-blended harmony and in another from the best constitution, the forms that are too tight and too much like mastery of slaves being oligarchic, and those that are too slack and soft being popularly ruled.

Chapter 4

But one should not regard democracy in such a simple   30 way as some people habitually do now, as being in place wherever the multitude is in authority (since in oligarchies and everywhere, the greater part is in authority) or regard oligarchy as being in place wherever few are in authority over the government. For if there were thirteen hundred people in all, and a thousand of them were rich and gave no share in ruling to the three hundred who were poor, even though they were free and like them in other respects, no one would claim they were ruled democratically. Likewise, if the poor were few but stronger than the rich who were greater in number, no one would refer to such a thing as

40 an oligarchy if the others, despite being rich, had no share
1290B in honors. So what ought to be said instead is that there is popular rule whenever the free are in authority and oligarchy whenever the rich are, but that the former happen incidentally to be many and the latter few, since there are a lot of free people but few rich ones. For otherwise, if ruling offices were distributed on the basis of size, as some claim they are in Ethiopia, or on the basis of beauty, that would be an oligarchy, since the number of beautiful or tall people is small. It is not sufficient, though, to define these forms of government by those criteria alone, but since there are a number of parts of both popular rule and oligarchy, it needs to be fur-

10 ther specified that when the free are few and rule a greater number who are not free, as in Apollonia on the Ionian Gulf, or in Thera, that is not popular rule either. For in each of these cities, those who were distinguished by high birth and were the first settlers of the colonies were in the positions of honor, even though they were few among many. Nor is it oligarchy if the rich rule because they are superior in number, as was formerly the case in Colophon, for before the war against the Lydians occurred, the majority held large estates there. Rather, there is democracy whenever those who are free and poor are greater in number and are in authority in the ruling office, and there is oligarchy whenever it is those

20 who are rich and better born and few.

So the fact that there is more than one form of government, and the reason why, have been stated. But let us go on to say that there are more forms than those mentioned, and say what they are and why, taking a starting point mentioned before. For we are agreed that every city has not just one part but more than one. It is the same as, if we intended to get a grasp of the species of animals, we would first separate out the things it is necessary for every animal to have (such as certain sense organs, something suited to work on and absorb food, such as a mouth and digestive tract, and in addition to these, parts by means of which each of the kinds moves). Then if there were only that many, but there were differences among them (I mean, for instance, a certain number of kinds of mouth and digestive tract and of sense organs, and also of parts suited to produce motion), then the number of combinations will necessarily make up the number of kinds of animals, since it is not possible for the same animal to have more than one variety of mouth or likewise of ears. So when all the possible linkages of these have been taken, they will produce species of animals, and exactly as many species of animals as there are combinations of necessary parts.

So it is the same way with the forms of government mentioned. For cities too are composed not of one but of many parts, as has been said repeatedly. One part is called farmers and deals with food and a second is the part called mechanical workers. This is the part that deals with the arts without which it is impossible for a city to be lived in, but while some of these arts have to be present by necessity, others are means to luxury or to living beautifully. A third involves the business of the marketplace, and by this I mean the part that occupies itself with sales and purchases and commerce and retailing, a fourth is the menial part, and a fifth class is the military defense, which, no less than those others, must necessarily be present if they are not going to be enslaved by any who come against them. Must it not be an impossibility for anything that is worth calling a city to be slavish by nature? A city is self-sufficient, and something slavish is not self-sufficient.

For this reason the way this matter is spoken of in the *Republic* is clever but not adequate. For Socrates claims a city is made up of four most necessary parts, and says these are a weaver, a farmer, a shoemaker, and a housebuilder, and then in turn, since these are not self-sufficient, adds a metal-worker and people to see to the necessary livestock, and then a merchant and a retailer. And these become the full total of his first city, as if every city were organized for the sake of necessities and not more so for the sake of what is beautiful,[118] and as if there was equal need for shoemak-

---

118   See the footnote to 1278b 23 above. Aristotle is referring to the passage

20 ers and farmers. He does not assign it a part for military
defense until, with its territory increasing and intruding on
its neighbors, they get themselves into war. But surely even
among the four people and however many are in association with them, it is necessary for there to be someone who
administers and judges what is just. So if one were to hold
that a soul is part of an animal more than a body is, then
things of this sort—something skilled at war, something to
take part in the judgment of justice, and in addition to these
something that deliberates, which is precisely the work of
political understanding—must be held to be part of cities
more than the things that extend as far as necessary use.
And whether these things are present in various separate
30 people or in the same persons makes no difference to the
argument, since it often turns out that the same people bear
arms and engage in farming. So if indeed the latter as well as
the former must be held to be parts of the city, it is obvious
that a heavy-armed force is a necessary part of a city.

A seventh part[119] consists of the people who are called
well off, and provides public services by means of its property. An eighth is the public-official part that does public
services in ruling offices, if indeed it is impossible for there
to be a city without rulers. So it is necessary for there to be
some people with the capacity to rule and be public servants
for the city either continuously or by turns in this sort of
service. And the remaining parts are the ones we just now
40 happened to single out, that deliberate and that judge matters of justice for people in disputes. So if these things need
to be done in cities, and be done in a beautiful and just man-
1291B ner, it is necessary for there to be some people who share the
virtue of citizens. Now it seems to most people that different
capacities are capable of being present in the same persons,
so that the same ones may be, for instance, military defenders and farmers and skilled workmen, or also engage in both

beginning in 369B of the *Republic*, in which Socrates describes what
Glaucon memorably calls a city of pigs. Socrates, as a first and mini-
mal hypothesis, imagines a city that satisfies only the simplest needs
of life and health; the inadequacy of that city provokes a spontaneous
response from the young men he is speaking to, who then take part in
searching for a more acceptable account.

119 No sixth part has been mentioned, but the end of Bk. VII, Chap. 8,
below, gives a similar list that includes priests.

deliberating and judging; and they all lay claim to virtue and believe themselves capable of filling most ruling offices. But for the same persons to be poor and rich is impossible. Hence these groups, the well-off and the needy, seem to be the principal parts of a city. Also, since for the most part the former are few and the latter many, these parts appear to be at the opposite extremes of the components of the city. So they also base the forms of government on the ascendancy of these parts, and there seem to be two forms, democracy and oligarchy.

Now it has been said above that there is more than one form of government, and for what reasons. Let us now state that there is more than one form of democracy and of oligarchy. And this is clear from the things that have been said. For there are a number of forms of populace, and a number of forms of those who are called eminent. One form of populace, for instance, consists of farmers, another of skilled workers, another of the group occupied with buying and selling in the marketplace, and another occupied with the sea, among whom one group is concerned with warfare, another with merchandise, another with passenger travel, and yet another with fishing. In many places a particular one of these groups is quite numerous, such as fishermen in Tarentum and Byzantium, battleship crews in Athens, merchant seamen in Aegina and Chios, and ferryboat crews in Tenedos. In addition to these there is the group of day-laborers, who have so little property that it is impossible for them to take time off, and also a free element not descended from citizens on both sides, and any other such form of multitude there may be. With the eminent people there are wealth, high birth, virtue, education, and various distinctions spoken of on the same basis.

A first sort of democracy, then, is one referred to most strongly on the basis of equality. The law in this sort of democracy declares that "equal" means that the needy are no more in ascendancy than the well-off, and that neither of the two is in authority but both are treated alike. For if in fact, as some people assume, freedom is most fully present in a democracy, and equality as well, the way in which this would be the case most of all would be for everyone to share alike to the fullest extent in the government. And since the

populace is the majority, and the opinion of the majority is authoritative, this must necessarily be a democracy. So this is one form of democracy. Another involves ruling offices
40 based on property assessments, but has these low; anyone who possesses the requisite amount has to be given the right
1292A to take part, but anyone who loses it takes no part. Another form of democracy has all citizens of undisputed descent take part, while the law rules. Another form of democracy has everyone take part in ruling offices, as long as they are citizens, while the law rules. Another form of democracy is the same in other respects, but the multitude, rather than the law, is in authority. This arises when decrees are authoritative and not laws, and happens because of demagogues. For in places ruled democratically under law, there can be no
10 demagogue, but the best citizens are in the forefront. But where the laws are not authoritative demagogues arise. For the populace becomes a monarch when it turns from many into a single composite, since the many are in authority not as particular persons but all together.

It is unclear in what sense Homer means "rule by many is not good," and whether he is speaking of this sort of rule or that in which there are several people who rule each on his own.[120] But this sort of popular rule, being monarchical, seeks to act like a monarch since it does not rule under law; it becomes like a master of slaves, and consequently servile flatterers are honored. This sort of popular rule is the analogue of tyranny among monarchies. Hence, too, their character is the same: both act like slavemasters over the
20 better sort of people, decrees are like the commands there, and a demagogue and a servile flatterer are the same and play analogous roles. Each of the two is especially strong with the respective kind of ruler—flatterers with tyrants and demagogues with populations of this sort. They are the ones who are responsible for the fact that decrees and not laws are authoritative, by referring everything to the populace. They end up becoming powerful by having the populace be in authority over everything, while they themselves have

---

120 The line quoted is spoken by Odysseus at II, 204 of the *Iliad*, when he has turned the Achaeans back from a disorderly mob into an army, and restored the supreme command to Agamemnon. Aristotle may find its application ambiguous in a political context, but he cites it with no such hesitation at the end of Bk. XII of the *Metaphysics*.

authority over the opinion of the populace, since the multitude is persuaded by them. Also, the ones who make accusations against officeholders claim the populace ought to
be the judge, and the invitation is cheerfully accepted, with
the result that all offices are utterly undone. One who claims   30
that this sort of democracy is no form of government at all
would seem to be making a reasonable objection. For where
laws do not rule, there is no government. The law ought to
rule over every general matter, while officeholders and the
particular government decide particular matters. So if democracy is one of the forms of government, it is clear that
this way of running it, in which everything is managed by
decrees, is not even democracy in the prevalent sense, since
no decree is capable of being general. So let the forms of democracy be distinguished in this way.

Chapter 5

As for forms of oligarchy, one has the ruling offices
based on property assessments so large that the poor, though   40
they are the majority, take no part, while anyone who owns
that much is allowed to take part in the government. It is
of another form when offices are filled from large property   1292B
assessments and they choose the remaining officials. (If they
do this from among them all, this seems to be more aristocratic; if only from among certain designated people, more
oligarchic.) It is a different form of oligarchy when a son succeeds his father, and a fourth when what was just mentioned
is the case and law does not rule, but the rulers do. This is
the counterpart among oligarchies of tyranny among monarchies, and among democracies, of the sort of democracy
we spoke of last. People call this sort of oligarchy a confed-   1292B
eracy of the powerful.

There are, then, this many forms of oligarchy and democracy, but one must not overlook the fact that it has turned
out in many places that, while the form of government resulting from the laws is not popular rule, it is still governed
in popular fashion because of custom and upbringing. Similarly, in turn, among other people, while the government as
a result of its laws inclines to the side of popular rule, by
upbringing and customs it is ruled oligarchically instead.
This turns out most often after changes in forms of govern-

ment. The people do not pass from one form to the other immediately, but are content at first to get the upper hand
20   on one another in small ways, so that the pre-existing laws remain while the group that has changed the government is in power.

Chapter 6

And the fact that there are this many forms of democracy and oligarchy is clear just from the things that were mentioned. For it is necessary either that all the parts of the populace mentioned share in the government, or that some do and some do not. Now when the part that farms and owns a modest estate is in authority in the government, they are governed by laws, because they have what it takes to live while they are working, but they are unable to take time off; consequently, they establish the law and convene only necessary assemblies. And others are allowed to take part
30   whenever they acquire the property assessment designated by the laws; by this provision, everyone who possesses it is allowed to take part. If it is not allowed at all for everyone to take part, it is oligarchic, but not[121] if they are allowed but it is impossible for them to take the time off because of a lack of revenue. So this is one form of democracy, for these reasons. A different form comes about from the next division, since it is possible for everyone who is an undisputed citizen by birth to be allowed to take part, while only those capable of taking the time off do so. Hence in this sort of democracy the laws rule because there is no revenue. A third form allows everyone who is free to take part in the government, al-
40   though they do not do so for the reason mentioned already, so that it is necessary for the law to rule in this form too. A
1293A   fourth form of democracy is one that arose in cities last in time. Because cities came to be much larger than they were in the beginning and an abundance of revenue was available, everyone takes part in the government on account of the ascendancy of the multitude, and they do share in it and do govern because even the poor are able to take the time off, since they get a fee. In fact this sort of multitude has the

---

121 Something is missing in the manuscripts, and Ross hesitantly suggests the "not." The "revenue" mentioned is explained below as public funds to pay for service in the assembly.

most leisure, since care for their private affairs does not encumber them in any way, while it does encumber the rich, so much so that they often do not participate in the assembly or in jury service. Hence the multitude of poor people, and not the laws, come to be in authority over the government.

So there are this many forms of democracy, of these sorts, on account of these necessities, and there are the following forms of oligarchy. When a greater number of people have estates, but of an inferior quality and not very big, that is the first form of oligarchy, since they confer the right to take part on anyone who possesses one, and because of the multitude of people participating in the administration, it is necessary for the law, rather than human beings, to be in authority. For they are so much farther removed from monarchy, having neither so much property that they can take time off and neglect it, nor so little that they have to be supported by the city, that they consider it a necessity that the law should rule them, and not they themselves. But if those who have estates are fewer than in the previous case, and the estates larger, the second form of oligarchy arises. For since they are stronger they expect to have the upper hand, and so they choose from the other citizens the ones who gain entry to the administration, but because they are not yet so strong that they can rule without law, they make a law to this effect. If the situation gets ratcheted up by their being fewer and having larger estates, a third stage of oligarchy arises, that in which they keep the ruling offices to themselves, by a law ordaining that the offices of those who die be inherited by their sons. But when the situation goes so far that it is strained to the limit by the bulk of their estates and their multitude of friends, this sort of confederacy of the powerful is close to monarchy, and human beings come to be in authority rather than the law. And this is the fourth form of oligarchy, the counterpart to the last form of democracy.

Chapter 7

There are still two forms of government besides democracy and oligarchy; one of them everyone speaks of, and it was mentioned as one of the four forms. (The four they speak of are monarchy, oligarchy, democracy, and fourth the form they call aristocracy.) But a fifth is the one referred to by the name common to them all (for they call it constitutional rule), though because it does not often arise, it escapes the notice of those (such as Plato) who attempt to count up the forms of government, and they deal with only four of 1293B the governments. Now it is beautifully appropriate to call the form we went over in our first discussions aristocracy. For it is only justice to refer to the form of government made up of those who are the best people simply on the basis of virtue, and not by some particular assumption about good men, as aristocracy, for in it alone the same person is a good man and a good citizen, while the people who are good in the others are so in relation to their own forms of government. Nevertheless, there are governments that have certain differences both from those that are oligarchically ruled and from the sort called constitutional rule, and they are called 10   aristocracies. For where office holders are chosen not just on the basis of wealth but also on the basis of excellence, this form of government differs from both and is called aristocratic. For even in governments in which virtue is not made a matter of common concern, there are still certain people who are well regarded and thought to be decent sorts. So where the government looks to wealth, virtue, and the general populace, as in Carthage, this is aristocratic; and this is the case also in those such as Sparta that look to only two things, to virtue and the populace, and where there is a mixture of these, of democracy and virtue. So besides the first and best sort of government, there are also these two forms 20   of aristocracy, and thirdly there are those forms of so-called constitutional rule that tip the scale more toward oligarchy.

Chapter 8

What remains is for us to speak about the form of government that has the name "constitutional rule," and about tyranny. We have adopted this order even though the former does not amount to a deviant form, and the aristocracies just mentioned do not either, because the truth is, they do all fall short of the form of government that is right in the highest degree, and then too because the forms that deviate from these (the ones we spoke of in the chapters at the beginning) tend to be counted in along with them. As for tyranny, it is reasonable for it to be made mention of last because it least

of all *is* a form of government, while the inquiry we are pur- **30**
suing is concerned with forms of government. So the reason
things have been put in this order has been stated, and it is
now up to us to make evident what has to do with constitutional rule. The meaning of it will be more clear when it is
distinguished from oligarchy and democracy, since constitutional rule, to put it simply, is a mixture of oligarchy and
democracy. But people are in the habit of calling those mixtures that lean more to the side of democracy constitutional
rule, while they call those that lean more toward oligarchy
aristocracies because education and high birth are more often found among those who are well off. Also, those who are
well off seem to have the things for the sake of which unjust
people commit injustice, and for that reason people refer
to them as "beautiful and good"[122] and eminent. So since   **40**
aristocracy is meant to assign the superior role to the best
among the citizens, people say of oligarchies too that they
draw more upon those who are beautiful and good. And it   **1294A**
seems to be an impossibility for a city to be well regulated if
it is not run along aristocratic lines but by its worst elements,
and likewise for a city that is not well regulated to be run
aristocratically. For there is no good regulation if the laws
are well laid down but not obeyed. Hence when the laws laid
down are obeyed, that should be thought of as one aspect of
a well-regulated condition, and when the laws people abide
by are beautifully laid down, that should be thought of as
another, since it is possible for laws to be obeyed even when
they are badly laid down. And "laws beautifully laid down"
admits of two senses, since they may be either the best possible or the best simply.

　　Aristocracy is thought to consist primarily in having   **10**
honors distributed in accord with virtue, since the distinguishing mark of aristocracy is virtue, of oligarchy wealth,
and of popular rule freedom. The enactment of what seems
good to the majority is present in them all, for in oligarchy
and aristocracy as well as among the populace, that which
seems good to the greater part of those taking part in the
government is authoritative. So in most cities the form of
constitutional rule is called by the wrong name,[123] since the

---

122　See the footnote to 1270b 24 above.

123　The translation follows Ross's editorial insertion. The text is unclear,

mixture it aims at is only of the well-off and the needy, or
of wealth and freedom, because in most places, in practice
those who are well off are held to occupy the place belonging to the beautiful and good. For since there are three things
20 disputing over equality in the government—freedom,
wealth, and virtue (since the fourth, which people call high
birth, goes with the latter two, for high birth is wealth and
virtue of ancient standing)—it is clear that the mixture of
the pair consisting of the well-off and the needy ought to
be called constitutional rule, while the mixture of the three,
compared to the others, most deserves the name aristocracy,
aside from its true and primary form.

It has been stated, then, that there are other forms of
government besides monarchy, democracy, and oligarchy,
and it is evident what these are like, and what differences aristocracies have among themselves, and constitutional rule
from aristocracy, and that these are not far apart from each
other.

Chapter 9

30   Following upon the things that have been said, let us
discuss the manner in which the form called constitutional
rule becomes distinct from democracy and oligarchy, and
how one ought to set it up. At the same time, the attributes by
which democracy and oligarchy are defined will also become
clear, since what needs to be done is to grasp the dividing line
between these and then make a composite of them by taking
a sort of jigsaw piece[124] from each of the two. And there are
three patterns for composition or mixture. One may in one

---

but I take the meaning of the argument in this paragraph to be that
politeia (constitutional rule) is a name that rightly applies to a form that
blends two criteria for holding office that can be constitutionally specified, property ownership and free birth. It is not a matter of definition
that excludes the third criterion, but the fact that virtue is different in
kind from the other two. Where someone from the poorer class can be
voted into higher office on the basis of merit, the government is a form
of aristocracy. But if those voting mistake the advantages of wealth for
virtue, the basis for higher office is still in fact the property qualification characteristic of constitutional rule.

124 The word *sumbolon*, usually translated "tally," referred to the irregu-
larly shaped halves of a broken coin divided between two parties to a
contract.

pattern take both of two things that each uses as law, as in the
case of judging. For in oligarchies, they assess a fine against
the well-off for not doing jury service and do not assign a fee
for the needy, while in democracies, they assign a fee for the   40
needy and no fine for the well-off. To have them both is a
common ground and mean between these forms, and hence
is suited to constitutional rule, since it is a mixture of both.   1294B
This then is one way of coupling them. Another is to take a
middle course between arrangements the two of them make,
as for serving in an assembly. Those who serve in one form
do so without any property qualification or a miniscule one,
those in the other with a large one; the common ground is
to have neither one, but a qualification intermediate between
the two. A third way, with a pair of arrangements, is to take
some parts of the oligarchic law and some parts of the democratic one. I mean, for instance, it seems democratic for offices
to be chosen by lot and oligarchic for them to be elected, and
democratic not to have a property qualification but oligar-   10
chic to have one. Accordingly, it is a mark of aristocracy or
constitutional rule to take one element from each, making the
offices elected as in an oligarchy, but free of a property qualification as in democracy.

   This, then, is the manner of mixing them, and what
marks out democracy and oligarchy as having been well
mixed is that it is possible to speak of the same form of government as democracy or oligarchy, since it is clear that it is
because they are beautifully mixed that people who speak
that way are led to do so. The mean also has this character,
since each of the extremes is evident in it, which is exactly
what happens in the Spartan form of government. For many
people try to speak of it as being a democracy, since its ar-   20
rangement includes a number of democratic features. First
of all, for example, in regard to the bringing up of children,
those of the rich are brought up like those of the poor, and
the manner in which they are educated is one for which the
children of the poor also have the means. And likewise in the
next stage of life, and once they become men, the same is true,
since there is no way in which a rich person is distinguished
from a poor one; what pertains to food is the same for everyone at the common meals, and the clothing rich people wear
is of such a sort as any poor person whatever is capable of
providing. What is more, of the two highest offices, the popu-   30

lace chooses the one and takes part in the other (since they choose the elders and participate in the ephorate). But others call it an oligarchy because it includes a number of oligarchic features; for instance all ruling offices are elected and none chosen by lot, and a small number have authority over penalties of death and exile, and there are many other such things. And it ought to be the case in a government that has been beautifully mixed that it seems to be both things and neither. And it ought to be preserved through itself and not by external means, and through itself not because those who want it that way are the majority (since this could be the case even in a bad form of government), but because none of the parts of

40   the city wants a different form of government at all. So the manner in which one ought to set up constitutional rule, and likewise the governments deserving the name of aristocracies, has now been stated.

Chapter 10

1295A   The thing left for us to speak of is tyranny, not because there is much to be said about it, but so that it may take its part in the inquiry, since we also set it down as a part of the array of forms of government. We delineated kingship in our first discussions, in which we made an examination, in regard to the kind of kingship most commonly spoken of, whether it is disadvantageous or an advantage to cities, and who should be set up as a king, where he should be drawn from, and how this should be done. And we separated out two forms of tyranny in the course of examining kingship, because their

10   power crosses over in a certain way toward kingship, since both these forms of rule are in accord with law. For among some of the barbarians, they choose supreme commanders as monarchs, and in the past among the ancient Greeks some monarchs, whom people called caretakers, came to power in this way. These have some differences from one another, but they were kingly in being under law and in having a sole ruler over willing subjects, but tyrannical in ruling according to their own will like a master over slaves. But there is a third form of tyranny, the one that seems to be tyranny in the highest sense and is the counterpart to full-scale kingship.

20   And this is necessarily the sort of tyranny there is whenever a monarchy is not subject to review and rules over all those

who are the ruler's equals and betters with a view to its own advantage and not that of those who are ruled. For this reason it is involuntary, since no free person willingly puts up with that sort of rule. So for the reasons given, there are these and this many forms of tyranny.

Chapter 11

What is the best form of government, and what is the best life for most cities and most human beings? The questions are posed not to those who measure by a standard of virtue that is beyond ordinary people, or by an education that requires a fortunate nature and resources, or by having in place a government one might wish for, but by a life that is possible for most people to share and a form of government which most cities are capable of taking part in. As for the governments that people call aristocracies, about which we were just speaking, some fall outside the reach of most cities, while others border on the form called constitutional rule, so that it is appropriate to speak of them both as though they were one. 30

Judgment about all these things is drawn from the same elements. For if it was beautifully said in the *Ethics* that the happy life is one in accord with unimpeded virtue, and that virtue is a mean,[125] then the mean in life, consisting of a mean condition every person is capable of attaining, would necessarily be best, and these same terms would necessarily also apply to the virtue and vice of a city and a government, since a form of government is one sort of life of a city. And in all cities, the city has three parts—those who are exceptionally well off, those who are exceptionally needy, and those 40 1295B

---

125 By referring to the mean (*to meson*), Aristotle is excluding intellectual excellence and speaking of virtue of character. The principal such virtues are courage, temperance, and justice. These are not attributes of a middling or mediocre sort of person, nor are they out of the reach of any person. They are means in the sense that they belong to a state of character that is not controlled by momentary impulses of fear, desire for pleasure, or greed, but has not overcome those impulses by substituting for them a rigid discipline of self-denial. The life of virtue, as Aristotle describes it in the *Nicomachean Ethics*, is a life of unimpeded self-fulfillment, lived through the power of choice. Anyone who lives it is called decent (*epieikês*) or good (*agathos*) by Aristotle; but there is another word, *spoudaios*, that he reserves for people of shining excellence. See Bk. III, Chap. 4, above, where Aristotle explicitly says that excellence as a citizen does not require intellectual virtue (1277a 14-16).

in the third group in between these. Now since it is agreed that measure and the mean are best,[126] it is clear that even with the gifts of fortune, a moderate possession is best of all. For that makes it easiest to be obedient to reason, whereas an extreme degree of beauty, strength, high birth, or wealth, or the opposites of these, an extreme degree of beggarliness or weakness or exceptional dishonor make it hard to follow
10 reason. For the one sort tend more to become insolent and vicious on a grand scale, while the other sort are too apt to become dishonest and succumb to petty vices; and acts of injustice stem from either insolence or dishonesty. Also, those in the middle range are least likely to avoid ruling or be eager to rule, and both these things are harmful to cities. And in addition to these things, those who have an overabundance of the goods of fortune—strength, wealth, friends, and other things of that sort—do not want to be ruled and do not even know how to. And this is already part of them straight from when they are children at home, for the result of luxury is that they do not get in the habit of being ruled even in their schoolrooms. But those who suffer from an extreme state of neediness in these things are too broken in spirit. Conse-quently, the latter sort of people do not know how to rule,
20 but only how to be ruled under a slavish rule, while the for-mer sort do not know how to be ruled in any way at all, but only how to rule the way slavemasters rule. So a city comes to consist of slaves and masters and not of free people, with one group resentful and the other contemptuous.

These things are the farthest removed from friendship and political association, for association has a friendly char-acter, since people do not want to associate with their en-emies even on a journey. A city is in fact meant to be made up of people who are equal and alike to the greatest possible extent, and this is present most of all among those in the middle range. Consequently, that city is necessarily the best governed which consists of those people out of whom we claim a city is naturally organized. And these are the most
30 secure of the citizens in a city. For they do not crave the

---

126 An inscription on the temple of Apollo at Delphi read "measure is best." As for wealth and poverty in particular, one may note Socrates' argument in the *Republic* (421C-422A) that both conditions blight hu-man lives.

things that belong to others the way the poor do, and others do not crave theirs the way the poor crave the things belonging to the rich. And by not being plotted against or plotting against others, they pass their lives free of danger. For this reason Phocylides made a beautiful prayer in saying "Many things are best for those in the middle; I want to be someone in the middle in a city."[127]

Therefore it is clear that the political association that makes use of the middle group is best, and also that the sort of cities that can be well governed are those in which the middle range is large, especially if it is more powerful than both the other parts, or if not, more powerful than one of the two, since by being added to that side it makes the scale tip and prevents the opposite excesses from happening. Hence the greatest good fortune is for those involved in the gov-   **40**
ernment to have property that is moderate and sufficient,   **1296A**
since wherever some people own a great many things and others none, what comes about is either extreme popular rule or unmixed oligarchy, or a tyranny arising from both excesses. For tyranny arises out of both the most reckless sort of democracy and oligarchy, but much less so out of the middle sorts or those close to them. We shall state the reason later in the chapters dealing with changes in forms of government. It is evident, though, that the middle form is best, since it alone is free of faction. For where the middle range is large, factions and schisms among the citizens occur least. And large cities are more free of faction for the same   **10**
reason, because the middle part is large. But in small cities it is easy to divide all the citizens into two groups, so that no middle range is left, and just about everyone is needy or well off. Democracies are also more stable than oligarchies because of the middle group, since there are more of them in democracies than in oligarchies, and they take a greater share of the honors. Whenever, in the absence of this group, the needy grow too great in number, things get into a bad condition and they are quickly ruined. One ought to take as a sign of this the fact that the best lawgivers are from the middle range of citizens. For Solon was one of these, as is   **20**
clear from his poetry, as were Lycurgus (for he was not a

---

127 A more elegant and thoughtful version of the same sentiment may be found in Socrates' prayer at the end of Plato's *Phaedrus*.

king) and Charondas and just about the greatest number of the others.

It is also clear from these things why most governments are either democracies or oligarchies. For since the middle group is often small in number in them, whichever group gets the upper hand, whether it is those who have property or the populace, always moves away from the middle and brings the government into line with its own members, so that it becomes either popular rule or oligarchy. In addition to these things, because of the occurrence of factions and battles with one another by the populace and those who are well off, whichever group turns out to be more power-

30 ful than the opposing side sets up a government that is not common or equal, but takes the upper hand in the government as its prize of victory, and makes it either a democracy or an oligarchy. Also, each of the two powers that have come into positions of leadership in Greece have looked to their own forms of government and set up either democracies or oligarchies in the cities, looking out not for the cities' advantage but for their own.[128] Consequently, for these reasons the middle form of government never occurs or only on few occasions and in few places. In the powers that have attained leadership up to now, only one man has allowed himself to

40 be persuaded to permit this sort of arrangement,[129] and by

1296B now a custom has even taken hold among those in the cities that they do not want equality, but either seek to rule or endure being mastered.

What the best form of government is, then, and for what reason, is clear from these things. And among the other forms, since we claim there is more than one sort of de-

---

128 The Athenian empire at sea and the Spartan alliance on land were buttressed by the local democratic or oligarchic factions, respectively, of their constituent cities, and they helped bring those groups to power. See Thucydides, *Peloponnesian War*, Bk. I, Chap. 19.

129 There is no agreement among scholars about who the one man is. Much of their speculation may be beside the point Aristotle is making here, which seems to apply only to Athenian and Spartan policy toward the cities allied with them. It is possible that he is thinking of Brasidas, the Spartan commander who told the people of Acanthus that his aim was to liberate them from the Athenians, not subject them to their own oligarchic party. See Thucydides, *Peloponnesian War*, Bk. IV, Chap. 86.

mocracy and more than one sort of oligarchy, which of them should be ranked first, second, and so on in succession for being better and worse, is not difficult to see now that the best form has been determined. For the one closest to this must always be better, while the one at a greater distance from the middle must be worse, so long as one is not judging on some hypothesis. And by "on some hypothesis" I mean   10
that often, though another form of government is more worthy of choice, nothing prevents a different form from being more advantageous to certain people.

Chapter 12

What form of government is advantageous for what people, and what sort for what sort of people, is the next thing to go over after what has been discussed. But first, the same point needs to be stated about all of them in general, namely that the part wanting the city's form of government to remain in place needs to be stronger than the part that does not want that. And every city is made up of quality and quantity. By quality I mean freedom, wealth, education, and high birth, and by quantity, superiority in number. And it is possible that, while the quality is present in one of the   20
parts out of which the city is organized, and the quantity in another part (the low born being greater in number than the high born, for instance, or the needy greater in number than the rich), the latter still does not exceed the former in quantity as much as it falls short in quality. In this case a comparative judgment of the one against the other needs to be made. And in a place where the number of the needy exceeds the proportion described, it is natural for there to be a democracy, and the particular form of democracy that applies to the excess in each population; if, for example, the number of farmers predominates, the first sort of democracy is natural, but if the number of mechanical workers and wage earners does, the last sort is, and similarly with the   30
others in between these. But in a place where the number of well off and eminent people exceeds in quality more than it falls short in quantity, oligarchy is natural, and in the same manner, the particular form of oligarchy that applies to the predominant part within the oligarchic group.

And the lawgiver always ought to include the middle

group in his form of government; if he lays down oligarchic laws, he should aim them at those in the middle, and
if he lays down democratic ones, he should bring them into
his laws. And in a place where the number of those in the
middle group exceeds either both extremes together, or
40   even just one of the two, it is possible for there to be lasting
1297A constitutional rule. For there is no fear that the rich would
ever conspire with the poor against them, since neither
side would ever want to be subject to the other one, and if
they were looking for a more communal arrangement, they
would not find any other besides this one. They would not
put up with ruling by turns because of their distrust of one
another; but the most trusted person everywhere is a neutral
arbiter, and the one in the middle is a neutral arbiter. A government will be more lasting to the degree that it is better
mixed. Even among those who want to produce aristocratic
governments, many go astray not only in giving the larger
10   role to those who are well off, but also in misleading the
populace.[130] For in the course of time a true evil will necessarily result from false goods, and the encroachments of the
rich are more destructive to the government than those of
the populace.

Chapter 13

The tricks people come up with for the sake of pretens-
es directed at the populace in constitutional rule are five in
number, having to do with the assembly, offices, lawcourts,
arms, and gymnastic training. With the assembly, the trick is
to allow everyone to be in the assembly, but to impose a fine
only on the well-off if they do not take part in it, or a much
20   greater one on them; with offices, it is to allow the needy
to decline them on oath of hardship, but not to allow those
who meet a property qualification to do so; with lawcourts,
it is to have a fine for well-off people who do not serve on
juries, but an exemption for the needy, or a large fine for the
former and a small one for the latter, as in Charondas's laws.

---

130 The following chapter details the tricks a badly mixed constitution
might use to limit the participation of the common people, while giving them the illusion of a role in the government. In Bk. X, Chap. 1, of
the *Nicomachean Ethics*, Aristotle makes an argument similar to the one
here, against those who think that the common people ought to be told
that pleasure is a bad thing.

In some places, everyone who signs up is allowed to be in the assembly and serve on juries, but people who sign up and do not serve in either the assembly or the courts incur large fines, so that they will avoid signing up because of the fine, and not serve in the assembly or courts because of not signing up. And they make laws along the same lines about bearing arms and doing gymnastic training. For the needy 30 are allowed not to possess arms, but there is a fine for the well-off for not possessing them, and there is no fine for the former if they do not do gymnastic training but there is a fine for the well-off, so that the latter take part because of the fine while the former take no part because of not fearing one. So these are oligarchic tricks used in legislation, but in democracies there are tricks opposite to these. For they provide a fee to the needy to serve in the assembly and on juries, and assign no fine for the well-off. So, obviously, if one wants to mix them justly, one ought to put together things from both sides, and provide a fee for one group and a fine for 40 the other, since by these means they would all participate, while by the other means the government comes to consist 1297B of only one side.

And the government ought to consist only of those bearing arms, but it is not possible simply to define a property qualification, and say that much needs to be available; instead, after investigating the maximum amount that so falls out that there will be more people taking part in the government than not taking part, one should assign that. For the poor are willing to keep calm even when they have no share in honors, so long as no one treats them insolently or takes away any of their property. But this is no easy thing, for it does not always turn out that those who take part in the administration are courteous people. And people are in 10 the habit, when there is war, of hesitating to serve, if they get no food and they are needy; if one provides them with food, though, they are willing to go to war.

In some places, the government is drawn not only from those who bear arms but also from those who have done so. Among the Malians, the government was drawn from these, though the offices were chosen from among the soldiers. And the first form of government that arose among the Greeks after the kingships was drawn from among the

warriors, and at first from among the cavalrymen, because war got its strength and superiority from the cavalrymen.
20   For a heavy-armed force is useless without organization, and among the ancients experience in such matters as formations was not to be found, so that the strength was in the cavalry. But as the cities grew and gained more strength in their armed men, more people took part in the government. And it is for this reason that what we now call constitutional rule, people of earlier times used to call democracy. It was reasonable for the ancient governments to be oligarchic and kingly, since, because of underpopulation, they did not have much of a middle group, and it, being small in number and weak in organization, put up with being ruled.

   The reason there are several forms of government,
30   then, and why there are others beyond the ones spoken of (since democracy is not one in number, and likewise with the rest), and also what their differences are and the reason they turn out that way, and in addition, which of the forms of government may be said to be best in most cases, and which of the other forms fits what sorts of people, have been stated.

Chapter 14

   And let us speak of the things that come next in turn, both in common and separately for each form of government, taking a start that applies to them all. Now in every form of government there are three parts about which a lawgiver of serious stature needs to make a study to see what is advantageous for each. When these are in a beautiful condition, the government is necessarily in a beautiful condition,
40   and forms of government have differences among themselves according to differences in these parts. One of these three parts is the answer to the question: what is it that de-
1298A   liberates about common concerns? The second is what has to do with offices, that is, which ones there ought to be and with authority over what matters, and what sort of choice ought to take place for them. And the third is, what is it that does the judging? The deliberative part is in authority over war and peace and making and dissolving alliances; laws; death, exile, and confiscation of property; and choosing and reviewing office holders. And necessarily, either all these

decisions are assigned to all the citizens or all to some (for instance to one or more offices, or different ones to different offices), or some of them to all and some to some.

Now for all the citizens to deliberate, and about all things, is characteristic of popular rule, since the populace seeks that sort of equality, but there are a number of ways for them all to decide. One way is by turns rather than all together, as is done in the constitution of Telecles the Milesian; and in other constitutions the collective administration convenes and deliberates, but everyone enters the offices by turns, from the tribes and their absolutely smallest parts, until it goes through everyone. In these cases, they all convene only for establishing laws and on matters pertaining to the constitution, and to hear proclamations from the officials. Another way is for all to deliberate together, but to convene only for elections of officials, lawmaking, matters of war and peace, and reviews of officials, while the officials, who are either elected from among them all or chosen by lot, deliberate on other matters assigned to each of them. Another way is for the citizens to meet about the officials and to review them, and deliberate about war and alliances, while on other matters, as many elected officials as possible manage affairs; such officials rule in those matters in which people with knowledge are necessary. And a fourth way is for everyone to convene and deliberate about everything, while the officials decide on nothing but only do the preparatory work; this is exactly the way the last form of democracy manages things now, the form we claim is analogous to an oligarchy that is a confederacy of the powerful and a monarchy that is tyrannical. All these, then, are democratic ways of proceeding.

For some people to deliberate about everything is oligarchic, and this has a number of different forms. For when people are chosen on the basis of moderate property qualifications, and are numerous because of the moderateness of that qualification, and they do not make changes where the law forbids it but follow the law, and anyone who meets the property qualification is allowed to take part, then such a government *is* an oligarchy but is, by being moderate, one that inclines toward constitutional rule. But when not everyone takes part in deliberating but only those who are

10

20

30

40

1298B

elected, but they rule in accord with law as in the preceding case, it is oligarchic. And when the very people who have the authority to deliberate choose themselves, or when a son succeeds his father, and they are in authority over the laws, this arrangement is necessarily oligarchic in the extreme. But when certain people are in authority over certain matters, when, for instance, everyone is in authority over war and peace and reviewing officials and the officials over everything else, and they are elected and not chosen by lot, the government is an aristocracy. And if elected people are in authority over some matters, but on other matters it is people chosen by lot, and chosen by lot either simply or from a predetermined group, or those elected and those chosen

10   by lot have authority in common, then in some cases this is constitutional rule inclining toward aristocracy and in others it is simply constitutional rule. The part that deliberates, then, is distinguished in relation to the forms of government in this way, and each government manages it according to the distinction described.

And for the sort of democracy that is nowadays considered to be a democracy most of all (I mean the sort in which the populace is in authority even over the laws), for the sake of deliberating better, it is advantageous to do the same thing that is done in oligarchies with the lawcourts. For they assign a fine to those they want to serve on juries to make sure they do serve, and popular governments assign a fee to the needy. It is to their advantage to do this for the

20   assemblies as well, for everyone will deliberate better when they deliberate in common, the populace with the eminent people, and they with the multitude. It is also advantageous for those who deliberate to be elected, or chosen by lot, in equal numbers from the parts, and advantageous too, if the popular part of the citizens far exceeds the other part in number, either not to give a fee to them all but only to as many as balance out the eminent citizens, or to eliminate the excess by lot. In oligarchies, it is advantageous either to draft in some assembly members from the populace or to provide for an official group of the sort there sometimes is in constitutional rule, which they call pre-councils or guardians of

30   the law, and to deal only with those matters these groups have deliberated on in advance. For this way the populace will take part in deliberating, but will have no power to

undo anything in the constitution. Also the populace might vote just on those things brought before them, or on nothing contrary to these, or else they might all contribute their advice while only the officials deliberate. And what ought to be done is the opposite way of what happens in constitutional rule: they ought to give the multitude authority to vote things down but no authority to vote them into effect, but let them be referred back to the officials. But in constitutional rule they do things upside-down, for the few have authority to vote things down and no authority to vote things into effect, but they always refer them back to the multitude. So on the deliberative and authoritative part of the government, let distinctions be made in this way.

Chapter 15

Next after these things is the division of offices. For this part of the government involves many differences in the number of offices, what they have authority over, and as far as time is concerned, how much belongs to each office (for some constitutions make them six months or less, others a year or more long-lasting), and whether the offices ought to be permanent or long-lasting or neither, or whether the same people ought to hold them multiple times or not the same person twice but only once, and also regarding the appointment of officials, from which groups they ought to come and by whom they ought to be chosen and how. In all these respects, one ought to be able to distinguish the number of ways things are capable of being done, and then fit the various sorts of ways to the forms of government they are advantageous to.

But it is not easy even to determine what things one ought to call offices, since the political association requires many people in charge of things, and not all of those who are elected or chosen by lot should be classed as ruling officials. For instance, first of all, there are priests, and this has to be classed as something different from the political offices. Sponsors of dramatic festivals are also elected, and so are heralds and ambassadors. Some public concerns are political, and either involve all the citizens in some action, as with a general over those in the military, or deal with a part, as with the overseers of women and children; others

40

1299A

10

20

relate to household management, for cities often elect grain-rationers,[131] and others are subsidiary positions to which cities that are well off appoint slaves. To put it simply, the positions that especially ought to be spoken of as ruling offices are those which are assigned certain matters on which to deliberate, decide, and give orders, and especially the last, since giving orders is more characteristic of a ruler. But while these things make virtually no difference in practice (for no verdict has ever been handed down on those who 30   dispute over the name), they do merit some further theoretical study.

What sorts of offices, and how many, are necessary if there is going to be a city, and what sorts, while not necessary, are still useful for excellent government, are questions one might raise instead in connection with every form of government, and especially about small cities. For in large ones, it is possible to assign one office for one job, and this ought to be done; for since there are many citizens, many people are able to enter office, so that some perform ruling functions at long intervals of time and others only once, and each job gets better care from someone whose sole business 1299B   it is than from someone busy with many things. But in small cities it is necessary to combine many offices into few, since with underpopulation it is not easy for many people to be in office. For who will their next successors be? Sometimes, though, small cities need the same offices and laws as large ones, except that, while the latter need the same offices filled often, in the former this need comes along at long intervals of time. Hence nothing prevents them from assigning an office many cares at the same time, since they will not get in the way of one another, and with their underpopulation it is 10   necessary for them to make the offices like skewer-lamps.[132] So if we can say how many offices it is necessary for there to be in every city, and how many are not necessary but ought to be there, someone who knows these things could more easily combine into a single office the sorts of official func-

---

131 Or possibly inspectors of weights and measures.

132 Presumably a roasting-spit made to double as a lamp-stand, for use on military campaigns. This is not quite the same sort of thing as the Delphic knife mentioned at 1252b 2, an all-purpose implement for carving, but something designed to combine two unrelated functions.

tions it is fitting to combine.

It is also fitting that the following point not be over-looked, namely, which sorts of things many local offices ought to look after, and which sorts a single office ought to have authority over everywhere—whether, for good or-der for example, there ought to be a market constable for the marketplace and another official for another place, or the same one everywhere. And there is also the matter of whether one ought to divide offices in relation to the action they are concerned with or in relation to people; I mean, for instance, whether there should be one office in charge of good order or different ones for children and women. And in relation to the forms of government, there is the matter of whether the kinds of offices also differ in each or have no difference—whether, for instance, the same offices are in au-thority in democracy, oligarchy, aristocracy, and monarchy, though not drawn from equal or similar people but from dif-ferent groups in the different ones, say from educated people in aristocracies, rich people in oligarchies, and free people in democracies, or some of the offices happen to be determined by those very differences, so that in some cases the same ones are advantageous and in other cases different ones. For it is fitting that the same offices be large in one place and small in another. But there are surely also some offices that are peculiar to the form of government, such as that of the pre-councilors; for this is not democratic—a council is suited to popular rule. There does need to be some sort of body that will take care of deliberating in advance for the populace, so it can be absorbed in its business, but if this is small in num-ber it is oligarchic; but it is necessary for pre-councilors to be few in number and hence oligarchic. But where both these offices are present, the pre-councilors serve as a check on the councilors, since the councilor is suited to popular rule and the pre-councilor to oligarchy. And the power of the council is also overturned in those sorts of democracies in which the populace itself convenes and transacts all business. This usually happens when there is an abundance of payment for those who serve in the assembly, since they have the free time to gather frequently and decide everything themselves. And the overseers of children and women, and any other officials there may be with authority for that sort of manage-ment, are aristocratic. They are not democratic (for how is

20

30

1300A

it possible to keep the women of the poor from going out?), or oligarchic (for the women of the oligarchs live in luxury).

10   Let this much be said about these matters for now; what needs to be done is to try to go over appointments of officials from the beginning. There are distinctions within three defining characteristics, which, when put together, necessarily take in all the ways of appointing them. One of these three is who the people are who appoint the officials, a second is whom those appointed are drawn from, and the remaining one is in what manner it is done. And there are three distinctions within each of these three. For either all or some of the citizens appoint them, and either from among all or from among some designated group (on the basis, for instance, of a property qualification, or of family, or virtue, or some other such thing, the way people were appointed among the Megarians from among those who came back together from exile and joined in fighting against the populace), and these things are done either by election or by lot.

20   And these things may in turn be paired together; I mean that some may appoint some offices while all appoint others, and some may be drawn from among all and others from among some, and some by election and others by lot.

Out of these, there will be six[133] ways within each distinction. For either all appoint from all by election, or all from all by lot, or all from some by election, or all from some by lot (and if from all, either by turns, for instance according to tribes, districts, or fraternal groups, until it goes through all the citizens, or else from all together), or also some are done one way and others another. If, in turn it is some who do the appointing, this is either from all by election, from all by lot, from some by election, from some by lot, or some one

30   way and others another—by which I mean in some cases from all by election and in others by lot, or in some cases from some by election and in others by lot. So there come to be twelve ways, apart from the two pairings. Three of these kinds of appointments are characteristic of popular rule: for

---

133   The manuscripts have the number four, but the text of this entire paragraph is uncertain, and exactly what is being counted when is unclear. The translation follows Ross's version, which incorporates a number of emendations. (There is, incidentally, a rare typographical error in a word in line 25 of the Oxford Classical Text, and an unpaired parenthesis in line 39.)

all to appoint from among all by election or lot or both, that is, some of the offices by lot and others by election. But for the appointments not to be made by all together, either from all or from some, either by lot or election or both, or some from all and some from some, either by lot or election or both (where by both I mean some by lot and some by election) is characteristic of constitutional rule. And for some to appoint from all by election or lot or both (with some offices by lot and others by election) inclines toward oligarchy, and more   40 toward oligarchy when it is by both; but for them to appoint some offices from among all and others from among some is characteristic of aristocratically inclined constitutional rule,   1300B or some by election and some by lot. For some to appoint from some by election is oligarchic, and similarly for some to appoint from some by lot (though this does not occur), and also for some to appoint from some by both means. But for some to appoint from all or all from some by election is aristocratic.

So the ways of appointing officials are this many in number, and distinguished in this way among the forms of government. Which are advantageous for which and how the appointments ought to take place will be evident along with the powers of the offices and what they are.[134] By the power of an office, I mean, for example, authority over rev-   10 enues or authority over defense, for a different form of power is involved in generalship, for instance, than in the office having authority over agreements in the marketplace.

Chapter 16

The judicial part is the remaining one of the three to discuss. And the ways of handling this need to be taken up on the same premise. And there are distinctions among lawcourts within three defining characteristics: from among whom their members are drawn, about what things they judge, and how they are appointed. By from among whom, I mean whether from all or from some, by about what things, the number of forms of lawcourts, and by how, whether by lot or by election. First, then, let the number of forms of lawcourts be distinguished. They are eight in number: one is

---

134 This is a reference to Bk. VI, Chap. 8, but there is no explicit discussion there of the questions postponed here.

20   for reviewing officials, another in case anyone commits any injustice against common interests, another for those things that bear on the constitution, a fourth for those disputing things having to do with penalties for both officials and private persons, a fifth having to do with private transactions having some magnitude, and besides these one for homicide and one pertaining to foreigners. And the forms of homicide court, whether consisting of the same judges or different ones, are for premeditated or involuntary homicides, for cases that are admitted but where there is dispute about whether they are just, a fourth for charges brought, on their return, against people exiled for homicide, as the court in Phreatto[135] in Athens is said to have been, though few courts

30   of that sort have turned up in all time even in large cities. Of the court for foreigners, one part is for foreigners against foreigners and the other for foreigners against native citizens. Also, besides all these, there is a form of court dealing with small transactions, those amounting to a drachma or five drachmas or a little more. For a decision has to be made about these cases too, but it does not require a multitude of judges.

But let what pertains to these courts, and those for homicides and foreigners, be put aside, and let us speak about the political ones, because when these are not beautifully handled, factional divisions arise and changes of government happen. And it is necessary either for all to decide on

40   all the matters that were distinguished, based on election or lot, or all on them all with some chosen by lot and others by election, or all on some of the same matters, either chosen

1301A   by lot or elected. These ways, then, are four in number, and there are as many more if they are decided by part of the citizenry. For those who judge about all things may in turn be drawn from some citizens by election, or about all things from some citizens by lot, or some of them by lot and others by election, or some courts dealing with these same things may consist of both allotted and elected citizens. These, then, as was said, are the ways corresponding to those that were

---

135   "In Phreatto" meant on the deck of a ship, from which the defendant addressed judges who stood on land in the Peiraeus, because the proceedings were official acts of Athens while the accused was not allowed to be in Athens. See Aristotle's *Constitution of Athens*, 57.

mentioned. Also, the same ones may be conjoined; I mean, for instance, some courts drawn from all, some from some, and others from both (if, for example, some drawn from all and some from some were members of the same court), and either by lot, by election, or both.

The number of ways it is possible to handle the law-courts has been stated. The first sorts of courts, those drawn from all and dealing with all things, are democratic; the second sorts, those drawn from some and dealing with all things, are oligarchic; and the third sorts, those drawn from all on some matters and from some on others, are aristocratic or suited to constitutional rule.

Book V

Chapter 1

Just about all the other topics we proposed have been discussed. The things that need to be looked into next after what has been discussed are the sources from which changes in forms of government arise, how many and of what sort they are, what kinds of destruction belong to each form, and into what sorts they are most likely to change from what sorts, as well as what kinds of preservation there are for them in common and separately for each, and also by what means each form of government could most appropriately be preserved. And one must first take as a starting point that many forms of government have come into being because, while all people speak with one voice about justice and proportional equality, they go astray about them, as was said earlier.[136] Popular rule came from people's supposing that they were equal simply if they were equal in any respect whatever (for because they are all alike free, they consider themselves equal simply). And oligarchy came from people's assuming they were wholly unequal if they were unequal in one particular respect (for because they are unequal in property they assume they are unequal simply). So then the one group claims, on the grounds that they are equal, that they deserve to take an equal part in all things, while the other group seeks to have a greater share on the grounds that they are unequal, since what is greater is unequal. So while their claims all have a certain justice, they are all off the mark if justice is taken in an unqualified sense. And for this reason, whenever one or the other group does not participate in the government in the manner of the assumption it happens to hold, they have factional conflict. Of

---

136 Book III, Chaps. 9 and 12.

all these, the ones who could divide off as a faction with the
40   most justice, but do so the least, are those who excel in virtue,
1301B for the most reasonable claim to be unequal simply would
belong to them alone. But there are some who, because they
excel on the basis of family, claim that owing to this sort of inequality they do not deserve equal treatment, since they seem
to be high-born people who have the virtue and wealth of
their ancestors.

These, then, so to speak, are the sources and springs of
faction, and people divide into factions as a result of them.
And changes come from them in two ways. Sometimes they
are directed at the form of government, to change from the
established one into another, such as into an oligarchy from a
democracy or a democracy from an oligarchy, or from these
10   into constitutional rule or aristocracy or from the latter into
the former; but sometimes they are not directed at the established form of government, and people choose to keep the
established one the same, but want this to be in their own
control, as with oligarchy or monarchy. They may also have
to do with more and less; for instance, if there is an oligarchy,
to change it into one that is run in a more oligarchic way, or
into one that is less so, or if there is a democracy, into one that
is run in a more or less democratic way, and similarly with
the rest of the forms of government, either to tighten or loos-
en them. They may also have to do with causing a change in
some part of the government, for example to set up or abolish
20   a certain office, the way some people say Lysander tried to do
away with the kingship in Sparta, and King Pausanias tried
to do away with the office of ephors; and at Epidamnus there
was a partial change in the form of government (for they put
in a council in place of the tribal leaders, but even so the ruling officials are the only members of the administration required to go into the meeting hall when an office is voted on,
and it was also oligarchic that there was one ruling official[137]
in this government). Everywhere, faction is due to inequality, if it does not belong to unequal people in a proportional
way (for a perpetual kingship is unequal if it is present among

---

137 This was an administrative position without any of the powers of a
monarch, according to Aristotle at 1287a 3-7 above. The point of the
parenthesis is that the introduction of the council amounted only to a
slight loosening of the oligarchy in the direction of democracy.

equals), since in all cases it is people seeking equality who engage in factional conflict.

But equality is of two kinds, one being in number and   30
the other according to merit. By "in number" I mean that which is the same and equal in multitude or magnitude, and by "according to merit" that which is in the same ratio. For instance, three exceeds two and the latter exceeds one equally according to number, but in ratio, *four* exceeds two and the latter exceeds one equally in ratio, since two is an equal part of four as one is of two, because both are halves. And while people are in agreement that what is just simply is what accords with merit, they differ in the way that was stated before, some believing that they are wholly equal if they are equal in any respect, and others considering themselves to merit all things unequally if they are unequal in some respect. Hence two forms of government come about most of all: popular   40
rule and oligarchy. For high birth and virtue are present in   1302A
few people, but those things in the greater number; for nowhere are there a hundred who are high born and good, but in many places many are well off. But for equality in everything to be assigned simply on either basis is a bad thing, and this is obvious from the way things turn out, for not one of the governments of these sorts is enduring. And the reason for this is that it is impossible not to meet some bad end after the first mistake is made at the beginning. That is why it is necessary to make use of numerical equality in some matters and equality of merit in others.

All the same, democracy is more stable and more free of faction than oligarchy. For in oligarchies, two sorts of fac-   10
tion arise, one among themselves and another against the populace, while in democracies there is only faction against the oligarchy, and whatever sort of faction there could be in the populace itself against itself that is even worthy of mention does not arise. Also, the form of government drawn from the middle range is closer to that of the populace than to that of the few, and it is the most stable of governments of these sorts.

Chapter 2

Since we are looking into the things from which factional conflicts and changes in forms of government come,

the general sources and causes of them need to be taken up first. And one may say these are pretty much three in
20   number, each of which needs to be distinguished in outline first. For one must understand what condition people are in when they engage in factional conflict, the end for the sake of which they do so, and thirdly what initial occasions arise for turmoil among citizens and factions against one another. And one must hold something we happen to have spoken of already to be the most general cause of their being disposed toward change. For those who aim at equality form factions if they believe that, despite being equal, they have less than those who hold the upper hand, while those who aim at inequality and predominance do so if they assume that, despite being unequal, they do not have more but an equal or lesser amount. (And there is a way in which it is just to desire these things, and a way in which it is unjust.)
30   Those who are in the lesser position form factions so they might be equal, and those who are equal in order to be in the greater position. What condition people are in when they form factions, then, has been stated. The things over which they form factions are profit and honor, and the opposites of these as well. For people also form factions in their cities to avoid dishonor and fines, on their own behalf or that of their friends. And the causes and sources of changes, which lead people to be disposed in the way described over the things mentioned, turn out to be in one sense seven in number, but in another sense more. Two of them are the same as the ones described, but not in the same way; for people are provoked
40   against one another by profit and honor not in order that
1302B   they might obtain them themselves, as was said before, but also because they see others getting more of these things, some justly and others unjustly. They are also provoked by insolence, fear, superiority, contempt, and disproportionate growth, and also in a different way[138] by canvassing for votes, not taking things seriously, small differences, and dissimilarity.

---

138 The preceding seven causes are motives that induce those out of power to seek change; the following four are contributing causes not always recognized as such by those in power. The next chapter describes them in more detail.

Chapter 3

Among these, it is pretty obvious what sort of power insolence and profit have, and how they are causes. For when those in ruling offices act insolently and take more than their share, people form factions both against one another and against the forms of government that gave them license to do so. And their taking more than their share comes sometimes from private persons and sometimes from public funds. And it is also clear in what manner honor has power, and how it is a cause of faction. For people form factions when they themselves are dishonored and see others honored; and these things happen unjustly when people are either honored or dishonored contrary to what they deserve, but justly when it is in accord with what they deserve. Faction comes from superiority whenever anyone (whether one person or more) is greater in power than what accords with the city and the power of its administration, since it is usual for a monarchy or confederacy of the powerful to arise out of such people. This is why people in some places, such as Argos and Athens, usually resort to ostracism, although it is better to see to it from the beginning that no one present in the city attains such great superiority, rather than allowing it to happen only to remedy it afterward. People form factions out of fear both when they have committed injustice and are afraid they will pay the penalty, and when they are about to suffer injustice and want to get in first before it happens to them, the way the prominent people in Rhodes organized against the populace because of the lawsuits brought against them. And people form factions and go on the attack on account of contempt in oligarchies, for example, when those who have no share in the government are greater in number, because they suppose themselves to be stronger, and in democracies when those who are well off become contemptuous of the disorder and unruliness. In Thebes, for instance, after the battle at Oenophyta, the democracy was destroyed by being badly governed, and that of the Megarians was overturned because of disorder and unruliness, and the same thing happened in Syracuse before the tyranny of Gelon, and to popular rule in Rhodes before the coup.

Changes in forms of government also occur because of disproportionate growth. For just as a body is composed

of parts and needs to grow in proportion so that its sym-
metry will be maintained, and if it does not it is destroyed
(as it would be if its foot were four yards long and the rest
of its body two feet tall), or sometimes it changes into the
shape of a different animal if it were to grow out of propor-
40   tion not just in size but qualitatively as well, so too is a city
1303A   composed of parts, an increase in any of which, such as the
multitude of needy people in democracies or constitutionally ruled governments, often goes unnoticed. And this happens sometimes because of chance events, as in Tarentum,
where many prominent people were defeated and killed by
the Iapygians a little after the Persian wars, and a democracy arose out of a constitutional government; and in Argos,
they were forced to take in some of the surrounding population because of those who were killed on the seventh[139] by
Cleomenes of Sparta; and in Athens, when they suffered
misfortunes on land, the prominent people became fewer,
10   because they served in the military on the basis of the citizen
registry around the time of the Spartan War.[140] This happens
in democracies too, but less so. For when more people come
to be well off or properties get larger, they change into oligarchies and confederacies of the powerful.

And forms of government change even without factional conflict, both as a result of canvassing for votes,[141] as
at Heraea (for this was why they made the offices be chosen by lot instead of elected, because they were choosing
those who were canvassed for), and as a result of not taking things seriously, when people allow those who are not
friendly to the government to come into offices of authority,
the way the oligarchy in Oreus was overturned when Her-

---

139   This was a great massacre which Argos barely survived; the number is
thought to refer to the day of the month it happened on.

140   The upper classes in Solon's constitution (see footnote to 1274a 22
above) filled the infantry and cavalry ranks, since they provided their
own heavy armor and horses; the lower classes were paid to serve as
rowers on battleships (triremes, powered by great numbers of oars).
So the Athenian successes at sea in the Peloponnesian War, and their
inferiority to the Spartans on land, changed the proportions of the
population.

141   The word (*eritheia*) is made from the word *erithos*, which meant day-
laborer; so the practice appears to have involved hiring people to get
out the vote for whoever paid them.

acleodorus became one of the officials, and reorganized the   20
oligarchy into constitutional rule and even democracy. They
also change little-by-little, by which I mean that often, when
people overlook something small, a great transformation in
customs comes about unnoticed, as in Ambracia there was a
small property qualification, but in the end people took office with none, on the view that the small one was so close to
none that it made no difference.

Dissimilarity of races also contributes to faction, until
they get their breathing in sync.[142] For just as a city does not
come into being from a random multitude of people, so too
it does not come into being at a random time. This is why,
up to now, those that have accepted joint colonists or later
settlers have in most cases split into factions. For instance,
the Achaeans colonized Sybaris jointly with the Troezenians,
but then, when the Achaeans became more numerous they   30
threw out the Troezenians, which was the source of the curse
that came upon the Sybarites. And at Thurii the Sybarites
split into factions with their joint colonists, for they thought
they deserved to have more because the territory was theirs,
and they were driven out.[143] And when the later settlers of
Byzantium were caught plotting against the Byzantines, the
latter threw them out by armed force. The Antissaeans also
threw out by armed force the exiled Chians they had allowed in, and when the Zanclaeans took in the Samians, the
refugees themselves threw *them* out. The people of Apollonia on the Black Sea got involved in factional conflict when
they brought in new settlers; the Syracusans, after the time
of the tyrants, when they made citizens of their foreign mer-   1303B
cenaries, split into factions and came into battle; and when
the people of Amphipolis took in settlers from among the
Chalcideans, most of them were thrown out by them. (In
oligarchies, the bulk of the people form factions in the belief that they are treated unjustly because they do not share

---

142   A proverbial expression about yoked horses, used in this same con-
      nection in Plato's *Laws*, 708D.

143   Sybaris was destroyed by a neighboring city, re-founded nearby by
      the survivors, and destroyed again. With the help of the Athenians,
      the Sybarites organized the new city of Thurii (planned by Hippoda-
      mus and given its laws by Protagoras) in the same region with a new,
      multiracial group of joint colonists. "Sybaritic" became a byword for
      luxury and laziness.

things equally, as was said before, despite being equal, and in democracies the prominent people do so because they do share things equally, despite not being equal.)

Sometimes, too, cities split into factions on account of territory, when the land is not naturally suited to be a single city, as at Clazomenae, where those at Chytrum opposed those on the island; so too with the people of Colophon and Notium. Even at Athens, the people living in the Peiraeus are not like those in town but more inclined to popular rule. For just as in war, crossings over ditches, even when they are very small, break up the battle lines, so, it seems, every difference makes a division. And the greatest division is perhaps that of virtue and vice; next is wealth and poverty, and so one with one greater than another, and one of them is the one mentioned.

Chapter 4

And while factions do not arise over small matters, they come from small occasions and produce divisions over large matters. And even small things gain strength especially when they arise among those in positions of authority, as happened in Syracuse, for example, in ancient times. For the form of government changed when two young men who were in ruling offices came into factional conflict over a matter erotic in origin. For when one of them was out of town, the other, who was his close friend, won over the boy he loved; he in turn, furious at the other, persuaded his wife to come to bed with him, and from that beginning they drew in everyone in the administration and split into factions. That is why it is necessary to be wary of such things when they are getting started, and break up factions among powerful leaders. The mistake comes at the beginning, and the beginning is said to be half of the whole,[144] so when there is even a small mistake at that point it is proportionally magnified in the other parts. In general, when there are factions among prominent people, they make the whole city join in the fun,[145] as happened in Hestiaea after the Persian wars

---

144 Or even more than half, as Aristotle says in the *Nicomachean Ethics* (1098b 7), in speaking of the importance of getting an inquiry started on the right track. Here the beginning (*archē*) has the double meaning of the first step in a series of events and the ruling portion of a city.

145 Aristotle apparently made up the word *sunapolauein* from *apolauein* (derive enjoyment), which had an established ironic usage.

when two brothers quarreled about the distribution of their inheritance; the one who was more needy, on the grounds that his brother was not declaring the value of the estate or of the treasure their father had found, drew the popular party in with him, while the other, who had great wealth, drew in the well-off. And in Delphi, a source of all later factions came from a quarrel stemming from a marriage. For 1304A a man who interpreted some mishap as he was coming for his bride as an omen went away without taking her, and her kin, taking this as a mortal insult, planted some sacred objects on him while he was sacrificing and then killed him as a sacrilegious thief. And in Mytilene, a source of many evils, and of the war against the Athenians in which Paches took over their city, arose from a factional squabble stemming from heiresses. For when Timophanes, one of the well-off citizens, died and left two daughters, Dexander, who was turned down and did not get them for his sons, started a factional conflict and stirred up the Athenians, of whose city 10 he was the representative. At Phocis too a factional conflict stemming from an heiress involved Mnaseas, the father of Mnason, and Euthycrates, the father of Onomarchus, and this conflict became the origin of the Sacred War for the Phocians. And at Epidamnus the form of government changed as a result of an engagement; for someone who had promised his daughter in marriage, when the father of her betrothed became one of the officials and fined him, joined in league with those who were excluded from the government because he felt he had been badly mistreated.

There are also changes into oligarchy or into popular or constitutional rule that result when a governing body or a portion of the city gets a good reputation for anything or grows in size. For example, the council of the Areopagus 20 seems to have made the government of Athens more strict after it got a good reputation in the Persian wars, and then in turn, when the mob of sailors was responsible for the victory at Salamis, which led to a position of leadership due to power at sea, it made the democracy stronger. And in Argos, when the prominent people got a good reputation for the battle against the Spartans in Mantinea, they tried to overturn the popular rule. And in Syracuse, when the populace was responsible for victory in the war against the Athenians they changed from constitutional rule to democracy. And in

30   Chalcis, the populace, along with the prominent people, deposed the tyrant Phoxus and immediately took hold of the government. And in Ambracia, in the same way again, the populace joined in throwing out the tyrant Periander with those who had attacked him, and brought the government around to itself. And in general, this must not be overlooked, that those who have been responsible for power, whether private persons, ruling bodies, tribes, or generally any part or group whatever, set factional conflict in motion. For either those who envy them for being honored initiate the conflict, or they themselves are unwilling to stay on an equal footing because of their distinction. And forms of government also change whenever the parts of the city that seem to be 1304B   opposed become equal to each other, as in the case of the wealthy and the populace, when there is no middle group, or a very small one. For if one or the other side has a much superior position, the remaining one is unwilling to take the risk against the side that is obviously stronger. And this is also why those who are outstanding in virtue do not cause any factional trouble to speak of, since they are few against many.

Universally, then, this is the way it is with the sources and causes of faction and change in all forms of government. And people sometimes change their forms of government by force, sometimes by deceit, and by force either right from 10   the beginning or by resorting to compulsion afterward. And deceit comes in two forms as well, for sometimes they pull off a complete deception at first and change the government while people are willing, then clamp down with force afterward when people are unwilling. There is the case, for example, of the Four Hundred,[146] who deceived the populace by claiming the king of Persia was going to provide money for the war against the Spartans, and tried to clamp down on the government after people bought the lie. But sometimes, after persuading people at the beginning, they persuade them again afterward and rule over willing persons.

In simple outline for all forms of government, then, changes end up occurring as a result of the things mentioned.

---

146   An oligarchic group that took power briefly in Athens late in the Peloponnesian War.

Chapter 5

But it is necessary to study the consequences of these things by dividing them up for each particular form of government. And democracies change most often because of the reckless behavior of demagogues.[147] In some cases, by making unjustified private accusations against those who have wealth, they cause them to unite (for a common fear brings even the worst enemies together); in other cases they incite the multitude in common. And one may see many occasions where this has happened in these ways. For in Cos the democracy changed when corrupt demagogues arose (for the prominent people organized against them), and in Rhodes as well; for the demagogues provided pay for public service and prevented paying what was due to the naval commanders, who were forced by the lawsuits brought against them to organize to overthrow the popular government.[148] And popular rule was also overthrown on account of demagogues in Heraclea immediately after it was colonized, for the prominent people were driven out by being unjustly treated at their hands, but then the exiles gathered together, came back, and overthrew the popular government. And the democracy in Megara was overthrown in pretty much the same way, for the demagogues expelled many of the prominent citizens so that they could confiscate their possessions, until they made so many exiles that they came back, were victorious in battle over the populace, and set up an oligarchy. The same thing also happened at Cyme in the case of the democracy that Thrasymachus overthrew. And one who studies the changes in other democracies would see this is pretty much the way they happen. For sometimes, by treating the prominent people unjustly in order to gratify the people, they drive them to organize by redistributing either

20

30

1305A

---

147 The word *dêmagôgos* originally applied to any leader of the populace, even to a statesman like Pericles who could rebuke the Athenians and never had to flatter them (see Thucydides, *Peloponnesian War*, Bk. II, Chap. 65). The two clauses of the following sentence illustrate the typical behavior that came to characterize the breed, in abuse of the legal process and rabble-rousing rhetoric.

148 The demagogues maintained their power by providing money for people to serve in the assembly, and paid for it by reneging on the money owed to those who had supplied the city with battleships, who in turn were sued by the shipbuilders.

their estates or their income through levies for public benefits; and sometimes they resort to slander so that they can confiscate the property of the rich.

In the old days, when the same person would become a demagogue and a general, popular rule changed into tyranny. For pretty much the greatest number of the early ty-
10 rants came from demagogues. And the reason this happened then but not now is that in those days the demagogues were drawn from those who served as generals and were not yet skilled at speaking, while nowadays, with the spread of rhetorical skill, those who are capable of speaking become demagogues, but due to their inexperience in warfare they do not attempt anything beyond that, unless some such thing has happened somewhere to a slight extent. And tyrannies also arose more often formerly than now because great offices were in the hands particular persons, as happened from the presidency in Miletus, for the president had authority over many great matters. Also, because in those days cities
20 were not large and the populace lived in their fields where they were busy with their work, the champions of the populace, when they were skilled at warfare, attempted tyranny. They all did this by winning the trust of the populace, and the means of winning trust was their hostility to the rich; in Athens, for instance, Peisistratus stirred up factional conflict against the people of the plain,[149] in Megara, Theagenes slaughtered the herds of the wealthy when he caught them grazing off their own lands by the river, and Dionysius earned his tyranny by denouncing Daphnaeus and the rich, using hostility to win trust as someone who was on the side of the people.

Democracies also change from the ancestral kind to the
30 latest sort. For where the offices are elected, and there is no property qualification, and the populace elects them, those who campaign for votes bring things to such a pass by their demagoguery that the populace is in authority even over the laws. A remedy, to prevent this from happening or make it happen less is for the tribes to choose the rulers, rather than the populace as a whole. Just about all the changes in democracies, then, happen for these reasons.

---

149 The rich landowners lived in the plain, and dominated the poor who lived on the coast; Peisistratus formed a third party of the poorest of the poor in the hills as his base of power.

Chapter 6

Oligarchies change most often in two most obvious ways. One occurs when they treat the multitude unjustly, for then any champion is sufficient, especially when it turns out that the leader comes from the oligarchy itself, as with Lygdamis in Naxos, who afterward became a tyrant over the Naxians. The source of faction takes different forms when it comes from others. For sometimes the overthrow comes from within the group of those who are well off themselves, but are not included in the ruling offices, when those who hold the honors are exceedingly few. This has happened, for instance, in Massalia, in Istrus, in Heraclea, and in other cities. For those who had no share in the offices kept causing commotion until first the older brothers, and later the younger ones also, got a share. For in some places a father and son cannot hold office at the same time, and in some an older and younger brother cannot. The oligarchy in Massalia became more like constitutional rule, the one in Istrus ended up turning into popular rule, and the one in Heraclea went from a smaller number of participants to six hundred. And in Cnidus the oligarchy changed when the prominent people formed factions among themselves because so few were taking part, and as was mentioned, a son could not take part if a father did, and none but the eldest if there were a number of brothers; and while their factions were in conflict the populace got involved, took up a champion from among the prominent people, and attacked and conquered them, since what is split by faction is weak. And in Erythrae, in the oligarchy of the Basilidae in ancient times, even though things were well looked-after by those in the government, the populace still changed the form of government because they were discontented at being ruled by so few.

Oligarchies are also changed from within their own ranks when they become demagogues out of rivalry. And demagoguery takes two forms, one of which is within the few themselves, for a demagogue may arise even when they are very few. For instance, in the Thirty in Athens, those around Charicles grew strong by demagoguery aimed at the Thirty,[150] and those around Phrynicus did so in the

40
1305B
10
20

---

150 A particularly brutal oligarchy that held power in Athens for less than a year following the end of the Peloponnesian War, and came to be known as the Thirty Tyrants.

same way among the Four Hundred. The other form occurs when those who are within the oligarchy aim their dema- goguery at the mob; in Larisa, for example, the guardians of
30   the citizens engaged in demagoguery with the mob because they were the ones who elected them. This happens in all those oligarchies in which those who elect the offices are not those from among whom the office holders come, but those who hold office come from large property qualifications or political clubs, while those who elect them are the citizens who bear arms or the populace. This is exactly what hap- pened in Abydos, and it happens wherever the lawcourts are not filled from the administration, for when people act like demagogues to get verdicts, they change the form of government, which happened also in Heraclea on the Black Sea. And it also happens whenever some draw the oligarchy into a smaller group, for those who seek an equal share are forced to bring in the populace as helpers.

40   Changes from an oligarchy also come about whenever oligarchs use up their private fortunes by living in dissipa- tion, for people of that sort seek to make innovations, and ei-
1306A ther attempt a tyranny themselves or back someone else in starting one, as Hipparinus did with Dionysius in Syracuse. In Amphipolis someone whose name was Cleotimus brought in people from Chalcidia as settlers, and when they came he incited them to factional conflict against those who were well off; and in Aegina, the man who made the deal with Chares[151] attempted to change the form of government for a reason of this sort. Sometimes they make some attempt to change things directly, but sometimes they steal common funds, with the result that either they or those who fight against the ones doing the stealing stir up faction among themselves, which happened at Apollonia on the Black Sea. When an oligarchy
10   is like-minded, it is not easily changed from within itself. The government in Pharsalus is a sign of this, for although they are few, they stay in authority over many because of the beau- tiful way they treat one another. But when they make another oligarchy within the oligarchy, they are overthrown. This hap- pens when, despite the fact the whole administration consists of few people, not all of those few share in the highest offices,

---

151 Chares was an Athenian general known to employ mercenaries, and Aegina is an island very near Athens.

which happened at one time in Elis; for though the government was held by few, very few of them got to be among the
elders, because they were permanently fixed at ninety members and the choice of them, like that of the elders in Sparta,[152]
favored the powerful.

A change can happen in oligarchies both in war and in   20
peace. In war it happens when they are forced to use mercenaries because of their distrust of the populace, for the
one who is given charge of them often becomes a tyrant, as
Timophanes did in Corinth, and when there are more than
one, they set themselves up as a confederacy of the powerful. Sometimes, out of fear of these things, they give the
multitude a share in the government because they are forced
to make use of the populace. But in peace, because of their
distrust of one another, they turn over their security to mercenaries and to a neutral official, who sometimes gets to be
in authority over both sides; this is what happened in Larisa
during the rule of the Aleuadae who surrounded Simus, and   30
in Abydos at the time of the political clubs, one of which was
that of Iphiades.

Factional conflicts also arise when some in the oligarchy are pushed out of the way by others and marginalized
through marriages or lawsuits. From causes related to marriage, there were, for example, the cases mentioned above,[153]
and also the oligarchy of the cavalry in Eretria which Di-
agoras overthrew when he was treated unjustly in the matter of a marriage. From a verdict in a lawcourt, there was
the factional conflict in Heraclea and the one in Thebes; the
punishment of those convicted on charges of adultery was
carried out justly but in a partisan spirit, against Eurytion by
judges in Heraclea, and against Archias by those in Thebes   1306B
(for their enemies carried their rivalry so far as to have them
bound on pillories in the marketplace). And many oligarchies have been overthrown by certain discontented members of the government because they were too much like
rule of a master over slaves, as with the oligarchy in Cnidus
and that in Chios.

Changes of the governments called constitutional rule

---

152 See the footnote to 1266a 1.

153 1304a 1-17.

and of oligarchies also happen by accident, in the ones in which those who deliberate, judge, and hold the other ruling offices are drawn from a property qualification. For often
10   when the qualification is set at first in due relation to present conditions so that few will take part in the oligarchy, or the middle group in constitutional rule, and prosperity comes along due to peace or to some other good fortune, it turns out that the same properties come to be worth many times the property qualification, so that everyone takes part in all the offices; sometimes the change happens in increments, little by little and unnoticed, but sometimes it happens quickly.

So by such causes oligarchies change and become split by faction. But in general both democracies and oligarchies sometimes alter not into opposite forms of government but
20   into varieties within the same kind, for instance from democracies and oligarchies under law into arbitrary[154] forms, or from the latter to the former.

Chapter 7

In aristocracies, factions arise in some cases because few have a share in the honors, which was also said to cause commotion in oligarchies, since aristocracy is in a certain way oligarchy (for in both the rulers are few, though they are not few for the same reason). Indeed, for these reasons, aristocracy is even thought to be oligarchy. And factional conflict necessarily happens most often when there is some group of people with the conceit that they are peers in virtue, such as the so-called "sons of the virgins" in Sparta (for
30   they were descended from the peers).[155] When they were caught plotting, they were sent off as colonists to Tarentum. Or it happens when some who are great and inferior to none in virtue are dishonored by some who are held in greater honor, as Lysander was by the kings, or when someone who

---

154 Aristotle's word is simply the adjective made from "authority" (*kurios*); he has described these governments in Book IV as democracies in which decrees are authoritative (1292a 6-7) and oligarchies in which the rulers are (1292b 6-7).

155 In the early aristocratic government of Sparta, members of the ruling Spartiate class were called "peers" (*homoioi*); during a long war with Messenia, many half-Spartiate sons were born to women who were not legitimately their mothers.

is of manly character has no share in the honors, such as Cinadon, who organized the attack on the Spartiates in the time of Agesilaus. It also happens when some become very poor and others become well off, which comes about most often during wars; and this happened in Sparta as a result of the Messenian war, as is clear from the poem of Tyrtaeus   1307A called "Law and Order," for some who felt the pinch from the war thought they were entitled to have a redistribution of the land. It also happens if someone is great and capable of being greater still, so that he might rule alone, as seems to have been the case in Sparta with the Pausanias who was a general in the Persian war, and in Carthage with Hanno.

Most often, constitutional governments and aristocracies are brought down by a deviation from justice in the constitution itself. For the source is the fact that democracy and oligarchy are not beautifully mixed in constitutional rule, or these with virtue in an aristocracy, but especially the two—   10 the two I am speaking of being popular rule and oligarchy. For it is these that constitutional governments, as well as many of those called aristocracies, try to mix. For aristocracies differ in this respect from the governments that are given the name constitutional, and for this reason the former are less stable and the latter more. For people call those that incline more toward oligarchy aristocracies, and those that incline more toward the multitude constitutional governments. This is why the latter sort are more secure than the former, since the greater number are stronger, and they are more content when they have an equal share; but those who are among the well-off, if the constitution gives them a superior position, seek occasions to behave insolently and take   20 more than their share. In general, whichever side the constitution inclines toward is the direction it changes toward, since either side will increase its own predominance; constitutional rule, for example, changes into popular rule, and aristocracy into oligarchy. But they also change into their opposites, for example aristocracy into popular rule (for the poorer people pull it around to the opposite direction when they think they are being treated unjustly), and constitutional rule into oligarchy (on the grounds that the only stable sort of equality is that in accord with merit, and having one's own due). What was mentioned happened in Thurii: because the offices were drawn from an excessive property

30 qualification, they changed to a smaller one and to more official positions, but because the prominent people acquired *all* the land in violation of the law (for the constitution was too oligarchic and consequently they were able to get the upper hand), the populace, having been trained in warfare, became stronger than the guards, until those who were in possession of the extra land gave it up. Also, since all aristocratic governments are oligarchic, the prominent people are more apt to take more than their share; even in Sparta, for example, landed estates are coming into few hands. And there is too much license for prominent people to do whatever they want and make marriage alliances with anyone they want, which is also why the city of the Locrians was ruined as a result of the marriage alliance with Dionysius,

40 which would not have happened in a democracy or even in an aristocracy that had been well mixed.

1307B It is especially aristocracies that change imperceptibly by being undone little by little, which was something mentioned in earlier remarks as applying universally to all forms of government, that even a small thing can be a cause of changes. For whenever they give up anything related to the constitution, it is easier after that to change another thing too that is a little larger, until they change the whole order of things. And this also happened in the government of Thurii. For there was a law that one could serve as a general at five year intervals, but when some of the younger men became skilled at war and well regarded among the multitude of guard troops, they grew contemptuous of those in charge

10 of affairs and considered it easy to overrule them, and they tried first to nullify this law so that the same people would be allowed to serve as generals continuously, since they saw that the populace would be eager to vote for them. Those among the officials who were assigned to this matter, who were called councilors, though they were determined at first to oppose this, were persuaded, on the assumption that once they had changed this law the rest of the constitution would be left alone; but later, when they wanted to prevent other changes, they could no longer do anything more, and the whole arrangement of the government changed into a confederacy of the powerful people who had undertaken to revolutionize things.

All forms of government are undone sometimes from   20
within themselves and sometimes from outside, when there
is an opposite form of government nearby, or far away but
having power. This is exactly what happened with the Athenians and Spartans, for the Athenians overthrew oligarchies
everywhere, and the Spartans overthrew popular rule. From
what sources changes of government and factional conflicts
come, then, has been pretty well stated.

Chapter 8

The next thing is to speak about the preservation of
a form of government, both in common and separately for
each form. And first of all, it is clear that if we understand
the things by which forms of government are destroyed, we
also grasp the things by which they are preserved. For opposite causes produce opposite effects, and destruction is   30
the opposite of preservation. In well-blended governments,
then, nothing is more necessary than to watch out for any
departure from the laws, and to be on guard especially in
small matters. For lawlessness creeps in unnoticed, in the
same way that a small expenditure frequently repeated
wastes away one's property. But the expense goes unnoticed
because it does not happen all together, for one's thinking
reasons falsely about the expenditures, as with the sophisti-
cal argument, "if each is small, then all are too." And while
there is a sense in which this is true, there is a sense in which
it is not, since the whole that is the all is not small, though it
is composed of small amounts. So this is one safeguard that
needs to be taken from the start. The next is not to put any   40
trust in contrivances for the purpose of tricking the multi-   1308A
tude, since they are completely discredited by events. The
sort of tricks we are speaking of that are used by governments have been described above.[156]

Another thing is to observe that not only some aristocracies but even some oligarchies endure, not because
the forms of government are stable but because those who
have come into office treat people well, the ones outside the
government and the ones in the administration, by doing
no injustice to the ones who have no share and by bring-

---

156   See the first paragraph of Bk. IV, Chap. 13.

ing those among them with a capacity for leadership into the government, and by not unjustly bringing the ambitious
10 into dishonor or being unjust to the masses for gain; among themselves, those who share in the government treat one another in a democratic way. For the equality that those who are democratically inclined seek for the multitude is not only just but advantageous for those who are alike. Hence, if there is a large number of people in the governing group, many legal provisions suited to popular rule are advantageous, such as having offices with six-month terms so that all those who are alike can take part. For those who are alike are already a sort of populace, which is also why demagogues often turn up among them, as was said earlier.[157] With that provision, oligarchies and aristocracies will be less likely to collapse
20 into confederacies of the powerful, since it is not easy for rulers to do as much harm in a short time as in a long one, seeing as how this is the reason tyrannies arise in oligarchies and democracies. For in each of the two it is those who are greatest who attempt tyranny, the demagogues in the one and the powerful in the other, or else those who hold the greatest offices, when they keep ruling for a long time.

And governments are preserved not only by having the things that would destroy them far off, but sometimes also by having them close. For when people are in fear they cling to the government more firmly. Consequently, those who are concerned for the government ought to foster sources of fear, so that people will guard the government and not over-
30 turn it, keeping watch like night watchmen, and they ought to make what is far off close. They also ought to try to watch out for rivalries and factions among their prominent people, and use the laws to keep watch on those who are outside the rivalry before they too get involved, since recognizing an evil when it is first coming into being is not a job for any random person but for a man who is politically adroit.

As for change in oligarchy and constitutional rule that comes from property assessments, when this happens because the assessments stay the same while currency becomes plentiful, it is advantageous to look at the total amount of
40 property in comparison to its past value—in those cities
1308B that make an annual valuation, at that time interval, and in

---

157   See 1305b 23-27 above.

larger cities every third or fifth year. And if the total is many times greater or less than before, at the time when property qualifications were set up in the constitution, it is advantageous for there to be a law to tighten or loosen the qualifications—if the total is in excess, tightening them by the same multiple, but if it comes short, loosening them and making each qualification smaller. For in oligarchies and constitutional governments that do not do this sort of thing, the latter end up becoming oligarchies and the former confederacies of the powerful in the one case, and in the other democracies come from constitutional governments, and constitutional   10
or popular rule from oligarchies.[158]

A provision that applies in common to popular rule and oligarchy, and to monarchy and every form of government, is not to elevate anyone too far out of proportion, but to try to bestow small honors over a long time rather than great ones in a short time (since people get corrupted, and not every man has it in him to withstand good fortune), or failing that, if they have given them all at once, they should at least surely not take them away again all at once, but gradually. Most of all, they should try by means of laws to keep things in such harmonious proportions that no one gets into a position greatly superior in power, in friends, or in money, or failing that, for postings[159] abroad to be made for them.

And since people also attempt revolutionary changes   20
because of their private lives, one ought to put in place a particular office that would supervise those who live in a manner detrimental to their form of government, to democracy in a democracy, to oligarchy in an oligarchy, and similarly in each of the other forms. And for the same reasons, one ought to watch out for any part of the city that is enjoying success at the time; and a remedy for this is always to put actions and offices in the hands of the opposing parts. I am speaking of decent people as being opposed to the multitude, and

---

158 In the case of a substantial reduction of the money supply, there is a *de facto* tightening of the qualifications for office, that requires a compensating loosening; in the other case, inflation makes those qualifications looser than originally intended, and requires a tightening.

159 This word (*parastasis*) could mean banishment, but is not one of the words Aristotle ordinarily uses for that. He seems here to be recommending a policy one step short of the ostracism he considers an undesirable last resort (1302b 18-21).

the needy as being opposed to the well-off. One ought to try either to mix together the multitude of the needy and
30   the element that is well off, or to increase the middle group, since this breaks up the factional conflicts that result from inequality.

But the greatest concern in every form of government is for both the laws and the rest of its management to be so arranged that there can be no profit made from the offices. This needs to be guarded against most of all in oligarchies. For most people are not so annoyed at being kept from holding office (but are even delighted for someone else to leave them free time for their private concerns) as they are when they believe the rulers are stealing common funds; then they have two grievances together, at not sharing the honors and not sharing the profits. In fact, the only way it is possible
40   for there to be democracy and aristocracy at the same time is if someone could manage to make this arrangement. For
1309A then it would be possible for the prominent people and the multitude to have what they want, both together. Having it open to everyone to hold office is democratic, but having the prominent people *be* in the offices is aristocratic, and this will be the case whenever there is no profit to be made from the offices. For the needy will not want to hold office because there is no profit in it, but will prefer to be at their private concerns, while the well-off will have the ability to hold office because they need nothing additional from the common funds; consequently, it will turn out that the needy become well off by keeping busy at their work, and the
10   prominent people will not be ruled by random persons. So to keep the common funds from being stolen, let the handover of money take place in the presence of all the citizens, and let written records be deposited with each fraternal organization, company, and tribe. And to keep office-holding free of profit, honors should be prescribed by law for those who earn good reputations.

And in democracies, the well-off ought to be spared, not only by not making redistributions of their property, but not even doing so with their incomes, which happens unnoticed in some governments; and it is better to prevent the rich, even when they want to do so, from taking on expensive public benefactions that are not useful, such as sponsor-

ing choruses, running torch races, and all the other things of   20
that sort. And in an oligarchy, great care ought to be taken
for the needy, and the offices from which an income can be
made should be assigned to them; if any of the well-off is
insolent to them, the penalties should be greater than if it
happened among his own kind. Inheritances should also not
go by bequest but by kinship, and the same person should
not get more than one inheritance. For by this means, estates
would be more even, and more of the needy could get a foot-
hold in affluence. And in both democracy and oligarchy, it is
advantageous to give those who have a lesser share than the
others in the government—the well-off in popular rule and
the needy in oligarchy—either equality or priority, except in   30
those offices that are in authority over the government; the
latter should be put only or predominantly in the hands of
those from within the government.

Chapter 9

Those who are going to rule in authoritative offices
should have three particular things: first, a love of the established form of government; next, a great capacity for the
kinds of work involved in ruling; and third, in each form of
government, the sort of virtue and justice that is relevant to
that form of government (for if what is just is not the same
thing in all the forms, it is necessary that justice too would be
different).[160] But there is a difficulty, when it turns out that all
these things are not present in the same person, as to how to   40
make the choice. If, for instance, there were someone skilled   1309B
as a general, but corrupt and no friend of the form of government, and a just person who was a friend, how should
the choice be made? And it seems one ought to look to two
things: which attributes all people share more widely, and

---

160 In Bk. III, Chap. 9, Aristotle discussed the way in which oligarchy and
     democracy are founded on true but incomplete conceptions of what
     is just. If justice as a state of character is a disposition to choose what
     is fair to everyone, and the basis of that fairness depends on what
     constitutes equality or inequality in the things people deserve, an at-
     tachment to the established form of government will color the way
     someone recognizes what ought to be done. It should be remembered,
     as Aristotle reminds us shortly below, that he considers oligarchy and
     democracy deviant forms of government, incapable of serving the
     common interest of all citizens.

which ones less widely. This is why, in the office of general, one should look to experience more so than virtue (for people share in generalship less and in decency more), but in the office of trustee or treasurer it is the other way around (for they require more virtue than the amount most people have, while the knowledge they involve is common to everyone). But someone might raise the question, if ability and a love
10 for the form of government are present, what need is there for virtue? For even the two will produce advantages. But is it not possible for those who have these two attributes to be without self-discipline? In that case, just as people do not serve their own interests even though they know them and love themselves, nothing would prevent some people from being in the same condition in relation to the common interest. The simple fact is that all those things in the laws that we speak of as advantageous to the government preserve the government, as does the oft-mentioned elementary matter of greatest importance to watch out for: that the group that wants the government will continue to be stronger than the group that does not want it.[161]

And besides all these things, there is something that must not be disregarded, which is disregarded at present in
20 the deviant forms of government: the mean. For many of the things that seem inclined toward popular rule are the undoing of democracies, and many that seem oligarchic undo oligarchies. People who suppose that one of these characteristics is the only virtue carry it to the extreme, in ignorance of the fact that, just as it is possible for a nose to deviate from the straightness that is most beautiful, toward being hooked or turned up, but still be beautiful and be graceful to the eye, though if one were to stretch it any further to the extreme, he would first of all be throwing out the fitting proportion of the part, and finally get to the point at which he would make it not even look like a nose, on account of its excess in one of the opposite directions and deficiency in the other.
30 And it is the same way with the other parts as well, and this

---

161 Aristotle has mentioned this twice above in slightly different forms, at 1296b 14-16 and 1297b 4-6, and will repeat it once more at 1320b 25-28 below. The point of the sentence here seems to be that defects in the human beings chosen to hold office can only be guarded against, in the final analysis, by the presence of good laws and a strong consensus in support of the government among the citizens.

happens with forms of government too. For it is possible for oligarchy and democracy to be in good enough shape even though they are departures from the best arrangement, but if one were to stretch either of them any further, he would first of all make the government worse, and finally make it not even a government. That is why this is something the law-giver and student of politics must not be ignorant of: which of the things that incline toward popular rule preserve democracy and which ones destroy it, and which oligarchic measures preserve or destroy oligarchy. For neither of them is capable of existing and enduring without the well-off and the multitude; but when a leveling out of wealth occurs, this form of government will necessarily be something different, so that by destroying [one class of citizens] by laws carried to an extreme, people would be destroying their forms of government.[162]

40

1310A

And people miss the mark in both democracies and oligarchies. The demagogues miss it in democracies in which the multitude is in authority over the laws, because they always turn one city into two by doing battle against the well-off, though they ought, on the contrary, to seem always to be speaking in defense of the well-off. And in oligarchies, the oligarchs ought to seem always to be speaking in defense of the populace, and the oaths-of-office they take should be the opposite of the ones oligarchs now take. For in some oligarchies they now swear "I will be committed to harm the populace and I will devise whatever harm I can," whereas they should both adopt and declare the opposite attitude, making their oaths carry the message: "I will do no injustice to the populace."

10

But of all the things that have been mentioned for making governments endure, the most important one, which everyone now belittles, is for people to be educated with a view to their form of government. For no benefit can come from the most beneficial laws, even when they have been approved

---

162 The analogy to the painter or sculptor who shapes a nose means that two kinds of extremes are being envisioned, a democracy that uses laws to make everyone poor and an oligarchy that uses them to make everyone rich. Either version would be a utopian vision like that of Phaleas (Bk. II, Chap. 7, above), rather than a practical arrangement like constitutional rule, which seeks to combine the contributions differing kinds of people can make to common political life.

unanimously by those involved in running the city, if people are not going to be habituated and educated in the form of government—in a popular spirit if the laws are of a popular sort, or in an oligarchic spirit if they are of an oligarchic sort. For if a lack of self-discipline is possible in one person, it is
20   possible also in a city. And being educated in the form of government does not mean doing things that please the oligarchs or the partisans of democracy, but doing things that make it possible for those who run the oligarchy or the democracy to do so. But as things stand, the sons of the rulers in oligarchies live in luxury while the sons of the needy become toughened by exercise and work, so that they are both more desirous and more capable of revolutionizing things. And in those democracies that seem to be the most democratic, people have set things up in opposition to their advantage, and the reason for this is that they use a bad definition of freedom. For there are two things by which democracy seems to be defined, by hav-
30   ing the majority in authority, and by freedom. For it seems that justice is what is equal, and whatever seems equal to the majority is authoritative, while doing whatever one wants is freedom. Consequently, in democracies of this sort, each person lives the way he wants, and "toward what end he pleases," as Euripides puts it.[163] But this is shoddy thinking. For one need not think that living with a view to his form of government is slavery, but security.

So, to put it simply, the causes from which forms of government change and are destroyed, and the means by which they are preserved and endure, are this many.

---

163   The source of the quotation is lost. Commentators speculate about what Aristotle would consider a good definition of freedom. In the context of this chapter, his two references to the lack of self-discipline (*akrasia*) suggest that he might say that freedom is or depends upon self-discipline (*en-krateia*). (Compare Plato's *Meno*, 86D, and *Gorgias*, 491D-494A.) That would mean that freedom is characterized more by the power to achieve an end than by a lack of limitation in choosing one. And by inference from the discussion of natural slavery in Bk. I, one may add that freedom depends on the capacity to deliberate (1260a 12) and to foresee by thinking (1252a 32). Aristotle provides an image of freedom and slavery in a household in the *Metaphysics* (1075a 19-22): those who are most free have the most responsibility, while the slaves for the most part act at random.

Chapter 10

What is left to go over has to do with monarchy, the causes from which it is destroyed, and the means by which   40
it is naturally preserved. And the things that happen in king-   1310B
ship and tyranny are pretty close to what has been described in the other forms of government. For kingship corresponds to aristocracy, and tyranny is made up of the last stages of oligarchy and democracy. That is why it is the most harmful to those who are ruled, because it is a combination of two evils, and has in it the deviations and mistakes of both forms of government. And the origin of each of the two forms of monarchy is directly opposite to the other. For kingship arose in support of decent people against the populace, and   10
a king is established from among decent people on the basis of superiority in virtue or in actions stemming from virtue, or on the basis of a superiority in this respect of a family, while a tyrant comes from the populace and the multitude in opposition to the prominent people, to prevent the popu-lace from suffering injustice at their hands. This is obvious from what has happened. For just about the greatest number of tyrants have come, one may say, from demagogues who won people's trust by slandering the prominent people. Those tyrants who took over when cities had already grown large did so in this manner, while the ones prior to these came from kings who deviated from traditions and desired a form of rule more suited to the mastery of slaves. Some also   20
came from people elected to supreme offices (for in ancient times, popular governments set up long-term offices of pub-lic service and public missions), or out of oligarchies that se-lected one particular person to be in authority over the high-est offices. All these means offered an easy road to success if only someone were to want it, through the power already available to some in the form of kingly rule and to others in positions of honor. Pheidon, for instance, in Argos, and oth-ers, set up as tyrants from existing kingships; Phalaris, and those in Ionia, did so from positions of honor; Panaetius in Leontini, Cypselus in Corinth, Peisistratus in Athens, Dio-   30
nysius in Syracuse, and others went the same way from their roles as demagogues.

And as we said, kingship is arranged in a way that corresponds to aristocracy, for it is based on merit, in the form of personal virtue, or family virtue, or high birth, or acts of beneficence, or these combined with ability. For all those who attained this honor had been benefactors of their cities or nations, or had the power to benefit them—some, such as Codros, by preventing them from being enslaved in war, others, such as Cyrus, by setting them free, or founding a city, or acquiring land the way the kings of the Spartans,

40   Macedonians, and Molossians did. A king has the intention
1311A of being a guardian, so that those who own property will suffer no injustice and the populace will suffer no insolent treatment, while tyranny, as has been said repeatedly, looks out for no common interest except for the sake of its private benefit. The tyrannical objective is what is pleasant; the kingly objective is what is beautiful. Hence the objects of tyrannical ambition are things of monetary value, while those of the kingly sort lead to honor instead. And the kingly guard is made up of citizens, while the tyrannical guard depends on foreigners.

It is clear that tyranny has in it the evils of both democ-
10   racy and oligarchy. From oligarchy it gets its end, which is wealth (for necessarily it is only in this way that it can maintain its guard and its luxury), and also its refusal to trust the multitude in any matter (which is why they carry out a confiscation of arms, and why mistreating the masses, driving them out of town, and scattering them is a common feature of both oligarchy and tyranny). And from democracy comes its making war on prominent people, its covert and overt destruction of them, and its exiling them as opponents of its designs and obstacles to its rule. For it does in fact turn out that plots originate from these people, some of whom want to rule
20   themselves, while others want not to be enslaved. This is the reason for Periander's advice to Thrasybulus about cutting off the ears of corn that stand out, that there is always a need to get rid of those who stand out among the citizens.[164]

So as has pretty much been said, one ought to regard the sources of changes as being the same in monarchies as in the other forms of government. For it is due to injustice, fear, and contempt that many of their subjects attack monarchies, and in the case of injustice it is especially due to insolence, though sometimes also to the seizure of private

---

164 The story is recounted more fully at 1284a 26–33 above.

property. And the ends sought are also the same in tyrannies and kingships as they are in the other cases, for a great   30
amount of the wealth and honor everyone desires belongs to
monarchs. Some of the attacks that take place are on the person of the rulers, but others are on the office. Those that are
due to insolence are on the person. And while insolence is of
many forms,[165] each of them ends up being a cause of anger;
and pretty much the greatest number of those who attack
out of anger do so for revenge and not for preeminence. The
attack on the sons of Peisistratus, for example, was due to
their humiliating Harmodius's sister and insulting Harmodius (for Harmodius attacked them on account of his sister,
and Aristogeiton on account of Harmodius).[166]

There was also a plot against Periander, the tyrant in   40
Ambracia, caused by his asking his boyfriend, while he was   1311B
drinking with him, whether he had gotten him pregnant yet.
The attack on Phillip by Pausanias was caused by his letting
him be insolently treated by those in Attalus's circle, and that
on Amyntus the Small by Derdas by his public ridicule of his
youthful passion. And there was also the attack on Evagoras
of Cyprus by the eunuch; he killed him because he was vio-
lated due to the fact that Evagoras's son had taken away his
wife. And many attacks have also occurred because certain
monarchs have subjected people to personal disgrace. An
example is the attack of Crataeus on Archelaus, for Crataeus
had always been disgusted over their intimate relations, so
that even a lesser pretext would have been sufficient—lesser   10

---

165 The word translated "insolence" is *hubris*. In Bk. II it was translated
     "outrage" (see 1267b 39 and note) when used as a category of crime.
     It never refers to a mere swelled head or to overreaching one's capaci-
     ties. Whether it is used for an attitude or for violent crime, it always
     signifies something gratuitously cruel directed against another per-
     son.

166 Harmodius and Aristogeiton were celebrated as liberators of Athens
     from the tyranny begun by Peisistratus. The story of their private
     motives is told by Thucydides (*Peloponnesian War*, VI, 54-59). One
     translator removes most of the following material up to 1311b 34 to
     a small-print appendix, considering it salacious gossip of no political
     importance, but it is the nature of tyranny to blur the line between
     private and public acts by subordinating all common interests to the
     impulses and whims of the ruler, and of monarchy to begin a slide to-
     ward tyranny by crossing that line. Aristotle's parenthetical remark at
     1312a 2-4 indicates his opinion that such stories may illustrate general
     truths even when they are not factually accurate.

than the fact that he gave him neither of his daughters, after agreeing to, but gave the elder to the king of Elimeia when he was hard pressed by a war against Sirras and Arrabaeus, and the younger to his own son Amyntas, supposing that would make it least likely that there would be trouble between Amyntas and his son by Cleopatra—but the source of their estrangement was the disgust he already bore toward him over their sexual involvement. And Hellanocrates the Larisaean also joined in the attack for the same reason, for since, after making use of his youthful passion, he did not keep his promise to restore him to his home, Hellanocrates

20   imagined the intercourse they had was not from any passionate desire but a humiliating act of insolence. And Python and Heracleides of Aenus killed Cotys to avenge their father, and Adamas revolted from Cotys for his violation of him, because, when he was a boy, he was castrated by his order. And many people have either killed or attempted to kill those who shared in a king's rule and power because they were angered at being subjected to personal affronts by beatings, taking this as an outrage. In Mytilene, for instance, where the descendents of Penthilus were going around hitting people with clubs, Megacles along with his friends attacked and destroyed them, and later Smerdes, after suf-

30   fering blows and being dragged away from his wife, killed another Penthilus. And Decamnichus became a leader of the attack on Archelaus and the first to incite the attackers, and the cause of his anger was that Archelaus had handed him over to the poet Euripides for whipping; Euripides was upset at something he had said about his bad breath.

And many others have been destroyed and plotted against for reasons of that sort, and similarly on account of fear. For just as this was one of the causes in other forms of government, it is in monarchies as well. An example is what happened to Xerxes, when Artapanes was frightened by the allegation that he had hanged Darius[167] without be-

40   ing ordered to by Xerxes, assuming he would be pardoned because Xerxes would have no memory of it due to his win-

1312A   ing and dining. And other instances have been due to contempt, as when someone saw Sardanapalus carding wool

---

167 Xerxes' eldest son and intended successor; Artapanes was captain of Xerxes' bodyguard.

with the women. (If those who tell these stories are telling the truth; but if this one is not true in his case, it could still be true about someone else.) And Dion attacked Dionysius the Younger because of his contempt for him, seeing that the citizens felt the same way and seeing Dionysius himself always drunk. Even some of a monarch's friends may attack him out of contempt; being trusted gives them the contemptuous attitude that they will be unobserved. Those who believe they have the power to seize the office also in a certain way make their attacks as a result of feeling contempt; they are contemptuous of the risk because they feel powerful, and readily make the attempt because of that power, the way generals attack their monarchs. Cyrus, for instance, attacked Astyages out of contempt for both his way of life and his power, because his power had wasted away while he himself lived in luxury; and Seuthes the Thracian attacked Amadocus, whose general he was. Some also attack out of a combination of these reasons, both out of contempt and for gain, for instance, as with Mithridates against Ariobarzanes. It is especially those who are daring by nature and hold military honors from their monarchs who make attempts for this reason, for bravery equipped with power makes for daring, and with both of these going for them, they make their attacks with the attitude that they will easily prevail.

In those who attack out of a love of honor, a reason of a different sort from those mentioned up to now is at work. Some people make their attempts against tyrants because they see the great profits they gain and the high positions of honor they hold, but this is not the spirit in which everyone who makes an attack out of a love of honor chooses to take that risk. While those others do so for the reason mentioned, there are those who make attempts against monarchs in the same way they would undertake any other extraordinary action that presented itself, through which they could become famous and noteworthy to others, because they want to acquire not a monarchy but glory. Those who are spurred by this motive are admittedly the fewest in number, for it is necessary to presuppose that they have no concern for their own safety in the event that they fail to bring off the action. They have to go into it with Dion's idea,[168] but it is not easy for that to be found in many people. For he took the field against Dionysius with a few men, declaring it as his attitude that, however far he was able to advance was a big enough part in the action for him to have, and if he ended up dying as soon as he had gone forward one small step of ground, that death would be a beautiful way for him to go.

40
1312B   One way in which tyranny is destroyed, just as in each of the other forms of government, is from outside, if some opposing government is stronger. For it is clearly the case that they will want to destroy it because of the opposition of their purposes, and all people do what they want to do if they have the power. And the forms of government opposed to tyranny are, on the one hand, popular rule, by Hesiod's principle of "potter versus potter" (since the last stage of democracy is tyranny),[169] and, on the other, kingship and aristocracy, because of the oppositeness of the form of government (which is why the Spartans overthrew most tyrannies, as did the Syracusans at the time when they were beautifully governed). But another way tyranny is destroyed is
10   from within itself, when those who have a part in it split into factions, as did Gelo's circle, and Dionysius's circle just recently. In the case of Gelo, this happened when Thrasybulus, the brother of Hiero, won over Gelo's son and pushed him toward pleasures so that he himself could rule, but their family conspired to keep the tyranny as a whole from being overthrown, but only Thrasybulus—but those who were in on the conspiracy with them, seeing they had the opportunity, threw them all out. Dion, an in-law of Dionysius who had the populace on his side, took the field against him, but was destroyed himself after he threw him out.

---

168 Aristotle's intended example seems to be the notion Dion articulates and declares, rather than his actual motive, since he has just said that Dionysius was an object of contempt, and he will shortly mention that Dion himself came to a similar inglorious end.

169 Aristotle characterizes extreme democracy in two ways in Bk. IV. When democracy is not bound by laws it is analogous to tyranny, with the majority becoming a single collective monarch that treats everyone else like slaves (1292a 6-18); and even under law, a democracy that does not protect the interests of property owners is at the last stage before being taken over by a tyrant (1296a 1-4). The reference to Hesiod has to do with the natural rivalry among those in the same business (*Works and Days* 25-26).

The reasons for which people most often attack tyrannies are two: hatred and contempt. One of these, hatred, is always there for tyrants, and many have brought on their **20** downfalls by being despised. A sign of this is that most who have acquired ruling positions have also maintained them, while of those who have inherited them, one might say they have all lost them immediately. Living lives devoted to enjoyment, they become easy objects of contempt and give their attackers many opportunities. Anger too ought to be counted as a part of hatred, for in its own way it becomes a cause of the same actions. In fact, it is often a stronger spur to action than hatred is, because angry people attack more intensely, since passion does not involve reasoning. (Anger for the most part is a consequence of the spiritedness **30** aroused by insolence, which was the reason the tyranny of the Peisistratid family was overthrown, and many others as well.) Hatred has more room in it for reasoning, for anger is felt with pain, so that thinking is not easy, while hostility is free of pain.[170] And putting it in summary, the same array of causes we have mentioned for the overthrow of unmixed and ultimate oligarchy and of extreme democracy need to be applied to tyranny as well, since these forms of government happen to be tyrannies divided up.

Kingship is least likely to be destroyed by things from outside, which is why it is also of long duration; in most cases its destruction ends up being from within itself. And it is de- **40** stroyed in two ways, one when those who have a part in the **1313A** kingship form factions, and the other way when kings try to run things in a more tyrannical manner, whenever they claim authority over more things and contrary to law. Kingships no longer arise nowadays, and if monarchies do arise, they are tyrannies instead. This is because kingship is rule over willing subjects, with authority over weightier matters, while

---

170 This comparison may seem backward to us if we think of hatred as simply the most intense negative feeling, but Aristotle describes it in Bk. II, Chap. 4, of the *Rhetoric* as the opposite of love (*philia*), understood as the desire for another person's good for that person's own sake. In II, 2 of the *Rhetoric*, he describes anger (*orgê*) in detail as the response of spiritedness (*thumos*) to insolence (*hubris*); when we ourselves or those close to us are belittled or cruelly treated by another person, we feel pain and a desire for revenge. Aristotle's last word there on the two feelings (1382a 13-15) is that, while hatred makes us want someone not to exist, anger makes us want him to suffer.

there are now many people who are alike, with no one distinguished enough to measure up to the gravity and worth of the office. So for this reason people do not willingly put up with it, and if someone were to take office by deception or force, that would already be considered a tyranny. In kingships based on family, one ought to set down as a cause of their destruction, over and above the ones that have been mentioned, the fact that many who inherit the position become easy objects of contempt and yet behave insolently, even though they do not have tyrannical power but only kingly honor; their overthrow has come easily. For as soon as the people become unwilling, he will cease to be a king, and be a tyrant over unwilling subjects. Monarchies, then, are destroyed for these reasons and others of the same sort.

Chapter 11

And it is clear that, to put it simply, they are preserved by opposite causes, and that with kingships in particular, this is done by bringing them to a state of greater moderation. For necessarily, the fewer things they have authority over, the longer time their rule as a whole remains in place. For they become less like slavemasters and more equitable in their characters, and are less envied by those they rule. This is the reason the kingship has lasted a long time among the Molossians, and also that of the Spartans, both because the office was divided into two parts from the beginning, and because Theopompus moderated it again, among other things by setting up the office of the ephors. For by making a subtraction from its power he added time to the kingship, so that in a certain way he made it not lesser but greater. And this is exactly the reply people say he made to his wife, when she asked if he was not ashamed to be passing on to his sons a lesser kingship than he inherited from his father. "No indeed," he said, "for I am passing on one that will last a longer time."

Tyrannies are preserved in two ways that are complete opposites. One of these is the traditional method by which most tyrants maintain control of their rule. People say that Periander of Corinth established many of these, but it is also possible that many things of the sort are taken over from the Persian empire. They are the things that were mentioned some time ago as tending toward preservation of tyranny

as much as possible, by cutting down those who stand out
and getting rid of those with proud thoughts, and not allowing common meals, clubs, education, or anything else   1313B
of that sort, but guarding against everything from which
two things customarily come—pride and trust—and not letting there be any schools or other collegial gatherings for
leisured pursuits, and doing everything that will keep all
the people as unknown to one another as possible (since familiarity breeds a greater degree of mutual trust). Another
measure is to require the townspeople to be always out in
the open and spend their time near the palace gates (since in
that way what they are doing would be least likely to go unnoticed, and they would get in the habit of thinking small as
a result of always living like slaves). And as many other Persian and barbarian practices of that sort as there may be are   10
tyrannical in character (since they all have the same power).
Another is for there to be spies, to try to keep whatever any
of his subjects happens to say or do from going unnoticed,
such as the so-called talebearers in Syracuse, and those
Hiero used to send out to listen in wherever any meeting
or gathering would be taking place (for people speak less
frankly when they fear creatures of that sort, and if they do
speak frankly they are less likely to go unnoticed). Another
measure is to stir up mutual slander and clashes of friends
against friends, the populace against the prominent people,
and the rich among themselves.

It is also characteristic of tyrants to make their subjects
poor, both so that they cannot maintain a militia, and so that   20
they are too busy looking after daily needs to have free time
to get into conspiracies. Examples of this may be found in
the pyramids of Egypt, the monumental offerings of the Cy-
pselids, the construction dedicated to Olympian Zeus by the
Peisistratids, and Polycrates' works among those at Samos
(for these all produce the same effect: poverty and a lack
of leisure among those who are ruled). Another tyrannical
measure is the imposition of property taxes, as in Syracuse
(for in five years in the time of Dionysius people ended up
paying in their entire property). A tyrant is also a warmon-
ger, so that people will be without leisure and be constantly in need of a leader. And whereas kingship is preserved   30
by its friends, it is characteristic of a tyrant to distrust his
friends most of all, because what everyone wants, they have

the most power to carry out.

And all the things that happen in the last stage of democracy apply to tyranny as well: female control over households, to get them to denounce their husbands, and permissiveness toward slaves for the same purpose. For slaves and women do not get into plots against tyrants, and when things go well for them they are necessarily favorably disposed toward tyrannies, and democracies as well, since the populace also tends toward being a monarch. This is also why a valued
40   person in both is the flatterer: in popular governments this is the demagogue, since a demagogue is a flatterer of the populace, and with tyrants it is those who hang around them in
1314A   a self-abasing manner, which is how flattery works. And it is for this reason that tyranny is friendly to corrupt people, since tyrants enjoy being flattered, and this is something no one who thinks like a free person would do. Decent people *are* friends; in other words, they do *not* flatter. And corrupt people are useful for corrupt employments—a nail hammered at a nail, as the proverb has it. And it is characteristic of a tyrant to take no pleasure in anyone dignified or free. For the tyrant considers himself to be the only person of that sort, and anyone who matches him in dignity and carries himself like a free person robs tyranny of what is exceptional and masterful about it. So tyrants hate them as if they were overturning their
10   rule. And it is also characteristic of a tyrant to use foreigners instead of citizens as companions at their meals and pastimes, on the assumption that the latter are their enemies while the former will not oppose them.

These things and their like are characteristic of tyranny and are safeguards of its rule, and there is no sort of vileness they leave out. One may say that they are all encompassed within three forms, for tyranny aims at three things. One is for its subjects to think small, since a small-souled person would not plot against anyone. A second is for them to distrust one another completely, since a tyranny cannot be overthrown until some people have trust among themselves. And this is the reason tyrants make war on decent
20   people as detrimental to their rule—not just because such people do not think they deserve to be ruled like slaves by a master, but also because they are trusted, among themselves and by others, and do not inform on their own kind or any-

one else. And the third aim is a lack of power for action, since no one attempts impossible things, and hence no one overthrows a tyranny if the power to do so is not there. So the ultimate terms into which the intentions of tyrants are reducible are just these three, since one may trace every tyrannical measure back to these underlying purposes: making the people not trust one another, making them have no power, and making them think small.

One means by which the preservation of tyrannies is carried out, then, is of the foregoing sort. But there is another way of taking care of it that is practically the opposite of the things that have been described. And it is possible to gather it from the way kingships are destroyed. For just as one means of destruction of kingship is to make its rule more tyrannical, by the same token, one means of preservation of tyranny is to make it more kingly, if the tyrant watches out for one thing only—his power—so that he can rule not only willing but also unwilling subjects, for if he lets go of that he also lets go of being a tyrant. But while this has to remain present as an underlying purpose, he should do some other things, and seem to do others, to play a kingly role in beautiful style. First of all, he should seem to be concerned about public funds, and not spend them on the sort of giveaways that most people are infuriated by when tyrants with sticky fingers take money from them, who do the work and bear the burdens, and give it lavishly to mistresses and foreigners and co-conspirators; he should render an account of what he takes and spends, which some tyrants have in fact done before now. For by administering things in this way, one might seem to be a household manager and not a tyrant. He need not be afraid of ever running out of money, since he has authority over the city. And this practice is also more advantageous to tyrants when they are away from home than to leave behind what they have gathered up, since the people standing guard would be less likely to seize power; when tyrants are out of the city, those on guard are more to be feared by them than the citizens, since the latter are out of the city with them, while the former remain behind. And next, he should make a display of collecting taxes and public service contributions for the sake of managing affairs and to use, if the need should ever arise, in times of war, and in all respects appear to be equipping himself as a guardian and treasurer of public and not of private funds.

30

40
1314B

10

And a tyrant should not appear harsh, but dignified, but
still the sort of person who, while not feared by those encoun-
20 ter him, would be respected instead. This, however, is no easy
thing to achieve if he is easily despised, which is why, even if
he makes no effort in the direction of the other virtues, he ought
to cultivate the military variety, and make a reputation of that
sort for himself. And not only should he not be seen treating
any of his subjects insolently, not even a young boy or girl, but
neither should any other member of his circle. And the women
of his household ought to behave the same way toward other
women, since many tyrannies have also been destroyed by
acts of insolence among women. And as far as the enjoyment
of bodily pleasures is concerned, he ought to do the opposite of
30 what some tyrants do now. For not only do they indulge in this
right from morning on and nonstop for days on end, but they
even want to be seen by others while acting this way so that
people will admire them as happy and blessed. It would be
best for him to be moderate in such matters, but failing that, he
should at least avoid being seen by others. For it is not the sober
and wakeful person who is easy to attack or easy to despise,
but the one who is drunk and drowsy. What needs to be done is
the opposite of practically everything that was said above. For
he ought to equip and order his city as though he were a trustee
and not a tyrant. In addition, he must always make a display of
taking matters related to the gods exceptionally seriously. For
40 people are less afraid of suffering any lawless treatment at the
1315A hands of such rulers if they consider them to be god-fearing
and mindful of the divine powers, and they are less likely to
plot against those they think have even the gods as allies. But
he ought to appear that way without being silly about it.[171]

Also, he ought to honor those who become good in
any respect in such a way that they would not believe they
could ever be more honored by citizens living freely under
laws, and he should hand out such honors himself, but have
punishments meted out by other officials and judges. But
a common safeguard for every monarchy is not to make
any one person great, or if any, then more than one, since

---

171 An example that Aristotle may have in mind is a stunt described by
Herodotus (*History*, I, 60) as the "silliest thing by far" he had ever
heard of. When Peisistratus was restored to his tyranny in Athens,
a tall woman in armor rode into town in a chariot, with heralds an-
nouncing that Athena herself was bringing him back.

they will keep an eye on one another. If he must after all **10**
make someone great, it should at least not be someone of
bold character, for a character of this sort is liable to take
any action as an opportunity for attack. And if it seems good
to dismiss anyone from a position of power, he should do
this by stages and not take away all his authority at once.
Furthermore, he should put a curb on himself against every
sort of insolent act, and against two kinds above all, corporal
punishment and molestation of the young. This is a precau-
tion that needs to be taken especially toward those who are
passionate about their honor. For while money-lovers take
it hard when there is a slight to their possessions, honor-
lovers and decent human beings feel that way about dis- **20**
honor. Hence he either ought not to engage in such acts, or
he must make a display of inflicting punishments in a paternal manner and not in order to demean, and of having
intimate relations with the young from erotic motives and
not licentiously. In general, he should buy off any appear-
ances of dishonor with greater honors. Of the people who
make attempts at destruction upon the person of the tyrant,
those who are most to be feared and need the most watching
are the ones who have no intention of preserving their own
lives when they destroy his. This is why he needs to be especially cautious about people who consider either themselves
or those they happen to care about to have been treated with
humiliating insolence, for those who attack out of spirited
anger are of no mind to be sparing of themselves. It is just as **30**
Heracleitus says, when he declares it is hard to fight against
spiritedness, for the price it pays is life.

And since cities are organized out of two parts, needy
human beings and those who are well off, in the best case
both ought to assume they are being kept safe by the tyrant's
rule and one group is suffering no injustice from the other;
but whichever of the two is stronger, private persons of that
class should especially be made part of his rule, since, if this
group is on the side of his interests, there will be no necessity
for the tyrant to resort to a freeing of slaves or a confiscation
of arms. For one of the two parts will be enough, when added to his power, to make it stronger than those who might **40**
attack it. To speak of such things for each case would be too
fussy. For the aim is obvious, that he ought not to appear **1315B**
to his subjects to be tyrannical, but managerial and kingly,

not someone who looks out for number one but a trustee, and appear to pursue the moderate things in life rather than the extremes, and also appear to be favoring the prominent people with his company while courting popularity with the masses. The necessary result of these measures is that not only will his rule be more beautiful and enviable, by virtue of ruling over people who are better and not debased and accomplishing this without being hated and feared, but also his rule will be longer-lasting; furthermore, he himself will either have his character in beautiful shape as far as virtue is
10   concerned, or be halfway decent, and not vicious but half-vicious.[172]

Chapter 12

And yet of all forms of government oligarchy and tyranny are the ones that last the shortest time. The tyranny of Orthagoras' descendants and Orthagoras himself in Sicyon went the longest time; it endured for a hundred years. The reason for this is that they treated their subjects moderately, and in many matters they slavishly observed the laws; because he became skilled at war, Cleisthenes was not easy to despise, and in most respects they took pains to behave like demagogues. It is said, at any rate, that Cleisthenes awarded a crown to someone whose judgment denied him a victory,
20   and some people claim the statue of a seated man in the marketplace is a portrait of the one who gave that judgment. People also claim that Peisistratus once submitted when summoned to the Areopagus to answer a charge. The second longest-lasting tyranny was that of the Cypselid family in Corinth, for it went on for seventy-three years and six months. Cypselus held the tyranny for thirty years, Periander for forty and a half, and Psammitichus, the son of Gor-

---

172 The last word of the chapter appears once in the *Nicomachean Ethics* (1152a 17), for someone who lacks self-restraint or self-discipline; such a person has decent intentions but can't carry them out. It seems to refer here to the opposite case; a tyrant who follows Aristotle's advice would be carrying out a bad intention in a moderate way. Commentators sometimes refer to this chapter as Aristotle's handbook for tyrants, and point to echoes of it in Machiavelli's *Prince*. Whatever the relation of the two writings may be, Aristotle concludes that, if the mask of virtue that is the likeliest road to successful tyranny does not become the face, at least the role the tyrant has to play lessens the damage his true character could cause.

gus, for three years. And the reasons for this are the same;
Cypselus was a demagogue and went throughout his reign
without a bodyguard, and while Periander was tyrannical
he was skilled at war. Third longest was the tyranny of the   30
Peisistratid family in Athens, though it was not continuous.
Peisistratus was banished from his tyrannies twice, so that
out of thirty-three years he reigned as tyrant for seventeen
of them, and his sons for eighteen more, so that it came to
thirty-five years in all. Of the rest, the longest was that of
Hiero and Gelo in Syracuse, and it did not last many years;
its total was two years short of twenty. Gelo was tyrant for
seven years and his life was ended in the eighth, Hiero for
ten, and Thrasybulus was thrown out in his eleventh month.
The bulk of tyrannies have all been of exceedingly short duration.

What concerns monarchies and other forms of gov-   40
ernment, then, in connection with the reasons they are destroyed or else preserved, has pretty well been covered for   1316A
them all. Their transformations are discussed by Socrates
in the *Republic*, though not in beautiful fashion.[173] With the
form of government that is best and first, he does not discuss
a change for it in particular. He claims the cause is that nothing lasts but everything goes through a cycle of changes, and
the start of these is "the point at which a root ratio of four to
three, mated with a multitude of five, produces two harmonies," and speaks of a time when this number becomes that
of a solid figure, his meaning being that nature at that time
generates people who are substandard and impervious to
education. As far as this point itself is concerned, what he   10
says is probably not bad, since it is possible for there to be
some people who are incapable of being educated or becoming excellent men, but why should this change be peculiar
to the form of government called best by him any more than
all the rest and everything that comes into being? And why
would it be a result of time, which is what he says changes

---

173 This discussion occupies Bk. VIII of Plato's *Republic*. It begins with the
     observation that the best human contrivance is still something that
     comes into being and must eventually decay, and then proceeds by
     showing that each subsequent defective form is at cross-purposes to
     itself. Socrates warns (545D-E) that his mathematical preamble is not
     to be taken seriously but is a playful and pretentious counterpart to a
     Homeric invocation of the Muses.

everything, and yet things that did not begin coming into being at the same time would change at the same time? If, say,
something came into being the day before the turnaround,
would it change at that same time anyway? And in addition,
what is the reason it changes from that form of government
to one of the Spartan kind? For it is more common for all the
20   forms to change into their opposites than into one closely related. And the same argument applies to the other changes.
For he says it changes from the Spartan form into an oligarchy, from that into a democracy, and from democracy into
a tyranny. And yet they also change the opposite way, from
popular rule into oligarchy for instance, and more often than
into monarchy.

Also, he does not say whether there will be a change
from tyranny, or if so, for what reason and into what form,
and the reason is that there was no easy way he could have
said this. It is indeterminate, since according to him it would
have to change into the first and best form; in that way it
30   would go on continuously in a circle. But a tyranny also
changes into a tyranny, the way the one in Sicyon went from
that of Myron to that of Cleisthenes, or into an oligarchy,
the way that of Antileon did in Chalcis, or into a democracy,
the way that of Gelo's family did in Syracuse, or into an aristocracy, the way that of Charilaus did in Sparta, as well as
one in Carthage.[174] And there are also changes into tyranny
from oligarchy, as with just about the greatest number of the
ancient ones in Sicily, into the tyranny of Panaetius in Leontini, into that of Cleander at Gela, into that of Anaxilaus in
Rhegium, and similarly in many other cities.

40   And it is absurd to suppose that the reason a government changes into an oligarchy is that those in its offices
1316B change into money-lovers and money-makers, and not that
those who have a great superiority in wealth believe it is
unjust for people with no property to have an equal share
in the city with the property owners. In many oligarchies,
those in office are not permitted to make any money and
there are laws to prevent it, whereas in democratically run

---

174   Some scholars have worried that the last phrase contradicts Aristotle's claim at 1272b 32-33 above that Carthage had no tyranny, but the
context there makes it clear that he means it never lapsed into tyranny
after the aristocracy was instituted.

Carthage they are money-makers and have not yet changed the form of government. And it is also absurd to claim an oligarchy is two cities, of the rich and the poor. For why would it be subject to this any more than the Spartan form of government, or any other whatsoever in which people do not all have equal property and are not all similarly good men? Even when no one gets any poorer than before, governments change nonetheless from oligarchy to popular rule if the number of needy people gets larger, and from popular rule to oligarchy if the well-off portion is stronger than the majority, and the latter are apathetic while the former are paying attention. And while there are many reasons for which the changes happen, he does not speak of any but one, that people become poor from wasteful living and building up debt at high interest, as if all or most of them were rich from the beginning. But this is false; instead, some of the leading people do start revolutions when they lose their property, but when others do, nothing drastic happens, and even if it does, it is no more likely that the change will be to popular rule than to any other form of government. What is more, if the leading people do not share the honors, or if they are treated unjustly or insolently, they start factions and change their forms of government even when they have not squandered all their wealth, on account of the license they have to do whatever they want, which he says is caused by too much freedom. And despite the fact that there is more than one kind of oligarchy and of democracy, Socrates discusses their changes as though each were one single thing.

Book VI

Chapter 1

How many different kinds there are of the deliberative and authoritative part of the government, and of arrangements concerning offices and lawcourts, and what they are, and which ones are adapted to which form of government, and also matters pertaining to the destruction and preservation of the forms of government, the sources they arise from and the causes for which they happen, have been stated above. And since there turn out to be a number of forms of democracy, and likewise of the other forms of government, it would be no less appropriate to examine anything that remains in connection with them, and at the same time give an account of the proper and advantageous procedure for each form. And a further point that needs to be examined   40
concerns the combinations of all the procedures that have   1317A
been mentioned, for when these are paired up they make the forms of government intertwine, so that there are oligarchic aristocracies and democratically inclined forms of constitutional rule. The pairings that I am saying need to be examined are the ones that have not been considered up to now—if, for instance, the deliberative part and the part dealing with selecting officials were arranged in a way adapted to oligarchy while the parts having to do with lawcourts were handled aristocratically, or the latter and what has to do with the deliberative part oligarchically and the part dealing with the selection of officials aristocratically, or if in any other manner not all the parts combined were the proper ones for the form of government.   10

What sort of democracy fits what sort of city, and likewise which sorts of oligarchies fit what sort of multitude,

and which of the remaining forms of government are advantageous for which people, have been stated above; all
the same, since it ought to be made clear not only which of
these forms of government are best for cities but also how
one ought to construct these and the others as well, let us
take this up briefly. And let us speak about democracy first,
for what concerns the opposite form of government will
become evident at the same time, and this is the one some
people call oligarchy. And for this inquiry, all the features of
20   popular rule, as well as those that are thought to go along
with democracy, need to be taken up. For it is from the combinations of these that the forms of democracy turn out to
arise, and the fact that there is more than one different type
of democracy. For there are two reasons why democracies
are of multiple kinds. The first is that mentioned earlier,
that populations are different. For there can be a multitude
of farmers or of mechanical workers and menial laborers,
and when the first of these is put together with the second,
and then the third with the combination of the two, not only
is there a difference in whether the democracy is better or
worse, but it is not even the same type. And the second rea-
30   son is the one we are speaking of now. For the things that go
along with democracies and are thought to be proper to this
form of government produce different types of democracies
when they are combined. Fewer will go along with one type,
more with another, and all of them with yet another. And
it is useful to recognize each of them, both with a view to
constructing whichever of them one happens to want, and
for reforming them. For those who set up governments seek
to bring together all the things that are proper to its underlying principle, but they are making a mistake when they
do this, as was said above in the discussions of the destruction and preservation of forms of government. Let us now
discuss their guiding beliefs, their character, and the things
they aim at.

Chapter 2

40   Now an underlying principle of a democratic form of
government is freedom. For this is what people are in the
1317B habit of saying, as though it were only in this form of government that they shared in freedom, since they claim every

democracy aims at this. And one sort of freedom is being ruled and ruling by turns. For the justice characteristic of popular rule is to have equality based on number rather than on merit, and where this is what is just, the multitude necessarily has authority, and whatever may seem good to the majority, that is final and that is justice. For they claim each of the citizens ought to have an equal say; consequently, in democracies the needy end up having more authority than those who are well off, for they are the greater number, and the opinion belonging to the greater number is authoritative. This, then, is one indication of freedom which all partisans of popular rule set down as a defining characteristic of their form of government. Another is to live the way one wants. For they claim this is the way freedom works, if what characterizes someone who is enslaved is to live the way one does *not* want. So this is a second defining characteristic of democracy, and from it comes the principle that people are not to be ruled, preferably not by anyone at all, but failing that, only by turns, and it contributes in this way to the sort of freedom that is based on equality.

If these are the underlying assumptions and the starting point is of this sort, the things suited to popular rule are of the following kinds: choosing all offices from among all people; having all the people rule over each, and each by turns rule over all; having either all the offices, or those not requiring experience or skill, chosen by lot; having the offices not be based on any property qualification, or on one as small as possible; not to have the same person hold any office twice, or only on rare occasions in few offices apart from those having to do with war; having either all offices or those that admit of it be of short duration; having everyone, or persons chosen from among them all, do the judging on all or most matters, and on the most important and most authoritative ones, such as reviews of officials, the constitution, and private contracts; having the assembly be in authority over all matters or the most important ones, while no office has authority over any matter, or as few as possible (and among offices, the one most suited to popular rule is a council, where there is no abundance of payment for everyone, since where there is they take away the power even of this office, for a populace that has an abundance of payment draws all decisions back to itself, as was said above[175] in the inquiry before this one); next, to provide payment, at best for all functions—assembly, lawcourts, and offices—but if not, for the authoritative offices, lawcourt, council, and assemblies, or at least those offices in which it is necessary to have common meals with one another; further, since oligar-

40   chy is delimited by family, wealth, and education, the opposites of these are thought to be suited to popular rule—lack of family background, poverty, and lack of cultivation; and

1318A   again in the case of offices, for none to be perpetual, and if any is left over from an ancient change of government, to strip away its power and change it from elected to chosen by lot.[176]

So these are the things that are common to democracies. But what is thought to be a democracy and popular rule in the highest sense results from what is agreed to be the democratic form of justice—that is, for everyone to have a numerically equal share. For the equal thing is for the needy not to rule to any greater extent than do those who are well off, and not to be the sole authority, but for all to rule and have authority on a numerically equal basis. For people

10   would regard this as the way that both equality and freedom would be present in the government.

Chapter 3

The next question this raises is how they are going to have equality. Should they divide off the property assessments of five hundred people from those of a thousand and give the thousand equal power with the five hundred? Or should they establish equality on this basis not in that way but by making that division and then taking equal numbers of people from the five hundred and from the thousand and let them be in authority over elections and lawcourts? Is this the most just form of government by the democratic standard of justice, or one based on the multitude instead? For the partisans of popular rule claim that whatever seems

---

175 See 1299b 30-1300a 4.

176 An example is the Athenian "king archon," who retained out of the powers of the original kings, only those of presiding over certain religious ceremonies and hearing indictments in cases of impiety and murder.

good to the greater number of people is just, while the oli-   20
garchs say it is whatever seems good to the greater amount
of wealth, since they claim things ought to be decided on
the basis of the extent of wealth. But both claims involve inequality and injustice. For if it is whatever the few decide,
there can be tyranny, since if one person also has more than
the rest of those who are well off, then by the oligarchic
standard of justice it is just for him to rule alone; but if it is
whatever the numerical majority decides, they will commit
injustice by confiscating the property of the wealthy minority, as was said above.[177]

What sort of thing both sides would agree would be
equality must be examined from the things they both define
as just. For they say that whatever seems good to the greater number of citizens ought to be authoritative, so let that   30
stand, though not as the whole story, but since there happen
to be two parts of which the city is composed, the rich and
the poor, let whatever seems good to both, or to a majority
of each part, be authoritative. And if opposite things seem
good to them, let it be whatever was decided by the greater
number *and* those who have the greater property assessment; for instance, if there were ten of the rich and twenty
of the more needy sort, and the matter was resolved by six
of the former and fifteen of the latter, four of the rich have
been joined with the poor and five of the poor with the rich.
So whichever side represents the greater property assessment when both groups have been added together on each
side, that side is authoritative. And if they fall out equal, this
ought to be regarded as a common difficulty, just as hap-   40
pens now when an assembly or a lawcourt comes up with a
split decision; for it needs to be settled by lot, or something   1318B
else of that sort needs to be done.

As far as equality and justice are concerned, even
though it may be difficult to discover the truth about them,
it is still easier to get to it than to persuade people of it when
they have the power to get the better of others. For it is always the weaker who seek equality and justice, while the
stronger pay no attention to them.

---

177 At the beginning of Bk. III, Chap. 10, where the same pair of arguments is made more fully.

Chapter 4

Of the four types of democracy there are, the best is the first one in the classification that was described in the discussions preceding these,[178] and this is also the most ancient of them all. But I am speaking of it as first in the way one would distinguish populations. For a population de-
10   voted to farming is best, so that it is possible to produce a democracy even where the multitude lives by farming and herding. For since they do not have much wealth they have no spare time and hence cannot often meet in assembly, and since they do[179] have the necessities they occupy their time with their work and do not desire what belongs to others; on the contrary, working is more pleasant to them than engaging in politics and office-holding, wherever there is no great profit from holding office. For most people have a greater desire for gain than for honor. An indication of this is that people used to put up with the ancient tyrannies and still put up with oligarchies if no one prevents them from work-
20   ing or takes anything from them, for some of them get rich quickly and the others avoid being poor. And if they have any desire for honor, being in authority over electing and reviewing officials fills the need; and among some populations, as in Mantinea, where they do not even take part in electing officials, except some of them chosen in turns from them all, but they are in authority over deliberating, this is sufficient for the mass of people. And one ought to consider even this to be a design for a democracy, since it was once that way in Mantinea.

Hence it is especially advantageous to the sort of democracy described above, and customarily a feature of it,
30   for everyone to elect and review officials and be jurors, but also for people chosen from a property qualification to hold the highest offices, and the higher the offices the higher the qualifications, or even if they do not come from property qualifications, for them to be capable persons. Those governed in this way are necessarily governed beautifully, since the offices will always be filled by the best people, with the populace willing and bearing no resentment against decent

---

178   See 1292b 22-1293a 10.

179   The manuscripts have the word "not" but Ross follows an earlier editor in omitting it.

rulers, and this arrangement is necessarily satisfactory to decent and prominent people, since they will not be ruled by those who are worse. And they will rule justly as a result of having others in authority over reviewing them. For being dependent on others, and not having license to do anything whatever that seems good to them, is advantageous. For a license to act however one wishes leaves one no capacity to guard against the baser element in every human being. So the necessary result is exactly what is most beneficial in governments: that decent people rule while being kept from going astray, while the multitude is not made any worse off.   **40**   **1319A**

It is plain that this is the best of the types of democracy, and also for what reason, namely because the populace is of a certain sort. And some of the laws laid down among many peoples in ancient times are entirely effective at providing a farming population, either by not permitting the owning of more than a certain acreage of land at all, or not within a certain distance from the city center or city limits.   **10**   And in ancient times it was laid down by law in many cities that one was not even permitted to sell the original land grants. And there is also a law which people say came from Oxylus that has an effect of that sort, that one may not lend money against any portion of any person's landed property. But these days, one needs to straighten things out by means of a law of the Aphytaeans, since it is useful for what we are speaking of. For even though they are many and have little land, they still all engage in farming; for they base their assessments not on whole properties but on parts they divide up so small that even the poor exceed the property qualification.

After a farming multitude, the best population is   **20**   found where people are herders and live off livestock. For their circumstances are in many ways very close to farming, and in matters particularly related to military actions, they are trained in their habits, useful in their bodies, and capable of living outdoors. But just about all the other sorts of multitudes, out of which the rest of the types of democracies are organized, are far inferior to these. For their way of life is debased, and there is no work depending on virtue that they put their hands to, whether the multitude consists of mechanical workers, the humans who inhabit the mar-

ketplace, or menial laborers. Moreover, because they hang around the marketplace and in town, a class of people of
30   this sort can easily attend the assembly virtually en masse, while those engaged in farming, because they are scattered around the territory, neither meet up nor feel any need for this sort of gathering. And where the territory also happens to be situated in such a way that it is far removed from the city, it is even easier for a serviceable democracy or constitutional government to be produced. For the multitude is constrained to have its dwellings in the fields, so if there is also a mob that inhabits the marketplace, one ought not to hold assemblies in the democracies without the multitude from the countryside.

How, then, one ought to provide for the best and first
40   sort of democracy, has been stated, and it is also clear how the others should be handled. For they ought to deviate in
1319B   stages, and always separate off the worse sort of multitude. As for the last stage, since everyone takes part, it is not possible for every city to sustain and not easy for it to endure if it is not well constituted in its laws and customs. (What things end up destroying this and the other forms of government have been pretty well described earlier for most cases.) In order to set up this sort of democracy and make the populace strong, their leaders customarily take in as many people as possible and make them citizens, not only those of lawful
10   birth but also those who are illegitimate and born of a citizen in either of the two ways—I mean from a father or mother; anything of that sort is more acceptable among this sort of populace. So this is the way demagogues are in the habit of providing for it; one ought, however, to take people in up to the point at which the multitude outnumbers the prominent people and the middle group and not go any further beyond that. For those who overdo it make the government too disorderly and provoke the prominent people into being more disgruntled at the democracy. This is exactly what ended up becoming responsible for factional conflict in Cyrene. For a small debased group can be overlooked, but one that gets large is right in front of the eyes.

20   Other such provisions useful for this sort of democracy are the ones used by Cleisthenes when he wanted to expand the democracy in Athens, and by those who set up the popu-

lar government in Cyrene. More and different tribes and fraternal groups ought to be formed and the rites of private religious cults ought to be incorporated into a few public ones,
and everything ought to be cleverly arranged to get all the
people to intermingle with one another as much as possible,
while their former habitual associations are broken up. And
all the tyrannical provisions also seem to be suited to popular rule; I mean, for instance, lack of control over slaves (and
this may be advantageous up to a point), and over women
and children, and looking the other way while anyone lives   30
however he wishes. For support for that sort of government
will be widespread, since most people find it more pleasant
to live an undisciplined life than a moderate one.[180]

Chapter 5

But setting up such a government is not the greatest or
only work of the lawgiver and of those who want to organize it; seeing that it is preserved is a greater one. For it is not
difficult for those under any form of government whatever
to make it last for one or two or three days. That is why one
ought to try to draw on the things that were studied above,
the various kinds of preservation and destruction that belong to the forms of government, to provide stability, guarding against the things that destroy governments while put-   40
ting in place the sort of laws, unwritten as well as written,   1320A
which include to the greatest extent the things that preserve
them. One ought to regard as conducive to popular rule or
to oligarchy not what makes the city be ruled in the most
democratic or oligarchic manner possible, but what makes
such rule last the longest time. Nowadays, demagogues
confiscate a lot of property through the lawcourts to gratify
the populace. So those who care about their form of government ought to act in opposition to this practice by making a
law that nothing taken from those who suffer adverse judg-

---

180 Aristotle argues in the *Nicomachean Ethics* (see especially Bk. VII,
Chap. 13) that pleasure is an indispensable ingredient of a satisfying
life, but that most people never develop far enough to discover the
truly satisfying pleasures. Discipline imposed in childhood by parents
or laws would be a necessary step toward developing the capacity for
moderation and for mature pleasures. The misunderstanding of pleasure is hence at the root of the "bad definition of freedom" Aristotle
mentions above at 1310a 25-36.

ments will be the people's property or go into public funds but into temple funds. For those who commit injustices will
10   be no less deterred, since they will be fined just as much, but the mob will be less apt to cast negative votes in their verdicts when they are not going to get anything out of them. Also, one always ought to make public lawsuits take place as little as possible, by discouraging those who bring frivolous lawsuits with large penalties. For they are in the habit of bringing suit not against members of the populace but against prominent people, but in the best case all the citizens ought to be well-disposed toward the government, or failing that, at least not regard those in authority as enemies.

And since democracies in their last stages take in a lot of people, and it is difficult for them to attend assemblies without pay, this situation, where there do not happen to be
20   revenues, is hostile to the prominent people. For the funds necessarily come from property taxes, confiscation, and corrupt lawcourts, which have overturned many democracies before now. Where there do not happen to be revenues, then, one ought to have few assemblies, and few days on which courts with many jurors meet. This carries the advantage that the rich will not be afraid of the expense, if the well-off do not get a juror's fee but the needy do, and it is also conducive to much better judging of lawsuits; for those who are well off are not willing to be absent from their private affairs for many days, but are willing for a short time. Where
30   there are revenues, one ought not to do what demagogues do now, which is to hand out the surplus; and as soon as the people get it, they ask for the same amounts again, since this sort of aid to the needy is a leaky jar. One who is truly an advocate of the people ought to see to it that the multitude is not too needy, since this is what is responsible for a democracy's being depraved. So policies need to be contrived in such a way that prosperity becomes long-lasting. And since this is also advantageous to those who are well off, one should give out to the needy surpluses accumulated from revenues in lump sums, especially if someone would be able to muster enough of a sum for owning a piece of land, or
1320B failing that, for capital to put into trade or farming. And if this is not possible for everyone, then one ought to distribute it in turns to tribes or to some other portion of the populace, and while this is going on, tax the well-off for the payment

for necessary meetings while excusing them from pointless public benefactions.[181]

It is by governing in this sort of way that the Carthaginians have won over the populace as a friend. For they are always sending out some members of the populace to the outlying towns and making them well off. And it is a mark of being refined and having good sense in prominent people for them to divide the needy among themselves and give them capital to turn to productive uses. And it is also a beautiful idea to do what the Tarantines do. For they make their property common for use by the needy and thus gain a favorable attitude among the multitude. They also made all their offices double, elected and chosen by lot, in order that the populace could take part in those of them chosen by lot and so they would be better governed by the ones that were elected. It is also possible to do this by having those chosen by lot and those who are elected take turns[182] in the same office. How one ought to provide for democracies, then, has been stated.

Chapter 6

And how one ought to provide for oligarchies is also pretty well evident from these things. One ought to put together each sort of oligarchy out of opposite elements by inference from the correspondingly opposite type of democracy. In the first and most well-blended of the oligarchies, which is close to what is called constitutional rule, one ought to divide up the property qualifications, making some lower and others higher—lower ones on the basis of which people will take part in offices dealing with necessities and higher ones for offices dealing with matters of greater authority. They ought to permit anyone who acquires the property qualification to take part in the government, using the qualification to bring in a multitude of the populace large enough

---

181 See 1309a 14-20 above.

182 The verb *merizein* would ordinarily mean "divide" or "partition," but if the Tarantine method was to have two people divide the functions of each office, the alternative seems to be a rotation in the manner of choosing a single office holder, and *kata meros* means "by turns." Taras was a colony of Sparta; on the common use of private property, see 1263a 21-40 above.

that with them they will be stronger than those not taking part, and in all cases they ought to take in the participants from the better portion of the populace. And they ought to
30   provide for the next sort of oligarchy in a similar way, but by tightening the qualification a little. As for the sort that is opposite to the last stage of democracy, the one that among oligarchies is most like a confederacy of the powerful and most tyrannical, it needs more precautions to the same extent that it is the worst sort. For just as bodies in good shape as far as health is concerned and ships with their crews in beautiful condition for sailing have room for more mistakes without being destroyed by them, while bodies in a sickly condition and rickety ships that are stuck with lousy crews are not capable of enduring even small mistakes, so too the
1321A   worst forms of government need the most precautions. So while a large population in general preserves democracies, since this is the opposite of what is just on the basis of merit, it is clear that oligarchy on the contrary needs to gain its preservation from good planning.

Chapter 7

As there are four main parts of the multitude, occupied in farming, mechanical work, the marketplace, and menial labor, there are also four groups useful in war, a cavalry, a heavy-armed force, a light-armed force, and a naval force. Where the land happens to be suited for horses, it is natu-
10   ral to build up a strong oligarchy. For the safety of the inhabitants is secured by this power, and the rearing of horses depends on people who own large estates. Where the land is suited for heavy-armed maneuvers, the next sort of oligarchy is natural, since a heavy-armed force is made up of the well-off rather than the needy. But light-armed and naval powers are entirely suited to popular rule. So these days, where this sort of multitude is large, when there is conflict, the oligarchs often come off worse in the struggle. But one ought to adopt a remedy for this used by generals who are skilled at war, who pair up an appropriate force of light-armed soldiers with their force of cavalry and heavy
20   armor. The reason popular parties prevail over the well-off in schisms is that it is easy for those who are lightly armed to challenge a force of cavalry and heavy armor. So while

setting up this sort of force from these people is setting it up against themselves, there needs to be a division made on the basis of age between those who are older and the young, and while their sons are still young they ought to teach them light-armed and unarmed tactics, and have a group picked from the boys to be fighters on their own side in actions.

And there ought to be a granting of a place in the administration to the multitude, either, as mentioned before, to those who acquire the property qualification, or as among the Thebans, to those who have stayed out of mechanical occupations for a certain length of time, or else as in Massalia, by making a selection of worthy candidates from among those in the administration and those outside it. But the most authoritative offices, which those within the government ought to hold onto, should have public service obligations attached to them so that the populace will be willing not to take part in them, and will have sympathy for their rulers as people paying a heavy price for their office. And it is fitting for those entering such offices to offer magnificent sacrifices and build something for public use, so that by sharing in the feasts and seeing the city adorned with monuments and buildings, the populace will be glad to see the government stay in power—and for the prominent people there will incidentally be a memorial of their expenditure. But this is not the way those involved in oligarchies do things now; they do the opposite. They look for monetary gains no less than for honor, and for this reason it is well said that these oligarchies are small-time democracies.

So let the matter of how one should set up democracies and oligarchies be determined in this way.

Chapter 8

Following what has been said, there is the matter of dividing the things related to offices in a beautiful way, as to their number, what they are, and what they deal with, as was said earlier.[183] For apart from the necessary offices it is impossible for there to be a city, and apart from those that lead to good arrangement and order it is impossible for it to be beautifully managed. But it is also necessary for there

183 This chapter picks up the discussion in Bk. IV, Chap. 15.

10   to be fewer offices in small cities and more in large ones, as was mentioned in that earlier passage, so which offices it is fitting to combine and which ones to separate ought not to be overlooked.

The first of the necessary matters is attention to the marketplace, in which there needs to be an office overseeing matters pertaining to contracts and orderly transactions. For in just about all cities people have to buy some things and sell others among themselves for necessary use, and this is the handiest way toward self-sufficiency, which is generally thought to be the reason people join into one government. Another kind of attention following this one and closely related to it has to do with public and private property in
20   town, so there can be orderliness, and also safety and repairs when buildings and roads are falling apart, and so people can be free of disputes over boundaries, and to take care of all other matters along similar lines to these. Most people call this sort of office policing, but it has a greater number of parts, and in more populous cities they appoint different people for different ones, such as repairers of the city walls, superintendents of the water supply, and harbor masters. And there is another office that is necessary and very much like that one, since it is concerned with the same things, but in the countryside and outside the town; some
30   people call these officials rural constables; others call them forest wardens.

So these are three kinds of attention to these necessary matters; and there is another office to which revenues from common sources are brought in, where they are kept safe and distributed to each administrative department. People call these officials receivers or treasurers. Another office is that in which private contracts and judgments of the lawcourts are required to be registered, and indictments and initial filings of lawsuits ought to come to these same officials. In some places they divide this into more than one office, but it is possible for[184] one office to be in authority over all these things. People call them sacred recorders, superintendents,
40   recorders, and other titles close to these.

---

184 Ross follows earlier editors who make this read "there are places where," but the manuscript text, followed here, seems to be an instance of "offices it is fitting to combine."

The next one after this is just about the most necessary and most troublesome of offices, that which deals with punishments against convicts and those posted on debtor lists, and with custody of persons. It is troublesome because it incurs great hostility, so where it is not possible get large gains out of it, people either do not consent to hold this office, or when they consent they are not willing to act in accord with the laws. But it is a necessary office, because no benefit comes from lawsuits over matters of justice when they cannot attain their end. So if it is impossible for people to live in common with one another if lawsuits cannot take place, it is also impossible where punishments cannot be carried out. For this reason it is better that this not be a single office but different people from different courts, and better to try to divide up the postings on the debtor lists the same way, and also for the ruling officials to carry out some of the punishments, and especially new officials rather than those already there, and among those in place, to have a different one doing the punishing from the others who made the adverse judgment, such as town constables in place of the market constables, and others in place of them. The less hostility there is to those doing the punishing, the more the punishments will attain their end. So there is a double hostility where there are the same people making the adverse judgments and doing the punishing, and where the same people do so in all cases they are enemies to everyone. Indeed in many places the group that guards prisoners is divided off from that which inflicts punishments, as with the so-called Eleven in Athens. So it is better to separate this function too, and to look for a clever way to deal with it as well. For it is no less necessary than the one mentioned, but it turns out that decent people avoid this office in particular, while it is not safe to give authority to corrupt ones. They need guarding themselves more than they are capable of guarding others. So there ought not to be a single office assigned to them, and the same one ought not to be in place continuously, but one drawn from among the young, where there is a corps of cadets or reserve guards, and different ones from among the officials ought to be put in charge of them in turns.

These offices are to be placed first, then, as being the most necessary; after these come offices that are no less

1322A

10

20

30

necessary, and ranked higher in status, since they require a good deal of experience and trust. Such would be the ones connected with the defense of the city, and the whole array of functions directed to military uses. In peace and war alike, there need to be people in charge of guarding gates and walls, and of reviewing and marshalling the citizens. The offices for all these functions are greater in number in some places and fewer in others; in small cities, for example, one office deals with them all. People call such officials generals or military commanders. And if there are cavalrymen, light-armed troops, archers, or a naval force, an additional office is sometimes set up for each of these, and people call them admirals, cavalry commanders, squadron leaders, and those assigned to sections under them are called battleship captains, platoon leaders, brigade commanders, and others for whatever parts there are of these. The whole of this attention to military matters is one in form. So this is how things stand with this office, but since some, if not in fact all, of the offices handle large amounts of public funds, it is necessary for there to be a different office that receives and audits their accounts while it does not handle any other matter. Some call these officials auditors, others accountants, examiners, or fiduciaries. Besides all these offices there is one that is the most authoritative of all. For the same office often guides things from start to finish, the one which, where the populace is in authority, presides over the multitude, since there has to be something that convenes the authoritative part of the government. In some places these officials are called precouncilors because they do the preliminary deliberating, but where the multitude is the authoritative element, the office is called a council instead.

So those offices dealing with political affairs are just about this many, but another form of attention is that paid to the gods. There are priests, for instance, and people in charge of matters related to temples, including preserving existing buildings and repairing those that are falling apart, as well as all the other things dedicated to the gods. In some places, in small cities for instance, this ends up being a single concern, but in some places there are many offices separate from the priesthood, such as managers of sacrifices, guardians of temples, and keepers of sacred funds. Closely connected with this is an a office reserved for all the public sac-

1322B

10

20

rifices that the law does not assign to the priests, but to those who have the honor of providing them from the civic hearth. Some people call them archons, others kings, and still others presidents.

So the necessary kinds of attention, put in summary   30
form, deal with the following things: matters of divinity and war, revenues and expenditures, the marketplace, the town, coasts, and countryside, and in connection with the lawcourts, the recording of contracts, carrying out of punishments, custody of prisoners, keeping of accounts and inspection and review of officials, and last are those that deal with the body that deliberates about common concerns. The kinds peculiar to cities with more leisure and greater prosperity and which are also mindful of good order, are overseers of women, guardians of the law, overseers of children, athletic directors, and in addition to these, supervision of   1323A
competitions in athletics and of dramatic contests dedicated to Dionysus, as well as any other such spectator events there may happen to be. Some of these offices are obviously not suited to popular governments, such as overseers of women and children, since the poor, being without slaves, need to use both women and children as attendants.

And of the three kinds of office by which particular governments choose their authoritative officials—guardians of the law, pre-councils, and councils—guardians of the law are suited to aristocracy, pre-councils to oligarchy, and councils to popular rule. On the subject of offices, then, just about   10
all of them have been spoken of in outline.

Book VII

Chapter 1

On the subject of the best form of government, it is necessary for anyone who is going to make an appropriate inquiry to determine first what way of life is most worthy of choice. For if this is unclear, it is necessarily also unclear what form of government is best. For it makes sense that those who do best in life would be those who are governed the best way their circumstances admit, provided nothing unforeseeable happens. This is why one must first have agreement about which way of life is most worthy of choice for practically everyone, and after that, whether this is the same or different for a life lived in common or separately. So if one believes that even the things said about the best life in our popular writings[185] are stated sufficiently, it is appropriate for them to be used now as well. And in regard to one distinction at least, it is certainly true that no one would dispute that, of the three classes of goods—external ones, those of the body, and those of the soul—all of them must belong to those who are blessedly happy. For no one would claim someone was blessed who did not have a bit of courage or moderation or justice or good judgment, but was afraid of the flies fluttering around him, did not hold himself back from any extremes when he felt a desire to eat or drink, ruined his dearest friends for a quarter, and likewise was as senseless and deluded in his thinking as any child or insane person. But as much as everyone would go along with these

20

30

---

185 These are writings addressed to an audience outside the school in which Aristotle taught. One example, containing some of the material he makes use of here, is the *Protrepticus*, an exhortation to philosophy of which extensive fragments have survived.

statements, they would also differ on the matter of amount and on their rankings of priority. For people regard it as sufficient to have any trace at all of virtue, but with wealth and possessions and power and prestige and everything of that sort, they seek a superabundance beyond any limits.

But we will point out to them that it is easy to get hold
40 of persuasive evidence about these matters right from the facts, by seeing that people do not acquire and safeguard the virtues by means of external things, but the latter by
1323B means of the former, and that living happily, whether this is found by human beings in enjoyment or in virtue or both, belongs to a greater extent to those who have set in order their character and thinking to the utmost and are moderate about the acquisition of external goods, than to those who have acquired more of the latter than they have any use for but come up short with the former.[186] But the same conclusion is easily taken in view by those who examine it through argument. For external things have a limit, as any instrumental thing does, and every useful thing is directed toward something; an excess of such things is necessarily
10 either harmful or of no benefit to those who have it. But each of the goods pertaining to the soul is more useful to exactly the same extent that it goes on increasing, if indeed one ought to speak of these things too not only as beautiful but also as useful. And in general it is clear that we will maintain that the best conditions of a variety of things in relation to one another follow the ranking of priority which is allotted to those things of which we say they are the conditions. So if the soul is a more valuable thing, both simply and for us, than both possessions and the body, then it is necessary that the best conditions of each have a relation corresponding to these things. Furthermore, it is the soul for the sake of which these things are naturally worthy of choice, and for the sake
20 of which all those who think soundly ought to choose them, and not the soul for their sake.

Let it be agreed by us, then, that just as much happiness falls to the lot of each person as he has of virtue and good

---

186 The translation does not capture the fact that twice in this sentence Aristotle reverses the usual words for latter and former (these and those) to convey the sense that goods of the soul are the ones nearer to us and external goods farther away.

judgment, and of action in accord with these, calling upon the god as our witness, who is happy and blessed through none of the external goods but through himself alone and by being of a certain sort in his nature. And it is for this reason that good luck is necessarily different from happiness, since chance and luck are responsible for the goods external to the soul, while no one is just or moderate by luck or through reliance on luck. And a corollary entailed by the same arguments is that the best city is one that is happy and gets along beautifully. But it is impossible for those who do not perform beautiful actions to get along beautifully, and there is no beautiful deed, whether of a man or of a city, apart from virtue and good judgment. And courage, justice, good judgment, and moderation in a city have the same power and form that every human being who is called courageous, just, sensible, and moderate participates in. So let these things, to this extent, be prefaced to our discussion. For it is not possible to forego touching on them, but to go through all the pertinent arguments in detail is not an option—that is a task requiring a different sort of study.[187] For now, let this much be assumed: that the best way of life, both separately for each person and in common for cities, is one equipped with virtue to such an extent that one can take part in the actions that proceed from virtue. As for those who dispute this, since we are leaving them aside in our present inquiry, a careful examination would need to be made later if anyone turns out not to be persuaded by what is said.

Chapter 2

Something that remains to be said is whether one should claim that happiness is the same or not the same in each one human being and in a city, but this is in fact obvious, since everyone would agree that they are the same. For those who regard living well as consisting in wealth in the case of one person also count a whole city as blessedly happy if it is wealthy; those who hold a tyrannical way of life in the highest honor would also claim that a city that rules the greatest number of other cities is the happiest; and

---

187 Or "a different kind of leisure." The *Nicomachean Ethics* as a whole is devoted to the question of how one ought to live, and treats it comprehensively.

if one accepts that a single person is happy by means of virtue, he will also claim that a city more excellent in virtue is happier. But then there are the following two questions that need examination. One is whether the life more worthy of choice is that lived by being governed in common and sharing in a city, or rather that of an outsider free of the bonds of political association. And the other, regardless of whether sharing in a city is worthy of choice for everyone or for most though not for some people, is which form of government and which way of arranging a city one ought to rank as best.

20   But since the latter question, and not the one about what is worthy of choice for each person, is a task that belongs to political thought and study, and this is the inquiry we have now undertaken, the other question would be off the subject while this task is on the track we are pursuing.

Now it is obvious that the best form of government would necessarily be that ordering by which anyone whatsoever could act the best and live blessedly. But among the very people who agree that the life involving virtue is most worthy of choice, there is disagreement about whether a political and active life is preferable, or rather one which is free of dependence on all external things, such as some sort of contemplative life, which some claim is the only sort for a

30   philosopher. For among those human beings who have been the most passionate to achieve distinction, in times past and in our own times, it is almost exclusively these two lives that they have manifestly chosen—the two I mean being the political and the philosophic. And which way the truth stands makes no small difference, for the person who judges well must organize things toward the better goal, for each human being as well as for the political association in common. Some people believe that ruling neighboring cities the way a master rules slaves carries with it an injustice of the most extreme kind, and that, while ruling them politically involves no injustice, it does constitute a hindrance to one's own well-being. But others arrive at an opinion which is practically

40   the opposite of the these—that the only life fit for a man is the active and political one, since actions stemming from every virtue are not found in private persons to a greater

1324B extent than in those who act and are governed in common. So this is the way some people take up the idea, but others claim that the only happy course for a government to take is that of mastery and tyranny. And among some peoples this is the measure of the laws and constitution: that they exercise mastery over their neighbors.

So while one might call most of the legal ordinances laid down by most peoples a hodgepodge, still if the laws anywhere do look toward some one thing, they all aim at being dominant, in the way that education and the bulk of the laws in Sparta and Crete are pretty much designed for wars. Moreover, in all nations that have the capacity to get the upper hand, this sort of power is held in honor, as among the Scythians, Persians, Thracians, and Celts. Among some of them, certain laws are even intended as incitements to this sort of virtue. Along these lines, people say that in Carthage, a man gets an array of bracelets equal to the number of military campaigns he has fought. And there was once a law in Macedonia that a man who had not killed anyone in war had to wear a horse's halter as a belt. Among the Scythians, one who has not killed anyone in war is not allowed to drink from a cup passed around at a certain banquet. Among the Iberians, a warlike nation, they place a ring of spikes in the ground around a man's tomb equal in number to the enemies he has destroyed. And there are many other such practices among other peoples, some imposed by laws, others by customs.

And yet, to those willing to examine the matter, it would perhaps seem too strange if this were a task for a student of the political art, to be able to see how to rule and master one's neighbors whether they are willing or unwilling. How could this, which is not even lawful, be relevant to the political art or that of a lawgiver? But ruling of a sort which is done unjustly as well as justly is not lawful, and dominating can be done unjustly. We certainly do not see this in the other kinds of knowledge; for it is not the job of a doctor or a helmsman to use force as well as persuasion on his patients or crewmen. But most people seem to think the art of mastering slaves is the political art, and the very thing each group claims is not just or advantageous when applied to themselves, they are not ashamed of practicing toward others. For they seek a just sort of rule among themselves but have no concern about things that are just for others. But it would be strange if there were not a natural distinction between what is meant to be mastered and what is not meant to be mastered; so if this is the way things are, one ought not to try to master everyone, but only those meant to

40   be mastered, just as one ought not to hunt human beings for a banquet or sacrifice, but something meant to be hunted for this purpose, and any wild animal that is fit to eat is meant

1325A to be hunted. And it would surely be possible for one city to be happy on its own, one that is beautifully governed of course, if it is possible for a city making use of excellent laws to be settled somewhere on its own, and the organization of its government would not be directed toward war or toward dominating enemies, for let it be assumed that nothing of that sort is there.

Therefore it is clear that, while all concerns directed toward war are to be considered beautiful things, they are not to be regarded as an end or as the highest of all things; they are for the sake of that. The job of an excellent lawgiver is to study, for a city, a race of human beings, or any other

10   association of people, how they can participate in a good life and in the happiness that is possible for them. There will, however, be differences among some of the ordinances prescribed, and one matter for the lawgiver's art to discern, if there are any neighbors present, is what sort of training needs to be undertaken in relation which groups of them, and how to make use of appropriate measures toward each. But this matter of what end the best form of government would be directed toward will get to its appropriate investigation later.[188]

Chapter 3

As for those who agree that the life most worthy of choice is one involving virtue, but differ about the pursuit of it, a reply needs to be made by us to both these groups. For the one group dismisses the worthiness of political offices,

20   in the belief that the life of a free person is the most choice-worthy of all, and is different from that of someone engaged in political life; the other believes that the latter is best, since it is impossible for someone who engages in no action to get along well, and that well-being and happiness are the same

---

188 This will begin in Chap. 13 of this book.

thing.[189] Both groups are right in some of the things they say and not right about others. One group says that the life of a free person is better than one devoted to mastery, and this is true, since there is nothing grand about using a slave as a slave; giving orders about necessities plays no part in beautiful deeds. To regard every sort of rule as being mastery, however, is not right, for the separation between rule over free people and rule over slaves is no less than that between what is itself free by nature and what is naturally a slave. **30** But distinctions about these things were made sufficiently in our first chapters.[190] And it is not true to praise inaction over action, for happiness is action, and the actions of just and moderate people also contain the fulfillment of many beautiful things.

And yet, when these things are distinguished in this way, one might assume that it is best to be in authority over everyone, since in that way one would be in charge of the greatest number of the most beautiful actions. So anyone with the power to rule ought not to give it up to his neighbor but take it away from him instead; and a father ought to feel no responsibility for his children, nor children for their father, nor anyone at all to anyone dear to him, nor should they pay any attention in that direction. The best thing is the **40** most worthy of choice, and acting well is best. And perhaps there is truth in their saying this, if the most choiceworthy **1325B** things there are would belong to people who resort to robbery and violence. But perhaps it is not possible for them to belong to such people, and this is a false assumption they are making. For there is no possibility for actions to be beautiful when they are those of someone who does not surpass others to the same extent that a man surpasses a woman, a father his children, or a master his slaves. So someone who commits offenses could not in any way put things right afterward to the same degree he has already deviated from virtue. For among people who are alike, what is beautiful and just consists in taking turns, since this is equal and alike. Inequality for equals and unlikeness for those who are alike is contrary to nature, and nothing contrary to nature is beau- **10**

---

189   "Getting along well" (*eu prattein*) and "well-being" (*eupragia*) are both
      based on the verb meaning to act.

190   Book I, Chaps. 4-7.

tiful. Hence if someone else is stronger in virtue and in the power to put the best things into action, the beautiful thing is to follow that person and the just thing is to obey him. But he needs to have not only virtue but also the power that will make him capable of action.

Then if these things are beautifully argued and happiness needs to be set down as well-being in action, the active life would be the best one, both for a whole city in common and for each person. But it is not necessary for what is active to be directed toward others, as some imagine, nor is it necessary that the only active thoughts are those that are for the sake of the consequences that come from acting; rather,
20   those acts of contemplation and thinking that are ends in themselves and for their own sake are much more active. For their end is well-being, so that it too is an action.[191] And even in the case of external actions, we speak of those who are master-planners of those actions by means of their thinking as *acting* in the most authoritative way. And certainly cities situated off by themselves that choose to live that way are not necessarily inactive, since it is also possible for action to take place among its parts, because the parts of a city have many kinds of interaction with one another. And this is similarly the case with human beings, for any one of them at all. For otherwise the god and the whole cosmos, which *have* no external actions over and above their own within them-
30   selves, could hardly be in a good condition. So it is obvious that the same way of life is necessarily best for each human being and for cities and human beings in common.

Chapter 4

Seeing as how the things just said about these matters have served as a preface, and what concerns the other forms of government has been studied by us earlier, the beginning of what remains is to speak first about what sorts of underlying conditions need to be present for the city that is to be

---

191 The argument here is still of the popular sort referred to at the beginning of Bk. VII, and parts of it are stated in a sketchy way, but the conclusion seems to be that the well-being of a human being comes to fulfillment only in the active exercise of all our powers. One might argue too that the greatest freedom depends upon the liberation of those powers, which put to work the greatest fullness of life. Compare this to *Metaphysics* 1072b 26-27: "the being-at-work of intellect is life."

organized the way one would wish. For it is not possible
for the best form of government to come into being without
the commensurate equipment. Hence it is necessary to take
for granted in advance many things as being the way they
are wished for, so long as none of these are impossible. I am
speaking, for instance, of what has to do with the multi-   40
tude of citizens and with the land. For in the same way that
other craftsmen, such as a weaver and a shipbuilder, need   1326A
to have material available that is suited to the work they do
(for the product that comes from their art must necessarily
be a more beautiful one to the same degree that this material
is better prepared), so too do the political craftsman and the
lawgiver need to have appropriate material available in a
suitable condition.

And the first piece of political equipment is the multitude of human beings, both how many there need to be
and what sorts by nature. And it is the same with the land,
both how much of it and what sort there needs to be. And
most people assume that the fitting thing is that a happy city
would be a great one; but if this is true, they are mistaken   10
about what sort of city is great and what sort small. They
judge a great one numerically by the multitude of inhabitants, but they need to look not to their multitude but rather
to their capacity. For there is also a certain work that belongs
to a city, so that city ought to be thought of as greatest which
is most capable of accomplishing this work. It is just as if one
were to say Hippocrates was greater, not as a human being
but as a doctor, than someone who surpassed him in the size
of his body. Even if one had to judge by looking to numerical
multitude, however, this ought not to be done in reference to
any random multitude (for it is perhaps necessary for cities
to have present in them a large number of slaves and resi-   20
dent aliens and foreigners), but to those who are part of the
city and belong among the proper parts out of which a city
is organized. For it is the superiority in multitude of these
inhabitants that is a sign of a great city; it is impossible for
a city to be great from which a large number of mechanical
workers, but few heavy-armed troops, comes marching out.
For a great city is not the same thing as populous one.

But this too is certainly obvious from the facts, that
it is difficult and perhaps impossible for a city that is too

populous to have good laws. Among the cities that seem to be beautifully governed, at any rate, we see not even one that fails to control the number of people. And this is clear
30 from the evidence of arguments as well. For law is a certain kind of ordering, and being under good law is necessarily a well-ordered condition, but a number that is too excessive is incapable of forming part of an order. That would surely be a task for a divine power, the one that holds together the totality of things, since beauty is ordinarily a matter of number and size. Hence a city too would necessarily be most beautiful insofar as the limiting factor mentioned is present along with size. But there is also a certain standard for the size for a city, just as there is for everything else—animals, plants, instruments. For each of these things will have the capacity that belongs to it when it is neither too small nor excessive in size; otherwise, it will in some cases be wholly deprived of
40 its nature, and in others be in poor condition. A ship as big as a hand, for instance, will not be a ship at all, and neither will
1326B one a quarter-mile long, and when it gets to a certain size it will do a poor job of sailing, on account of either smallness or excessiveness. Likewise, with a city, an aggregate of too few people is not self-sufficient (but a city is self-sufficient), while one that consists of too many is self-sufficient in necessities the way a nation is, but is not a city, for it is not easy for there to be a government in it. Who is going to be general of a multitude that is too excessive, and who without a voice like Stentor's[192] is going to be its herald? Hence the first city is necessarily the one with a number large enough to be the first multitude that is self-sufficient for living well in a politi-
10 cal association. And it is possible for one that exceeds this one in multitude to be a greater city, but this is not possible without limit, as we said.

And it is easy to see from the facts what the limit of the excess is. For the actions of the city are those of either the rulers or the ruled, and the job of a ruler is command and decision. For making decisions about matters of justice, and for distributing offices as well, it is necessary for the citizens to know one another and know what sort of people they are, since wherever this turns out not to be the case, matters

---

192 Stentor's voice, according to *Iliad* V, 786, was as loud as that of fifty other men.

involving offices and decisions necessarily come out badly. For in both cases no justice is to be had from doing things off the top of one's head, which is obviously exactly what one finds in places that are too populous. What is more, it is easy for foreigners and resident aliens to take part in the government, since it is not difficult for them to go unnoticed in the excess of the multitude. Accordingly, it is clear that the best limit for a city is this: the greatest excess of multitude over self-sufficiency of life that is easily taken in at one view. So let what has to do with the size of a city be determined in this way.

Chapter 5

Matters that concern the land are very similar. As for what sort it should be, it is clear that everyone would recommend the kind that is most self-sufficient. And this would necessarily be one that grows all sorts of things, since that which has everything available and lacks nothing is self-sufficient. In quantity and size, it should be big enough that the inhabitants can live at leisure in a manner that combines freedom and moderation. Whether we are stating this limit beautifully or not is something that needs to be examined with more precision later, when it comes time to make mention of property in general and abundance of wealth, and of how and in what manner this is related to the use of it.[193] For there are many disputes involved in this investigation on account of people who would pull it in the direction of one or the other extreme way of life, some toward frugality and others toward luxury.

But the conformation of the land is not difficult to speak of (though on some particulars one ought to pay additional heed to those who are experienced at generalship); it should be hard for enemies to penetrate but easy for the people themselves to exit. Also, just as we claimed that the multitude of human beings ought to be easy to take in at one view, so too should the land, since a land that is easily taken in at one view is one that is easy to defend. And if one should make the placement of the city as one would wish, it

20

30

40

1327A

---

193 This promise, like several more that follow in Bks. VII and VIII, is not fulfilled in any later passage. In the present instance, Bk. I, Chaps. 8-11, on provisioning seem closest to what is described.

is appropriate for it to be beautifully situated in relation to both the sea and the land. One limiting factor is what was mentioned, that there ought to be passageway to all regions for defensive troops; the remaining one is that there ought to be easy transportation for conveyances carrying crops that are grown, and also building material made of wood and
10   any other such product the land happens to have.

Chapter 6

As far as access to the sea is concerned, people happen to have many disputes about whether this is beneficial or harmful to cities with good laws. For they claim that being open to a variety foreigners raised under other laws is detrimental to good order, as is overpopulation. For they say the use of the sea results in a multitude of traders who export and import goods, and an overpopulation that is adverse to being beautifully governed. Now if these things do not result, there is no doubt that it is better, both for safety and for easy
20   availability of necessities, for a city and its territory to have a share of seacoast. For in order to endure wars more easily, those who are going to survive need to be well defended on both fronts, by land and by sea; and for inflicting harm on their attackers, if they do not have the power to do so on both fronts, those who have a share in both will still have more opportunity to do so on one of the two. And the ability to import those things that happen not to be present among them, and to export those they have in excess, are both necessities. For a city needs to be a market for itself, though not for others; cities that hold themselves out as a marketplace for everyone
30   do that for the sake of revenue. But a city that ought to keep out of that sort of profit seeking ought not to have that sort of market either. And since we now see many territories and cities that have ports and harbors available that are well situated by nature in relation to the city, so that they do not dwell in the town itself but not too far away either, but are commanded by walls and other such defenses, it is evident that if any good result turns out to come from access to them, this good will belong to the city, while any harmful consequence there may be can easily be guarded against by laws that spell out and limit which people ought and ought not to be inter-
40   mingled with one another.

On the subject of naval power, there is no doubt that it is best for it to be present to a certain extent. For people need 1327B to be feared and to have the power to mount a defense, not only for themselves but also for some of their neighbors, on the sea just as on land. But as for the extent and size of this power, that needs to be considered in relation to the way of life of the city. For if it is going to pursue a life devoted to leadership and politics, then it will be necessary for this power to be present in a manner commensurate with its actions. But it is not necessary for cities to have the overpopulation that comes in with a mob of sailors, since they ought not to be any part of the city. For the fighting force on board 10 is a group of free men from the infantry, which has command and control of the ship. And if there is a multitude of people available who live on and farm the land outside the city, there is necessarily also a plentiful supply of sailors.[194] And we see that this is the case now among some people, such as those in the city of Heraclea, for they fill up numerous battleships despite having a city more moderate in size than others.

So let the matters that have to do with lands, harbors, cities, and the sea, as well as with naval power, be determined in this way.

Chapter 7

We stated above what limit there should be on the number of citizens, but let us now discuss what sort of peo- 20 ple they ought to be by nature. And one may discern this pretty well by looking at those cities among the Greeks that are well regarded as well as at the way the whole inhabited world is differentiated by nations. For the nations in cold regions, particularly those in Europe, are full of spiritedness but deficient in thinking and art, which is why they are more successful at staying free, but are nonpolitical and not capable of ruling their neighbors. But those in Asia, though they have an aptitude for thinking and art in their souls, are unspirited, which is why they stay subject and enslaved. But

---

194 Aristotle's point is that the large number of manual laborers needed to row triremes, the fast ships with three banks of oars that had dominated naval warfare since the Persian War, did not require the expansion in the number of full citizens that took place in Athens.

30   just as the race of Greeks is in the middle in terms of places, it likewise has a share in both temperaments, for it is both spirited and thoughtful; this is why it both stays free and is best governed, and it is capable of ruling everyone if it were to unite in a single government. And the same distinction holds among the Greek peoples in relation to one another, since some have a one-sided nature while others are well blended of both these capacities.

It is clear, then, that people who are going to be easily led toward virtue by a lawgiver need to be both thoughtful and spirited. For with the very thing that some people claim
40   needs to be present in guardians,[195] that they be friendly to those they know and fierce toward those they do not know, it is spiritedness that produces the friendliness, since this is
1328A   the capacity in the soul by which we feel friendship. A sign of this is that spiritedness is aroused more against one's intimates and friends than against strangers when one feels slighted. And this is why Archilochus, when complaining about his friends, appropriately addresses this remark to his spirit: "it is at the hands of your friends that you are choked with rage." Both ruling and freedom have their source in this capacity for all people, for spiritedness is a spur toward ruling and refuses to be beaten. But it is not beautifully said that such people are harsh toward strangers, for they should
10   not be that way toward anyone, and great-souled people are not fierce by nature but only in response to those who are unjust. But they feel this way even more strongly toward their intimate friends, as was said above, when they believe they have been treated unjustly by them. And this happens reasonably, for with people whom they assume owe them a good turn, they believe that on top of the harm, they have been robbed of this kindness. This is why it is said that "harsh are the battles of brothers," and "those who have loved extravagantly hate extravagantly."

What pertains to those who take part in the government, then, how many should be present and of what sort they should be by nature, and also what pertains to how

---

195 The reference is to Plato's *Republic*, where spiritedness (*thumos*) is identified as the quality that allows a human soul to be unified, and by analogy as the disposition that can be harnessed to hold a city together.

much and what sort of land there should be, have been determined in a rough sort of way. (For one ought not to look   20
for the same precision there is in arguments in things that
come by way of perception.)[196]

Chapter 8

Since, just as with other things organized by nature,
those things without which the whole could not exist are
not parts of the organized whole, it is clear that not all the
things that need to be available to cities ought to be counted as parts of a city, nor of any other association of which
anything one in kind is organized. For those who are part
of the association have to have something in common that
is one and the same, whether they participate in it equally
or unequally; this is either food, for instance, or an amount
of land, or else it is some other such thing. But whenever
one thing is for the sake of this, and another is that for the
sake of which it is, these things have nothing in common   30
other than the fact that one produces what the other takes
up. I mean, for example, common to every instrument and
craftsman in comparison to the product that comes into being, for there is no common thing that comes into being in a
house as compared to a housebuilder, but the art possessed
by housebuilders is for the sake of the house. Hence, while
cities need property, the property is no part of the city, while
many parts of its property are ensouled.[197] But a city is an association of people who are alike, for the sake of the best life
they are capable of. And since the best thing is happiness,
and this is the being-at-work of virtue and some complete
way of putting it into practice, and it so happens that some

---

196 Chapters 1-3 of Bk. VII consisted of general assumptions drawn from
      popular writings, and Chaps. 4-7 are based on broad observation of
      facts. The arguments to which he is referring here would presumably
      start from purely logical and theoretical premises, as do those of such
      people as Phaleas, Hippodamas, and the Athenian Stranger in Plato's
      Laws (all discussed in Bk. II) who claimed to have determined the best
      arrangements for a city with mathematical precision. Aristotle's own
      arguments for the best general design of a city occupy the remainder
      of Bk. VII, with the exclusion of the first half of Chap. 10.

197 These many parts would include livestock, but also, of more relevance
      to this argument, slaves. See Bk. I, Chap. 4 above. Aristotle considers
      the slave part of the master but not of the city.

40   people are capable of sharing in it while others have little or no capacity, it is clear that this is the reason why more than one form of city and variety of government arises. For since

1328B   each group hunts for this in a different way and by different means, this produces different ways of life and forms of government.

How many of these parts there are without which a city could not exist needs to be examined, since the things we say are parts of the city would necessarily also be present among them. So the number of functions it has needs to be grasped, since this will be clear from these. In the first place it needs to have food; then arts, since living requires many instruments; thirdly arms, since it is necessary for those in the association to bear arms among themselves for ruling on account of those who are disobedient, as well as against

10   those from outside who try to do them injustice; also, a convenient source of money that they can have available both for uses among themselves and for military expenses; fifth but also first, the attention to the divine that people call the priestly function; and sixth in number and most necessary of all, judgment about what is advantageous and just in their dealings with one another. These, then, are the functions that one might say every city requires. For a city is not a random multitude but is, as we claim, self-sufficient for life, and if any of these things happens to be lacking, it is impossible for that association to be simply self-sufficient. Accordingly,

20   it is necessary for a city to be organized for the exercise of these functions. Therefore there need to be a multitude of farmers who will provide the food, artisans, a fighting force, a well-off element, priests, and deciders of what is necessary and advantageous.[198]

Chapter 9

Now that these distinctions have been made, what remains to be considered is whether all these functions ought

---

198   In Bk. IV, Chap. 4, Aristotle made a similar list as a basis for discussing the varieties of democratic government. The primary difference between the two lists is the omission here of the people who engage in trade in the marketplace and the menial and manual laborers who have no skills. What he says about sea-traders and oarsmen in Chap. 6 of this book, that they are not and should not be full citizens of a well-governed city, would apply in general to these classes.

to be shared by everyone (since it is possible for all the same people to be farmers and artisans who also deliberate and judge), or different people ought to be assumed for each of the functions mentioned, or whether by necessity some of these are particular while others are common. And this is not the same in every form of government. For as we have said, it is possible for everyone to share in all of them, and   30
also for not everyone to share in them all but only certain people in certain ones. For this is in fact what makes the forms of government different, since in democracies everyone has a share in everything, while in oligarchies the opposite is the case. But since we happen to be examining the best form of government, and this is the one that would let the city be the most happy, and it was said above that it is impossible for happiness to be present apart from virtue, it is obvious from these things that in the city that is most beautifully governed, and that possesses just men in an unqualified sense and not under some supposition, the citizens need to live a life that is devoted neither to the mechanical   40
trades nor to the trade of the marketplace. For a life of that sort is ill-bred and not conducive to virtue. Indeed, those who are going to be citizens ought not to be farmers either,   1329A
since they need leisure both for the formation of virtue and for political activities.

But since the military force and the group that deliberates questions of advantage and decides questions of justice are included in the city and are obviously parts of it in the highest degree, should these be set down as different or should both functions be assigned to the same people? But this is obvious too, that in a certain sense they should go to the same people and in a certain sense to different ones. For insofar as each of these functions has a different peak time of life, and one requires judgment while the other requires power, they should go to different people, but insofar as it is an impossibility that those with the power to use force   10
and resist it will put up with being ruled all the time, for this reason they should go to the same ones. For those who have control of the arms are also in control of whether the government endures or not. What remains, then, is for the government to assign both these functions to the same people but not at the same time. Just as power is naturally present in younger people and judgment in older ones, it is advanta-

geous and also just for these functions to be distributed on the same basis to them both, for this division is what is in accordance with merit. But there needs to be ownership of property among them too, since it is necessary for citizens to have an ample supply, and these people are citizens. For the group of mechanical craftsmen does not take part in the
20   city, nor does any other class whose craftsmanship is not directed at producing virtue. This is evident from the assumption that happiness is necessarily present alongside virtue, and a city needs to be called happy not by people who look at some part of it, but by those who look at all the citizens. And it is obvious that these people need to have ownership of property, if it is necessary for the farmers to be slaves or barbarians living in the surrounding area.

Of the enumerated functions, the remaining one is the class of priests, and the arrangement suitable for them is also obvious. No farmer or mechanical worker ought to be ordained as a priest, since it is fitting for the gods to be
30   honored by citizens. And since the citizen group has been divided into two parts, one bearing arms and the other deliberating, and it is fitting for those who are weary after the passage of time to be assigned the service of the gods and to have a rest, it is to them that the priesthoods should be assigned.

So those without whom a city cannot be organized, and how many of them are parts of the city, have been described. For farmers and artisans and the whole class of menial workers are necessarily present in cities, but it is the arms-bearing and deliberating groups that are parts of the city. Each of these is separate, some permanently and others by turns.

Chapter 10
40   It seems to be well-known, not just to present-day and recent political philosophers, that the city ought to be divid-
1329B   ed into separate classes and that the fighting and farming groups ought to be distinct. For this way of doing things is still in place even now in Egypt, and things are this way in Crete; Sesostris laid down the laws this way in Egypt, so it is claimed, and Minos in Crete. And the arrangement for common meals seems to be ancient as well, those in Crete

having come along in the kingship of Minos, while the ones in Italy seem to be much more ancient than these. For those who preserve the stories of that region claim that a certain Italus settled there and became king of Oenotria, and on account of him they changed the name they were called to Italians instead of Oenotrians, and as much of that peninsula of Europe as is bounded by the gulfs of Scylletium and Lametus,[199] which are a half-day's journey apart from each other, got the name Italy. And they say this Italus made the Oenotrians farmers, when they had been nomads, farmers, gave them other laws, and was the first to institute common meals. Hence even today some of those descended from him observe the common meals and some of his laws. The Opicans, who were formerly and still are called by the name Ausonians, lived on the Tyrrhenian side, while the Chonians lived on the Iapygian and Ionian side, which is called Siritis, and the Chonians were of the Oenotrian race. So the arrangement for common meals started there first, while the separation into classes of the citizen population came from Egypt, for the kingship of Sesostris stretches much further back in time than that of Minos.

Indeed, one ought to regard just about everything else too as having been discovered repeatedly over long stretches of time, or rather infinitely many times.[200] For it is likely that need itself teaches the necessities, and it is reasonable that

---

199 That is, the toe of the boot that projects south from the present-day Isthmus of Calabria.

200 It is well-known that Aristotle denied the possibility that anything could be actually infinite, but there is one sort of case that may appear to be an exception. He demonstrates in Bk. VIII, Chap. 1 of the *Physics* that there could not ever have been a first motion, so that the number of cycles of bodies in the heavens prior to any given time is always literally infinite. In a number of places (e. g. *On The Heavens* 270b 19-20), he extends the same conclusion to cycles of human discoveries, repeatedly lost through natural catastrophes and regained through the re-emergence of the full development of human nature. These cases are not exceptions to Aristotle's understanding of potential infinity, though; the totality of prior revolutions of the moon, for instance, is not present all at once in fact or in thought any more than the totality of its future revolutions, or the totality of points on a line segment. It is only if we think a line is made out of points, or that past time exists as some sort of container, that we are tempted to consider such collections actually infinite. See Aristotle's final refutation of Zeno's paradoxes in *Physics* VIII, 8.

once these are present the things that tend toward refine-
30 ment and affluence get an increase. So one must suppose it
is the same way with things pertaining to forms of government as well. The facts about Egypt are an indication that
these are all ancient, for they are thought to be the most ancient people, and they have always had laws and a political
arrangement. For this reason one ought to adopt the things
that have been discovered satisfactorily, and try to find the
ones that have been left out.

Now it was said earlier that the land ought to belong to
those who bear arms and take part in the government, and
why the farmers ought to be distinct from them, and also
how much and what sort of land there ought to be. So what
40 needs to stated first has to do with its distribution and with
the farmers, who and what sort of people they should be,
1330A since we claim property ought not to be held in common the
way some have said, but ought to become common in use as
among friends, and none of the citizens ought to be in need
of food. As for common meals, everyone agrees it is useful
to have them in cities that are set up well; we shall say later
why we agree with this too.[201] And all the citizens ought to
take part in them, but it is not easy for the needy to contribute a prescribed portion from their own resources and still
provide for the rest of their households. And expenses that
have to do with the gods are also a common responsibil-
10 ity of the whole city. It is necessary, then, to divide the land
into two parts, and for one to be common while the other
is made up of private estates, and to divide each of these in
two again; of the common land, one part ought to be devoted to public services connected with the gods and the other
to the expense of the common meals, and of the land made
up of private estates, one part ought to be near the outlying area and the other near the town, so that everyone will
have a stake in both places with two allotments apportioned
to each. Doing things this way has features of equality and
justice, and is more conducive to like-mindedness about
border wars. For where this provision is not in place, some

---

201 This is generally considered one of those unfulfilled promises that began early in Chap. 5 of this book, but one might infer from 1331a 40-b
1 that Aristotle has in mind the beneficial effect on the manners of
younger people of being present with their elders and rulers at meals.

think that hostility along the borders is a matter of little im-   20
portance while others concentrate on it too much and make
it an ugly situation. For this reason there is a law among
some peoples that those neighboring on border cities cannot
participate in deliberation about wars against them, on the
grounds that their private interest makes them incapable of
doing a beautiful job of deliberating.

For the foregoing reasons, then, it is necessary to divide
the land in this way. But those who are going to do the farming ought in the best case, if things are to be as one wishes, to
be slaves, and neither all of the same race nor high-spirited,
since that way they would be useful at their work and also
safe from revolting. Second best would be for them to be
barbarians from surrounding populations who are close in
nature to the attributes mentioned. Those among them on   30
private lands ought to be the private property of the owners
of the estates, while those on common land ought to be common property. Later we will discuss the way one ought to
treat slaves, and why it is better to offer freedom as a reward
to all slaves.[202]

Chapter 11

It was said above that the city ought to have common access by all possible means to the mainland, the sea,
and the whole territory alike. If its layout in reference to
itself is to be as one would wish, one ought to be looking
at four things in making the wish. First at health, since this
is a necessity. For cities that have an exposure to the east
and to the winds that blow from the direction of the ris-   40
ing sun are healthier. Second best is an exposure protected

---

202 There is no such later discussion. The discussion of the treatment of
     slaves in Bk. I, Chap. 13 applies directly to natural slaves, who lack
     the mental capacity to direct their own lives, but may have some ap-
     plication to those who are slaves only because they or their ancestors
     were conquered in war. He says in Bk. I, Chap. 6 that enslavement of
     the latter is not only unjust but disadvantageous to all concerned. His
     recommendation about offering freedom to slaves may be a way of
     redressing this situation, rather than a merely practical policy to en-
     courage harder work and assistance in time of war. Aristotle's will is
     preserved in Diogenes Laertius's *Lives of the Eminent Philosophers* (Bk.
     V, Chap. 1); it provides for freeing all his slaves, certain ones immedi-
     ately and all the rest when they reach an appropriate age, if they merit
     freedom.

from the north wind, since these cities have easier winters.
1330B For the rest, it should be beautifully situated for political and military actions. For military ones, it should be easy for the inhabitants themselves to exit but hard for opponents to approach and surround. It should have plenty of its own water-sources available and especially springs, but if it does not, this can be procured by the construction of reservoirs for rainwater so large and capacious that they never run out when the people are cut off from their land by war. And seeing as how thought needs to be taken for the health of the inhabitants, which is involved in having the place lie on a
10   certain sort of ground and facing beautifully in a certain direction, and a second consideration is to use healthy kinds of water, to have concern for this as well is not beside the point. For those things that we are exposed to most and most often with the body contribute most to our state of health, and the effect of the wind and waters is of such a nature. For just this reason, in cities that use good judgment, a distinction needs to be made, if all the springs are not alike and those of a healthy sort are not copious, and waters for drinking and those for other use need to be kept separate.

As for fortified positions, what is advantageous is not the same in all forms of government. A high citadel, for instance, is
20   suited to an oligarchy or monarchy, but a fortification on level ground to a democracy, and neither one to an aristocracy but a number of strong positions instead. And the placement of private dwellings is considered more pleasing and more useful for other activities when it is clean-cut in the modern style of Hippodamus,[203] but the opposite, the way things used to be in ancient times, is more useful for wartime security. For that style makes it hard for foreigners to find a way in or to do reconnaissance when they are attacking. Hence the placement ought to have a share of both these styles, for this is possible if one builds, the way farmers do with vines, what some call clusters,
30   in order to make the city clean-cut not as a whole but in part and in places. For this will put it in beautiful shape for both security and orderly appearance.

---

203 This innovation of Hippodamus is the first thing Aristotle mentions about him in Bk. II, Chap. 8 above. The verb used there (*katatemnein*) implies that the land is carved up by straight lines into a clean-cut (*eutomos*) grid. We might call the style Cartesian.

As far as walls are concerned, those who claim that cities with any pretension to virtue ought not to have them are making assumptions that are too old-fashioned, especially when they see this refuted by fact in the case of those who prided themselves on that.[204] It is not a beautiful thing, against those who are similar in kind and not much different in number, to try to be kept safe by a fortification of walls, but since it can also turn out that the superiority of the attackers is greater than the virtue that is only human and present only in a few, if the city ought to be kept safe and not suffer injury or be insulted, the safest fortification by walls ought to be considered the utmost in warcraft, and especially so nowadays when discoveries about missiles and engines for sieges have been brought to a state of precision. To regard it as unworthy for cities to put walls around themselves is like seeking out a territory easy to penetrate and stripping it of mountainous regions, and also like not putting walls around private houses on the grounds that it would be an unmanly thing for the inhabitants to do. But one should by no means overlook the fact that those with walls surrounding their city have the option to treat their cities both ways, either as having walls or as not having them, while those who do not possess them do not have that option. So if this is the way it is, not only should walls be built around the city, they should also be carefully maintained so that they will be in a suitable condition for the city with a view to both an orderly appearance and their military uses, and especially those that have recently been discovered. For just as the concern of the attackers is the means by which they will get the upper hand, the defenders too, though they have made some discoveries, need to go on looking for others and investigating the subject philosophically.[205] For people will not even try to attack in the first place against those who are well prepared.

40

1331A

10

---

204 Sparta, which had no walls because it had confidence in its men, was humiliated in battle by the Thebans when Aristotle was a young man.

205 In fact, Archimedes, who lived about a century after Aristotle's time, devoted himself to contemplative mathematical investigations which yielded numerous discoveries of defensive weapons against sieges. Among these were catapults with adjustable trajectories, machines for firing missiles in bunches through holes in city walls, and cranes that could be used from within the walls to destroy ships at a distance outside them.

Chapter 12

Since the multitude of citizens needs to be divided
up for the common meals, and since the walls need to be
interspersed with guardhouses and towers at convenient
intervals, it is clear that these facts call for providing some
of the common meals in these guardhouses. So one might
organize these meals this way, but it is fitting to have the
common meals for the highest-ranking official groups in
the same places that serve as dwellings dedicated to the
gods—those that the law, or else some prophesy of the Delphic oracle, does not restrict to separate use as holy places.
Such a place could be any that is sufficiently conspicuous for
the excellence of its location and better fortified in comparison with the neighboring parts of the city. And below this
place it is fitting for there to be an assembly ground[206] set
aside of the sort they customarily have in Thessaly, which
they call "free," that is, one that has to be kept clear of all
commercial wares, and which no mechanical tradesman or
farmer or any other such person may approach unless summoned by the rulers. The place would be popular if there
were also an arrangement there for recreation areas for older
people, for it fits the decency of this sort of activity for it to
be divided according to age, and for some of the rulers to
spend time among the younger people, while the older ones
to spend time among the rulers. For being present under the
eyes of the rulers most of all engenders true respect and the
sort of fear that befits free people. The market for commercial wares ought to be different from this assembly ground
and in a separate place, having a location where it is easy to
bring together everything sent in by sea and land.

And since the foremost group in the city is divided into
priests and rulers, it is appropriate to have an arrangement
for common meals for the priests too in the sacred buildings.
Those official groups that give their attention to contracts,
legal indictments, summonses and other administration of
that sort, and also those involved in the rural constabulary
as well as in what is called municipal policing, ought to be

---

206 The word is *agora*, which came to mean a marketplace but originally
meant a gathering where public speeches were made. One translator
renders it here as "public square." Aristotle is recommending that political and leisure activities be combined in one place while business is
conducted elsewhere.

set up near an assembly ground and in some common meeting area, and the marketplace for necessities is a place of that
sort. For we are reserving the upper assembly ground for
using leisure, and that one for necessary activities. The arrangement that has been described should also be assigned
for the things in the countryside, for there too it is necessary
to have guardhouses for security and common meals for the
officials whom some call forest wardens and others call rural
constables, and also shrines need to be distributed through
the countryside, some for gods and others for heroes. But
it is idle to go on at length now speaking about such things
and giving precise details. For the difficult thing in such   20
matters is not thinking up but carrying out, since talk is the
work of our wishes while results are the work of chance.[207]
So let anything more about such matters be dismissed for
now.

Chapter 13

As for the form of government itself, what and what
sorts of things ought to go into the organization of a city
that is going to be blessedly happy and beautifully governed
need to be stated. And seeing as how well-being in all matters consists in two things, one of which is for the target and
end of the actions to be rightly set out while the other is to
discover the actions that are conducive to the end, it is possible for these to be either out of harmony with each other   30
or in harmony. For sometimes the target is beautifully set up
but people go astray in the way they act in order to hit it, at
other times they accomplish everything that leads to the end
but the end they proposed was a bad one, and at still other
times they go wrong in both. With doctoring, for instance,
sometimes they fail to do a beautiful job of judging what sort
of condition the healthy body ought to be in and also fail to
accomplish the things that would produce the standard they
themselves laid down. But both of these have to be mastered

---

207 It has been observed that Aristotle uses rhymes (*noêsai/poiêsai* and *eu-
chês/tuchês*) in the two antitheses here. When such antitheses are metri-
cally balanced, as they frequently are in the speeches of Isocrates, and
in those of Gorgias before him, Aristotle considers them the height of
rhetorical elegance. See his *Rhetoric*, Bk. III, the second half of Chap. 9.
It may be unnecessary to point out that elegance of style is not a quality Aristotle strives for in the *Politics*.

in the arts and forms of knowledge, the end and the actions leading to the end. Now the fact that everyone aims at living
40 well and being happy is obvious, but some have the opportunity to achieve these while others do not, due to some
1332A chance or to nature. For living beautifully also requires certain equipment, but less of this for people whose inherent condition is better and more for those in whom it is worse. But others from the outset do not seek happiness in the right way, even though the opportunity for it belongs to them.

And since our proposed task is to get a look at the best form of government, and this is the one by which a city would be best governed, and the one governed best is that in which there is the greatest possibility for the city to be happy, it is clear that the question of what happiness is must not be passed over. And we claim, and have so determined in the *Ethics*, if any of the arguments there is helpful, that it is the
10 being-at-work and putting to use of complete virtue, and this not in any conditional sense but unconditionally. By conditionally I mean what is necessary; by unconditionally I mean what is beautiful.[208] An example may be seen in what pertains to just actions, for just acts of retribution and punishment do stem from virtue but are matters of necessity, and they have beauty on condition of necessity. For it would be more worthy of choice for a man or a city to have no need of any such acts. But actions to bestow honors or abundance are of the highest beauty unconditionally. For the other sort is the removal of something bad, but actions of this sort are just the opposite, since they are acts that prepare for and give rise to good things. A man of serious moral stature would cope with
20 poverty and disease and other strokes of bad luck in a beautiful way, but the state of being blessedly happy consists in the opposites of these things. For this too was determined in the writings on ethics, that someone of serious moral stature is the sort of person who, because of virtue, finds things good that are unconditionally good. But it is clear that the uses to which such a person puts these good things will necessarily be unconditionally serious and beautiful as well; this is why human beings consider external goods to be the causes of happiness, as if they were to give the credit for a shining ex-

---

208 See 1278b 15-30 above, and the footnote there. The definition of happiness is arrived at in Bk. I, Chap. 7 of the *Nicomachean Ethics*.

ample of beautiful harp-playing to the harp rather than to the artistry of the one playing it.

Accordingly, it is a consequence of what has been said that it is necessary for some things to be present already and for others to be provided by the lawgiver. Hence, for the or- **30** ganization of the city to be as we wish in matters of which luck is in control is merely a matter of wishing, for we assign the control of what is already present to luck. But for the city to be of excellent stature is no longer a product of luck but of knowledge and choice. And certainly a city is excellent by having the citizens who take part in the government be excellent, and for us, all the citizens take part in the government. Therefore, this is what needs to be investigated: how a man becomes excellent. For even if all of them are capable of being excellent without each of the citizens being so, the latter is more worthy of choice; for by having each be excellent, it follows that all are.

Now certainly people become good and excellent by means of three things, and these three are nature, habit, and **40** reason. For it is necessary to have a nature in the first place, as a human being and not any of the other animals, and thus have a body and soul of a certain sort. But in some cases hav- **1332B** ing the nature is of no benefit, since habits make it change. For there are some things that develop in two directions by nature, for worse or for better as a result of habits. Now while the other animals live by nature most of all, and in some small respects also by habits, a human being also lives by reason, for he alone has reason. So these things need to be in harmony. For people do many things contrary to their habits and their nature on account of reason, if they are persuaded that it is better for them to be otherwise. The sort of nature people ought to have if they are going to be easily molded by the lawgiver, we have determined earlier.[209] The job that remains from that point is one of education. For people learn some things by being habituated and other things by listening.[210] **10**

---

209 As a combination of thoughtfulness and spiritedness, in Chap. 7 of this book.

210 The word translated "reason" in this passage is *logos*. The references to persuasion and to learning by listening point to its fundamental meaning of the capacity for intelligible speech. The same word is used above at 1253 7-18, where our political nature is traced to the possibilities opened up by speech.

Chapter 14

But since every political association is organized out of rulers and ruled, this needs to be considered: whether the rulers and ruled ought to be distinct throughout life, or the same group of people. For it is clear that their education will also have to go along with this division. Now if the one sort differed from the rest as much as we believe gods and heroes differ from human beings, having such a great superiority
20   right from the start in body, and thus also in soul, that the superiority of the rulers was beyond dispute and obvious to those who are ruled, it is clear that it would be better for the same people to rule all the time and for the others to be ruled once and for all. But since it is not easy to accept this premise, and there are no kings with as big a difference from their subjects as Skylax claims is the case in India,[211] it is obvious that for many reasons it is necessary for everyone to share alike in ruling and being ruled by turns. For the equitable thing in the case of people who are alike is for the same thing to apply to them, and it is difficult for a form of government to endure if it is organized contrary to what is just. For all those
30   in the countryside who want to start a revolution will be on the side of the subject population, and the idea that the people in the governing group could be so many in number that they would be stronger than all of those is one of the things in the class of impossibilities. It is, however, certainly beyond dispute that the rulers ought to be superior to those who are ruled. So how this is going to be achieved, and how they will share things, needs to be considered by the lawgiver. And this was dealt with above, for nature has provided the distinction by making a younger and older part in something that is itself the same in kind, and between them it is fitting for one part to be ruled and for the other to rule. And no one resents being ruled on account of his age or considers himself above it,
40   especially when that favor is going to be returned when he reaches the appropriate age.

Therefore it must be said that there is a sense in which those who rule and those who are ruled are the same people,

---

211   Skylax was sent by Darius, king of Persia, to explore India; he brought back reports of one tribe with ears so long they could wrap up in them like blankets, another that absorbed nutrients by smelling because they had no mouths, and other such believe-it-or-not tales.

and a sense in which they are different. So it is also neces- 1333A
sary for there to be a sense in which their education is the
same and a sense in which it is different. For people say that
anyone who is going to do a beautiful job of ruling needs
to be ruled first. And, as was said in our first discussions,[212]
rule is either for the sake of the one ruling or for the sake of
the one ruled. We claim that one of these forms is mastery of
slaves while the other is appropriate to people who are free.
But there is a difference in some cases between things that
are commanded based not on the deeds but on their end.
For this reason, it is a beautiful thing for free young persons
to perform many of the services that are held to be servile
tasks. For as far as what is beautiful or not beautiful is concerned, actions differ not so much in themselves as in the 10
end for the sake of which they are performed. And since we
claim that the same virtue belongs to a citizen and to a ruler
as to the best man, and that the same person ought to be
ruled first and rule later, the business of the lawgiver ought
to be this: how and through what pursuits men can become
good, and what the end is at which the best life aims.

Now there is a distinction between two parts of the
soul, one of which has reason in its own right, while the
other, which does not have it in its own right, is capable of
listening to reason. The virtues for which a man is said to be
good in any way belong, we claim, to these parts. To those
who make the distinction the way we assert it, there is no 20
unclarity about how one should state where the end is more
appropriately to be found. For the worse is always for the
sake of the better—this is obvious in things that come from
art and from nature alike—and the better part is the one that
has reason. And this is also divided in two, in the way we
habitually make the distinction, for there is practical reason
on the one hand, contemplative reason on the other, so it
is plainly necessary that this part of the soul be divided in
the same way. And we shall speak of their activities as being in proportion to them, and say that activities of a part
that is better by nature must be more worthy of choice for
people who are capable of attaining all of them or two of
them. For the most choiceworthy thing for each person is 30
always that which is the highest he can attain. And all of life

---

212 In Bk. III, Chap. 4.

is divided as well, into business and leisure, and into war and peace, and among actions, some are necessary and useful while others are beautiful. Among these, the choice must be the same as with the parts of the soul and the activities of them: war must be for the sake of peace, business for the sake of leisure, and necessary and useful actions for the sake of beautiful ones. Laws made by a political ruler should be made, then, by one who takes all these things in view, in accordance with the parts of the soul and their activities, and

40   giving priority to what is better and to ends. And the same thing applies to ways of life and to choices among objects of concern, for one ought to be capable of conducting business

1333B   and war, but even more so of living in peace and occupying one's leisure, and one ought to perform necessary and useful actions, but even more so beautiful ones. So it is with these aims that people ought to be educated, both while they are still children and through all the other stages of life in which they have need of education.

But those who are now thought to be best governed among the Greeks, and those lawgivers who set up these forms of government, obviously did not organize the things involved in their governments with a view to the best end, or design their laws and education with a view to all the

10   virtues; they have instead made them sink to the level of the virtues vulgarly thought to be useful and more conducive to gaining the upper hand. And in a spirit much like theirs, some later writers have declared the same opinion. For they praise the Spartan government and admire the aim of the lawgiver for making all the laws with a view to dominance and war. What they say is easily refutable by argument and has now been refuted by the facts as well. For in the same way that most human beings think mastery over many people is happiness because a large supply of the goods of fortune comes with it, Thibron and each of the others who

20   write about the government of the Spartans display admiration for their lawgiver because being trained for dangers led them to rule many people. And yet now at any rate, since ruling is no longer possible for the Spartans, it is clear that they are not happy and their lawgiver was not a good one.

But this is absurd, if, despite the fact that they abided by his laws and there was no impediment to carrying out those laws, they have abandoned a beautiful way of living. But these writers are not right in their assumption about the kind of rule which the lawgiver ought to hold in public esteem. For rule over free people is a more beautiful thing than ruling in the manner of a master of slaves, and involves greater virtue. And further, this is not the reason one ought to regard a city as happy and praise its lawgiver, that he   30 trained them to be dominant in order to rule their neighbors; these things in fact have the potential for great harm. For it is clear that this is something any of the citizens capable of it will have to try to pursue as well, to have the power to rule his own city. This is the very thing the Spartans accuse King Pausanias[213] of doing, even when he held so high a position of honor. Nothing in arguments to that effect is appropriate to political life or beneficial or true. The same things are best both privately and in common, and it is these that the lawgiver ought to instill in the souls of human beings. This is not the purpose for which he ought to pay attention to a training for military skills, that his people should impose   40 slavery on those who do not deserve it, but primarily so that they themselves will not be enslaved by others, secondly in order that they may seek a position of leadership for the   1334A benefit of those who are ruled, and thirdly to gain mastery over those who deserve to be slaves. Events bear witness to the arguments that a lawgiver ought to be more diligent about designing matters pertaining to military skills, and all the rest of his lawmaking, for the sake of living in leisure and for peacetime. For most cities of this kind stay safe while they are at war but once imperial rule has been acquired they come to ruin. When they keep the peace, they lose their hard edge, like iron, and the one responsible for this is the lawgiver who has not educated them to have what it takes to live at leisure.   10

---

213 This is not the Pausanias who distinguished himself as a commander during the Persian War and disgraced himself as a traitor afterward, but the later Spartan whom Aristotle mentions at 1301b 20-21 for attempting to abolish the office of the ephors, and whom Aristotle distinguishes by the title of king.

Chapter 15

But since the end for human beings appears to be the same in common and in private, and it is necessary that the same standard apply to the best man and the best form of government, it is obvious that the virtues that are for leisure need to be present. For, as has been said often, peace is the end at which war aims, and leisure is that of business. And among the virtues that are for leisure and passing one's time, there are some whose work is done at leisure and some through being busy. For many necessities have to be present in order for one to have the opportunity to be at leisure; this is why
20   it is appropriate for a city to be moderate, courageous, and capable of endurance. For as the proverb goes, there is no leisure for slaves, and those who do not have the capacity to face dangers courageously are the slaves of those who attack them. So there is need for courage and endurance when one is busy, and for philosophy when one is at leisure, while moderation and justice are needed at both times, and even more in those who are living at peace and at leisure. For war forces people to be just and moderate, while the enjoyment of good fortune and the leisure that accompanies peace tend instead to make them insolent. So a good deal of justice and modera-
30   tion is needed by those who seem to be the best off and to be enjoying all the blessings of those, if there are any, who dwell, as the poets say, in the isles of the blessed. It is they most of all who will need philosophy and moderation and justice, to the extent that they have more leisure among an unstinting supply of such good things.

So it is obvious why a city that is going to be happy and be of excellent stature needs to partake of these virtues. For it is shameful for people to be incapable of making use of good things, and even more so to be incapable of making use of them when at leisure, and to display themselves as good when busy and at war but slavish when at peace and at lei-
40   sure. That is why one ought not to train for virtue the way the
1334B Spartans' city does. For the reason they surpass others is not that they do not consider the same things everyone else does to be the greatest of goods, but that they believe these goods are more effectively gained by means of one particular virtue. But since [they consider] these goods and the enjoyment of them to be greater than that which comes from the virtues,

[they train only for the virtue that seems to be useful for them. That there ought to be training for virtue as a whole,] and for its own sake, is obvious from the foregoing discussion.[214] So the things that need to be looked into are the manner and means by which this will be accomplished.

We arrived at a distinction above, that there is need for nature, habit, and reason.[215] And among these, it was determined earlier what sort of nature people ought to have, but it remains to look into whether they ought to be educated first by reason, or first by habits. For these things ought to be   10
harmonious with each other in an optimal harmony. For it is possible to have mistaken the best hypothesis by one's reason, and to be led astray in the same direction by one's habits. And this at least is clear first of all, that, as in other cases, our birth is from a starting point, and the end that comes from a starting point is the starting point for another end; but in us, reason and intellect are nature's end, so that it is for them that birth and the concern with habits ought to be a preparation. Next, just as soul and body are two, so too do we observe two parts of the soul, one irrational and the other having reason, and the active conditions of these parts are two in number; one of them is desire and the other the activity of intellect.   20
And just as the body is prior to the soul in coming into being, so too is the irrational part prior to that having reason. This is obvious, since spiritedness and willfulness, and desire as well, are present in children right when they are born, while reasoning and intellect come in naturally as they go on. Hence attention to the body necessarily comes first, before attention to the soul, and attention to desire comes next, though the attention to desire is for the sake of intellect, and attention to the body for the sake of the soul.

Chapter 16

So if the lawgiver needs to see to it from the start that the bodies of those who are brought up turn out best, the   30
first thing attention needs to be paid to is mating, and what sorts of people should enter into marital relations with each

---

214   There is a gap in the manuscripts. The bracketed parts of the translation follow a reconstruction by the commentator Newman, which is given in the critical apparatus of Ross's edition.

215   The argument now picks up from the end of Chap. 13 of this book.

other and when. And he ought to make laws about this kind of association with an eye to the people themselves and also to their time of life, so that they may decline in age together at the same stages and their capacities will not be out of harmony, with the man still capable of generating and the woman incapable, or the woman capable and the man not. For these things make for divisions and disagreements between them. Next, there should be laws about the succession

40   of their children, for the children ought not to be left too far behind their fathers in age (for acts of gratitude from the

1335A children, or of assistance from the fathers, are of no benefit when the latter are too old), nor be too close in age. That involves a lot of irritation, since such children have less of a feeling of respect, as they would for those in the same stage of life, and their closeness in age breeds complaints about the running of the household. A further point, which brings us back to where we started, is that there should be laws to provide that the bodies of the offspring be suited to the wishes of the lawgiver.

Just about all these things result from paying attention to one matter. For since, speaking for the most part, the number of seventy years at most marks the end of generation in

10   men, and fifty in women, the beginning of mating ought to be at an age that ends up at these times. And coupling by the young is a bad thing for producing children. For in all animals, the offspring of the young are imperfect and they are more likely to bear females and offspring small in form, so this same thing necessarily happens among human beings too. And there is evidence of this, for in those cities in which it is the local custom for a young man and young woman to mate, people's bodies are imperfect and small. Also, young women have harder labor in childbirth, and more of them die. And some say this sort of thing is the reason why the

20   oracle came to the Troezenians, that many were dying because women who were too young were getting married, and it was not related to the cultivation of crops.[216] Also, it contributes to moderation for marriages to be made when the women are older, for they seem to be more promiscuous when they have gotten used to intercourse while young.

---

216 "Do not plow the young furrow" was first interpreted to mean they were not leaving unplanted fields fallow long enough.

And the bodies of males seem to be stunted in growth if they have intercourse while the seed is still growing, for there is a definite time for this too, beyond which it no longer remains abundant. Hence it is fitting for women to mate around the age of eighteen, and men at thirty-seven or a little before.[217] **30** For at such ages mating will take place in those whose bodies are at their peak, and they will decline together to the end of childbearing at well-coordinated times. Also, if birth takes place right away, as is reasonable to expect, the succession of children will occur when they are at the beginning of *their* prime and their fathers' ages have already used up about the number of seventy years.

When mating ought to take place, then, has been stated; as for the season, the times people ought to use are the ones most people do use now, and beautifully so, marking out winter as the time for this conjugal union to take place. And from that point they ought to look at what is said about childbearing by doctors and naturalists; the doctors say **40** enough about the right occasions for their bodies, and the **1335B** naturalists about winds, approving of northern rather than southern ones. What sorts of bodies it would be most beneficial for them to have for the sake of their offspring is a topic more appropriate to those who pause to pay attention to matters of childrearing; to speak of it now even in outline is sufficient. For the conditioning of athletes is not useful for the fitness appropriate to a citizen for the sake of health or childbearing, and neither is a regimen that is overly fastidious and unsuited to hard work; what is useful is the mean between them. One ought to have a condition formed by hard work but not by violent exertions, or exertions in only **10** one direction like those involved in the conditioning of athletes, but directed toward the activities of free people. And these exertions ought to be undertaken by men and women alike. Pregnant women too should take care of their bodies and not be idle or adopt a meager diet. And this is easy for the lawgiver to bring about by requiring them to take some sort of walk every day for worshipping the deities to whom the honors related to birth are assigned. As far as their think-

217 The translation follows an editor who adds "before" to the end of this sentence, rather than the one preferred by Ross who shifts "or little" to the end of the previous sentence.

ing goes, however, as opposed to their bodies, it is fitting for
them to remain idle, since developing embryos obviously
draw benefit from the one carrying them the way plants do
20   from the earth. On the matter of disposing of or rearing the
ones that are born, let there be a law that no defective infant
should be raised, while an arrangement based on customs
forbids disposing of any of those born merely because of
the number of children. The number of children produced
ought to be limited, but if conception takes place for any of
those who continue having intercourse beyond that number,
an abortion ought to be induced before the power of perception arises in addition to life. For what is or is not sanctioned
by divine law will be determined on the basis of perception
as well as life.

And since the beginning of the age when they should
start mating has been determined for a man and for a woman, let the length of time also be marked out that is fitting for
them to serve the public interest in the matter of childbear-
30   ing. For the offspring of those who are older, like the offspring of those who are younger, and born imperfect in both
their bodies and their thinking capacities, and the offspring
of people in old age are feeble; hence, let the time be limited
to correspond with the peak of the thinking capacity. And
in most men this is around the time of fifty years, as certain
poets who measure age in seven-year intervals have said. So
when they get four or five years beyond this age they ought
to be released from bringing children into the world; obviously, for the time that remains, they ought to be engaging
in intercourse for the sake of health or for some other such
reason. As for intercourse with another woman, or another
40   man, let it simply be a violation of what is beautiful if one
openly takes part in it in any way with anyone when one is
a husband and bears that name. And if one openly does any
1336A such thing during the time of child rearing, let him be punished with a loss of honor appropriate to his offense.

Chapter 17

Whatever sort of food it may be that is fed to children
once they are born ought to be regarded as making a great
difference to the capacity of their bodies. To those who examine the matter, both in other animals and in the nations in

which there is a concern to produce a military kind of conditioning, it is apparent that a diet rich in milk is best suited to their bodies, and one with less wine because of diseases. Also, it benefits them to engage in all the exercise possible in those of such an age. But so that their limbs will not be deformed on account of their softness, some nations even now use certain mechanical implements on such people which make the body straight. And it also benefits their souls to begin instilling habits right from when they are small children, since this is of the utmost usefulness both for health and for military activities. This is why there is a custom among many of the barbarians for some of them to immerse newborns in a cold river, and for others, like the Celts, to dress them in light clothing. For in all matters in which it is possible to instill habits it is better to instill them right when children are starting out, and form habits by a gradual approach. And the condition of children is naturally well suited because of its warmth to a training for the cold.

So in the first stage, it is beneficial for attention to be given to this sort of thing, and to matters closely related to this. And at the age next after this one, up to five years, during which it is not a beautiful idea ever to draw them toward any sort of learning or toward necessary work, so as not to impede their growth, they ought to get enough exercise to keep their bodies from being idle, which one should provide for them by means of play as well as other activities. And their forms of play ought not to be unsuited to free people and neither burdensome nor lax. As for the sorts of stories and tales children of this age ought to hear, let that be a concern for those officials people call overseers of children. For all such things ought to prepare the way for their later pursuits, which is why many forms of play ought to be imitations of things that will be serious concerns later on. But those in the *Laws* who prevent children from straining and bawling are not right to forbid these things, because they are beneficial to their growth. For they turn out in a certain way to be exercise for their bodies. For holding one's breath produces strength for people who do work, which results also for children who strain their lungs.

And the way they spend their time needs to be looked into by the overseers of children, especially to see that they

1336B will be among slaves as little as possible. For at this age, and up to seven years, it is a necessity for them to have their rearing at home. So it is reasonable to expect that even at such an age they will be getting the influence of a slavish attitude from the things they hear and see. So the lawgiver needs to banish filthy language from the city entirely, as he would anything else, for from easily speaking of any shameful thing one comes to do something like it. It ought, then, to be banished especially from among the young, so they will not say or hear any such thing. And if anyone openly says or does anything that is forbidden, a free person who is

10   not yet considered worthy of reclining at the common meals should be punished with a deprivation of honors and with beatings, and one older than that age, for his slavish behavior, with a loss of the honors due a free person. And since we are banishing speaking about any such thing, it is obvious that this should also apply to looking at unseemly pictures and plays. So let it be a concern of the officials that there is no statue or painting at all that represents such an act, except in places devoted to certain gods of the sort whom custom permits even scandalous mockery. In addition to these things, custom allows people of an appropriate age to do honor to the gods on behalf of their children and wives as

20   well as on their own behalf. But it needs to be set down in law that younger men cannot be spectators at lampoons or comedies until they reach the age at which they begin reclining at meals and partaking of strong drink; education will make them impervious to all manner of harm that comes from such things.

So for now we have made this discussion in cursory fashion; later one ought to pause to make further distinctions, first considering difficulties about whether it ought or ought not to be done and in what manner. We have mentioned as much as necessary for the present occasion. For perhaps the sort of thing Theodorus, the actor who appeared in tragedies, used to say was not a bad point, that he never

30   allowed anyone to come on stage before him, not even any of the worthless actors, because the spectators get comfortable with what they hear first. And this same thing happens in our dealings with human beings and with things, for we always like the first ones better. This is why one ought to make all things that are base foreign to the young, and es-

pecially any of them that involve either vice or malice. But when they have passed through five years, for the two years up to seven, they ought to become spectators at the lessons they themselves will need to learn. And then there are two ages for which it is necessary to divide up their education: that from seven years up to adolescence, and that from ado- **40** lescence up to twenty-one years. For those who divide up the ages in seven-year intervals are for the most part not getting it wrong, but one ought to follow nature's dividing **1337A** point; for every sort of art and education is meant to fill in what nature leaves out. So the first thing to be examined is whether any arrangement needs to be made about the children, the next is whether it is beneficial to make their care a public concern or something undertaken in a private manner (which is what happens even now in most cities), and the third is what sort of care this ought to be.

Book VIII

Chapter 1

Now the fact that a lawgiver needs to make the education of the young a matter of concern, no one would dispute. For in the cities where this does not happen, their forms of government suffer for it, since people need to be educated with a view to each form. For the type of character that is at home in each form of government is the habitual safeguard of the constitution and sets it up in the first place—a democratic character a democratic constitution, an oligarchic character an oligarchic one. And a better character is always responsible for a better government. And for all capacities and arts there are things related to their work that need to be taught beforehand and made into habits beforehand, and so it is clear that this also applies to the actions belonging to virtue. And since there is one end at which the city as a whole aims, it is obvious that there must necessarily also be one and the same education for all the people, and that the concern for this must be public and not private, the way each person now takes care of his own children, and teaches them whatever private lessons seem like a good idea. But training for common concerns needs to be made common as well. At the same time, one should not even regard any of the citizens as belonging to himself, but all of them as belonging to the city, since each is a part of the city.[218] And the concern for each part naturally looks to the concern for the whole. And one might praise the Spartans in this regard, since they take their children the most seriously, and make that a matter of common concern.

20

30

Chapter 2
So it is obvious that laws need to be made about educa-

---

218 This claim is explained and defended at 1252b 27-1253a 29 above.

tion and that this needs to be made a common concern. But what the education is going to be and how people should be educated ought not to be overlooked. For at present there are disputes about its functions. For all people do not assume that the young ought to learn the same things in connection with either virtue or the best life, and it is not obvious even whether it is more appropriate for it to be directed toward thinking or

40   toward the character of the soul. A survey of the education one stumbles across yields a disorderly array, and it is not at all clear whether one ought to train people in matters useful for life, things conducive to virtue, or exceptional studies, since all

1337B   these have found some who judge in their favor. About matters related to virtue there is no agreement at all. Right off, the virtue that people honor is not the same for them all, so it is only to be expected that they will differ over the training for it as well. It is not unclear that people ought to be taught some useful things that are necessary, but not all of them, since tasks belonging to free people and to those who are not free are obviously distinct; it is clear that they ought to take part in those useful tasks that will not make someone taking part in them debased. And one ought to regard as debasing that task, that art, or that study that

10   causes the body or the thinking of free people to end up useless for the purposes and actions that belong to virtue. Hence we refer to as debasing those arts of a sort that put the body into a worse condition, and also all forms of labor for wages, since they cause one's thinking to be unleisured and demeaned.[219] And while it is not unsuited to a free person to have a share,

---

219   The word translated here as "debased" or "debasing" (*banausos*) is the same word used throughout the earlier books of the *Politics* for mechanical activities or trades. The connection between the two meanings is elaborated in this passage from Adam Smith's *Wealth of Nations* (Bk. V, Chap. 1, Part III, Art. 2, pages 734-735 of the 1965 Modern Library edition): "The man whose life is spent in performing a few simple operations, of which the effects too are, perhaps, always the same, has no occasion to exert his understanding…He naturally loses, therefore, the habit of such exertion, and generally becomes as stupid and ignorant as it is possible for a human creature to become. The torpor of his mind renders him, not only incapable of relishing or bearing a part in any rational conversation, but of conceiving any generous, noble, or tender sentiment, and consequently of forming any just judgment concerning many even of the ordinary duties of private life. Of the great and extensive interests of his country he is altogether incapable of judging; and unless very particular pains have been taken to render him otherwise, he is equally incapable of defending his country in war." Smith argues that the right sort of education can ameliorate the stultifying effects of lives spent in such occupations.

up to a certain point, in some of the kinds of knowledge among the liberal arts, sticking with them too far in pursuit of perfect mastery is also liable to bring the kinds of harm mentioned. But that for the sake of which one does or learns something makes a great difference as well; what is done for one's own sake or that of friends, or on account of virtue, is not unsuited to a free person, but someone who does that same thing on account of others[220] might often seem to be acting in a menial or slavish manner.

Chapter 3

The ordinary kinds of studies these days tend in different directions, as was said above, but there are pretty much four things in which people are customarily educated: letters, gymnastics, music, and fourth, for some people, drawing—skill at letters and drawing on the grounds that they are useful for life with numerous applications, and gymnastic training on the grounds that it prepares the way for courage. But one might already raise questions about skill at music. For most people these days take part in it for the sake of pleasure, but those who originally assigned it to education did so because, as has been said more than once, nature itself strives not only to be busy in the right way but also to be capable of being at leisure in a beautiful way. For this one principle governs everything, so let us speak about it again. If one has need of both, but being at leisure is more worthy of choice and more an end than being busy, what needs to be sought out is what one ought to spend one's leisure doing. Surely not playing, for then play would necessarily be the end at which our life aims. But if that is impossible,[221] and playful amusements ought to be made use of in the course of occupation with business instead (for someone who is working needs relaxation, and play is for the sake of relaxation, and being busy is accompanied by work and stress), one ought for that reason to watch for the right times for the use of playful amusement to be brought in, as if one

---

220 To pursue studies in order to gain money from others by professional teaching, or in a competitive spirit that seeks their honor, would be at least unleisured and narrowing, and in any case not what a city is seeking to instill in all its citizens.

221 See the discussion of this in *Nicomachean Ethics*, Bk. X, Chap. 6.

were applying it medicinally. For this sort of motion of the 1338A soul is a relief, and the pleasure of it brings relaxation. Being at leisure, on the other hand, is thought to have in itself pleasure, happiness, and a blessed way of living. And this is not present in people occupied in business but in those who are at leisure. For a person who is busy is busied for the sake of some end he assumes is not present, while happiness is an end which everyone conceives of as accompanied not by pain but by pleasure. They do not, however, all go on to place this pleasure in the same category, but each in accord with their several kinds and with the active disposition that belongs to them; and the best person sets it down as the best pleasure and the one derived from the most beautiful things.

10   And so it is obvious that one ought to learn certain things and be educated for the leisure in the course of one's life, and that these teachings and studies are for their own sake, while those for occupation with business are assumed to be necessities and for the sake of other things. And this is why those who came before us assigned music a place in education not as necessary (since there is nothing of the sort about it) nor even as useful (in the way letters are for provisioning and household management as well as for learning and also for many political activities, and drawing too is thought to be useful for discriminating more beautifully among the works of artisans), nor in turn as gymnastic train- 20 ing is conducive to health and strength (for we do not see either of these coming from skill at music). What remains, then, is that it is for the part of life one spends in leisure, which is obviously what people introduce it for. For they assign this as its place, which they conceive of as being the way of life suited to free people. This is exactly what Homer was writing about in these words: "the one whom they call to the bountiful banquet"—going on to speak of other people "who call for a singer who gives delight to everyone."[222] And in other lines Odysseus says this is the best way of spending time, when human beings are glad-hearted and "banqueters 30 sitting in rows in a hall are listening to a singer."

It is obvious, then, that there is some education which

---

222 *Odyssey* XVII, 385; Aristotle slightly alters the line, and the preceding line he quotes is not in our texts. The following words of Odysseus are from IX, 7-8.

people need to give their sons not because it useful or necessary, but because it is suited to freedom and is beautiful.
Whether there is one such education or a greater number,
what these may be, and how they are to be taught are things
that must be spoken of later. At the moment we have come
far enough down the road that we have some additional evidence from the ordinary topics of education among the ancients; for music makes this clear. And it is also obvious that
children ought to be taught some of the useful things, such as
the study of letters, not just because of their usefulness, but
also on account of the many other studies that become pos-   **40**
sible by means of them. Similarly, they should also be taught
drawing not so they will avoid mistakes in their private purchases and not be cheated in buying and selling furniture, but   **1338B**
rather because it makes them able to see the beauty of bodies.
To be looking for utility everywhere is the least fitting thing
for people who are great-souled[223] and free. And since it is
obvious education must make use of habits and apply to the
body before it uses reason and applies to one's thinking, it is
clear from these things that children should be turned over to
the arts of gymnastic and athletic training, since the former
makes the conditioning of the body be a certain way and the
latter provides it with activity.

Chapter 4

Now of those cities that are thought to show the most   **10**
concern for their children nowadays, some instill in them a
type of conditioning suited to competitive athletics, and do
serious damage to the form and growth of their bodies; the
Spartans have not made this mistake, but their exercises turn
out people of a brutal kind, on the assumption that this is the
most advantageous way to produce courage. And yet, as has
been said repeatedly, care should not be taken with one's
eye on a single virtue and especially not on that one. And
even if they do have their eye on that virtue, they do not find
it. For in the other animals and foreign nations we see that

---

223 Greatness of soul is discussed at length in Bk. IV, Chap. 3 of the *Nicomachean Ethics*, where Aristotle begins with its common use to describe
proud, honor-loving people, but transforms its meaning dialectically.
In the *Posterior Analytics*, 97b 14-26, he says the word *megalopsuchos* may
apply not only to the proud but also to people like Socrates who are
above caring about the things that depend on good and bad fortune.

courage does not go along with those who are most savage, but with those of a more restrained temperament like that

20   of lions. There are many nations that are reckless about killing and about cannibalism, such as the Achaeans around the Black Sea, and the Heniochi, and there are other mainland nations that are either similar to these or more extreme; they are good at plundering, but have not a bit of courage. Also, with the Spartans themselves, we know that they held superiority over everyone else as long as they kept up their passion for exercise, but these days they come up short of others, whether they are competing in gymnastics or in warfare. For they stood out not because they were giving their youth this type of gymnastic exercise, but because they alone were doing training while facing others who were doing none.

30   So one must give the leading role to what is beautiful and not to what is brutal. For no wolf or any other wild animal would struggle with any beautiful danger; it is rather a good man who would.[224] But those who abandon their children to go too far in these directions, while leaving them with no guidance in necessary things, are turning out truly debased people and making them useful for only one political task, and worse than others for that one, as the argument makes clear. For it is necessary to judge them not by their earlier deeds but by those of the present day, for now they have rivals in education where before they had none.

It is agreed, then, that gymnastic training ought to be

40   used, and how it ought to be used. For up to adolescence, a lighter regimen ought to be employed, avoiding a restricted diet and compulsory workouts so that there will be no hin-

1339A   drance to growth. No small indication that they can lead to this result is the fact that, in the Olympic competitions, one might find some two or three instances in which the same people won victories as both men and boys because training youths saps their strength by compulsory exercises. But once they have gone on to other studies for three years after adolescence, at

---

224   In Bk. III, Chaps. 6-7 of the *Nicomachean Ethics*, Aristotle defines courage as a settled disposition to choose to face danger when that is a beautiful thing to do. In Chap. 8 he goes on to distinguish courage from a number of things that resemble it and are frequently mistaken for it, one of which is the spiritedness that is found also in wild animals; courageous human beings are spirited, but not all spirited human beings are courageous.

that time it is fitting to impose workouts and compulsory diet-
ing during their next stage of life. For one ought not to be doing
hard work with one's thinking and with the body at the same
time, since each of the two kinds of exertion has an opposite
effect by its nature; exertion of the body is an impediment to   10
thinking, and exertion of thinking to the body.

Chapter 5

On the topic of music, while we dealt with some difficulties in the discussion above, it is beautifully appropriate
to move forward by taking them up again now, so that they
might be a sort of lead-in to the arguments one might make
in elucidation of it. For it is not easy to determine about it,
either what power it has or for what purpose one ought to
take part in it—whether for play and relaxation, like sleep
and strong drink (for in their own right, these are not things
of serious worth, but they are pleasant, and at the same time
a respite from care, as Euripides says,[225] which is why people
put it in their ranks and treat them all alike, sleep, strong   20
drink, and music, and also place dancing among them); or
whether it ought instead to be assumed that music is conducive in some way to virtue, on the grounds that it is a potent
thing, and just as gymnastic training brings the body into a
certain condition, music makes one's character be in a certain condition by habituating people to a capacity to enjoy
things rightly[226]; or whether it makes some contribution to a
way of life and a wise judgment, since this also needs to be
set down as third among the things that are said.

Now it is not unclear that one ought not to be educating
the young for the sake of play; they are not playing when they
are learning, since learning comes with pain. And surely it is
not fitting to attribute a way of life to children at ages such as   30
theirs, since a state of completion is not present in anything that
is incomplete. But perhaps it might be thought that the serious
occupations of children are for the sake of playfulness when
they have become men and attained their completion. But if
that is the sort of thing it is for, why would they need to learn

---

225 *Bacchae*, line 381

226 This alternative is argued vividly by Socrates in Plato's *Republic*, 401D
and following.

music, rather than participate in it vicariously, like the kings of the Persians and Medes, through the pleasure and learning of other people who perform it? For it is a necessity that those who make this very thing their work and art will carry it out better than people who give it their attention only long enough to learn it. If they had to do the work of such things themselves,
40   they would also have to prepare themselves for the business involved in cooking tasty food, which is absurd. And the same difficulty holds even if it is capable of making their characters better. Why would they have to learn these things themselves,
1339B instead of enjoying them rightly and being capable of judging them by listening to others, the way the Spartans do? For they, without learning music, are still capable, so they claim, of judging between songs that are wholesome and unwholesome. And the same argument applies if music is to be used to enhance the joy of living and a way of life suited to freedom. Why do they need to learn it themselves and not enjoy it while others practice it? We have only to consider the conception we have of the gods. Zeus himself does not sing or play the lyre to accompany poets; we even call the sort of people who do that
10   mechanical artisans and the action unmanly, unless someone is drunk or playing around.

But perhaps these things need to be examined later. What needs to be inquired about first is whether music should be put into an education or not, and what power it has out of the three kinds we raised questions about: education, play, or a way of life.[227] It makes good sense to assign it to them all, and it does appear to play a part in each. For play is for the sake of relaxation, and relaxation is necessarily pleasant, since it is a sort of remedy for the pain that results from exertions; and by general agreement, a way of life ought to be not only beautiful but pleasant as well, since be-
20   ing happy derives from both of these. And we all claim that music is one of the most pleasant things, whether it is instrumental or with a vocal part. (Musaeus, at any rate, claims "singing is the most pleasant thing for mortals," which is why it makes good sense for people to include it in their parties and gatherings as something with the power to glad-

---

227 The three labels are shorthand reminders of the role of music in character development, as a source of diversion, and as part of the central activity in which life finds its completion.

den their hearts.) So on this basis too, one might take it that the younger generation ought to be educated in it. For those pleasures that are harmless are fitting means not only to the end but also to relaxation. And since it turns out that human beings are at their end on few occasions, but relax and indulge in playful activities on many, not so much for anything more, but just on account of their pleasure, it would 30 be useful to give them a little rest in the pleasures that come from music.

It turns out, though, that human beings make the playful activities an end. For the end too, perhaps, involves a certain pleasure, but not just any random pleasure, and while seeking the former people take the latter as if it were the former, because it has a certain similarity to the end at which actions aim. For the end is not chosen for the sake of anything in the future, and these sorts of pleasures are not for the sake of anything in the future either, but because of things that have already happened, such as exertions and pain. One might, then, plausibly assume that it is for this reason that people look for happiness to come from these pleasures, but 40 as for taking part in music, it seems likely that it is not for this reason alone but also because of its usefulness for relaxation. The question must be asked, however, whether this may be 1340A merely incidental, while the nature of music is more honorable than can be attributed to the use mentioned, and one ought to partake of it not just for the pleasure that comes from it, which it shares with other things and of which everyone has a sense (for music does have a certain natural pleasure, which is why the use of it is beloved to all ages and all types of character), but to see whether it also contributes in any way to one's character and to the soul. And this would clearly be so if, by means of it, we become people of certain kinds in respect to our characters.

But the fact that we do become people of certain kinds is surely obvious by many means, and not least through the melodies composed by Olympus; for by general agree- 10 ment, these cause the soul to be divinely inspired, and divine inspiration is an attribute of the character in one's soul. Moreover, all those who listen to imitative performances are affected sympathetically, even apart from their rhythms

and melodies.[228] And since music is incidentally one of the
pleasant things, and virtue has to do with enjoying, loving,
and hating in the right way, one plainly ought to learn and
be habituated to nothing so much as to making right judgments about and taking delight in decent kinds of character
and beautiful actions. And there are, in rhythms and melo-
20 dies most of all, likenesses of the true natures of anger and
gentleness, and also of courage and moderation and all the
opposites of these and the other states of character. And
this is clear from the facts, for we experience a change in
the soul when we listen to such things. But the habituation
to feel pain and take delight in their likenesses comes close
to being in the same relation to the original things. If, for
instance, someone delights in contemplating the image of
something for no other reason than just for its form, it necessarily follows from this that the contemplation of the thing
itself, whose image he is contemplating, will be pleasing.
But no likeness to states of character happens to be present
30 in other kinds of sense perception such as objects of touch
and taste, and it is present only slightly in objects of sight.
For there are figures that have this sort of quality, though to
a small extent, and everyone shares this sort of perception,[229]
yet these are not *likenesses* of states of character; instead, the
gestures and colors that come with them are indications of
states of character, and they are distinctive marks in those
who experience them. Nevertheless, to the extent that there
is a difference in the contemplation of these things as well,
the young ought not to look at the works of Pauson but at
those of Polygnotus[230] and any other painters and sculptors

228 In Chap. 1 of the *Poetics*, Aristotle associates epic and dramatic poetry
with flute and harp music as arts that imitate character and action by
means of rhythm, speech, and harmony. The melodies traditionally attributed to Olympus were for the flute. The word "imitation" (*mimêsis*)
has no implication of deficiency, and in all these arts, what is imitated
is invisible. The motions of a soul and the choices that give shape to
action can be discussed and understood, but they can be contemplated
direct and whole only through the imagination, which is the medium
in which these imitative arts present and disclose the human image.

229 Ross follows an earlier emendation by inserting the word "not" before "everyone," but the manuscript reading seems to make better sense, as long as
one takes the following *eti* to mean "yet" rather than "furthermore."

230 In Chap. 2 of the *Poetics*, Aristotle says that Pauson painted people
who are worse than most of us, and Polygnotus people who are better.

there may be who are good at depicting character.

But in melodies themselves, there *are* images of states of character. And this is obvious, for the nature of their modes is divergent immediately in such a way that listeners are put into a different state and do not have the same experience with each of them; in response to some, people are in a more mournful and grave mood, as with the so-called Mixolydian, but in response to others, such as the relaxed modes,[231] they are in a softer frame of mind, and in response to one of them they are in the especially moderate and settled condition that the Dorian is unique among the modes in producing,[232] while the Phrygian makes them inspired. These things are beautifully said by those who have reflected philosophically on this sort of education, for they draw the evidence for their statements from the facts themselves. And the same thing holds in the case of rhythms, for some have a steadier character while others are lively, and among the latter some involve cruder motions while others are more suited to free people. So it is obvious from these things that music has the power to make the character of the soul be of a certain sort, and if it has the power to do that, it is clear that it needs to be channeled and the young should be educated in it. And the teaching of music is well fitted to their nature at such an age, for at their age, the young do not willing submit to anything unsweetened, and music is a natural sweetener. And there also seems to be a certain kinship in us to harmonies and rhythms, which is why many of the wise claim that the soul either is a harmony or contains harmony.

Chapter 6

But the question we raised above, whether or not they ought to learn it by singing and hands-on practice, must now be discussed. And it is not unclear that whether they them-

40

1340B

10

20

---

231 Particular tunings of the Ionian and Lydian modes used at drinking parties, according to Glaucon in Plato's *Republic* (398E).

232 This was the mode of Sparta's martial music. Plutarch writes in his life of Lycurgus (Chap. 22, Sec. 3): "It was at once a magnificent and terrible sight to see them march on to the tune of their flutes, without any disorder in their ranks, any discomposure in their minds, or change in their countenances, calmly and cheerfully moving with the music to the deadly fight. Men, in this temper, were not likely to be possessed with fear or any transport of fury, but with the deliberate valor of hope and assurance." (Dryden translation)

selves take part in the activities makes a great difference to
what sorts of people they become. For one of the things that
is difficult if not impossible is for people who have not taken
part in activities to become serious judges of them. In addition, children need to have something to keep them occupied, and the rattle Archytas came up with, which people
give to children so that while they are using it they will not
be breaking things around the house, ought to be considered
a beautiful idea, since a young person is not capable of be-
30   ing calm. So while this is fitting for children in their infancy,
education is a rattle for young people when they are older.[233]
So it is obvious from such considerations that they ought
to be educated in music in such a way that they take part
in the activities. And it is not difficult to distinguish what
is or is not appropriate at different ages, or to refute those
who claim this concern is for mechanical artisans. First of all,
since people need to take part in the activities for the sake of
judging them, they should engage in those activities while
they are young; then when they get older, they can give up
the activities and be competent to judge what is beautiful
and enjoy it rightly on account of the learning they did in
40   their youth. As for the complaint some people make that
music makes people mechanical artisans, this is not difficult
to refute by considering the extent to which those who are
1341A being educated for political virtue ought to take part in the
activities, and the sorts of melodies and rhythms they ought
to take part in, and also the instruments their lessons ought
to be made on, for even this is likely to make a difference.
For the refutation of the complaint is contained in these details. For nothing prevents certain kinds of music from having the alleged effect. Obviously, then, the way it is learned
ought not to be an impediment to actions later in life, and

---

233 Archytas's rattle is thought to have been something like a castanet
mounted on a stick, with pieces that clapped together when it was
shaken. This way of holding an infant's attention would suggest a first
and crudest semblance of a musical instrument. In Bk. VII of the *Physics* (247b 17-248a 9), Aristotle describes the most important kind of
learning as a process of calming down out of our native state of disorder, so that our innate powers of understanding and knowing can be
engaged by the world and do their work. While this is a replacement
of one natural condition by another, it may require help from other
people. This suggests that the role of a musical education in forming
character has the additional effect of allowing the intellect to emerge.

ought not to make the body mechanical and useless for military and political training, but ought to be designed for learning beforehand and uses later. And this could happen in the learning of music if they did not put their effort into things meant for professional competitions, those wonderful and extraordinary works that have now been taken up in the competitions and adopted from them into education, but worked on things not of that sort, and just up to the point at which they become capable of enjoying beautiful melodies and rhythms and not merely the common sort of music that is enjoyed even by some of the other animals, and also by the multitude of slaves and children.

And it is also clear from these things what sorts of instruments should be used. Flutes should not be brought into their education, and neither should any other professional instrument such as a harp or anything else of that sort there may be, but whichever ones of them will make people good listeners, either in their musical education or in any other kind. It is also the case that the flute is not adapted to imitating character but more to arousing intense feeling; consequently, it should be used on the sorts of occasions on which contemplating a spectacle has a power that is cathartic[234] rather than for learning. And let us add another point that is incidentally opposed to the use of flute-playing for education, the fact that it prevents speaking. This is why it was a beautiful idea for those of earlier times to reject the use of it as unsuitable for the young or for free people, even though they had used it at first. For when they came to have more leisure because of their prosperity and prided themselves more on virtue, and also got lofty notions as a result of their deeds both before and after the Persian Wars, they began to dabble in every kind of learning, making no distinctions but seeking them all. It was for this reason that they brought flute-playing into their lessons. For even in Sparta a certain choral leader used to play the flute for the chorus himself, and in Athens flute-playing used to be all the rage, so much so that most of the free citizens, just about, took part in it. This is evident from the plaque Thrasip-

---

234 This is the kind of power Aristotle attributes to tragedy in Chap. 6 of the *Poetics*; in Chap. 4 of that work he suggests that the defining mark of comedy is to reveal something ridiculous in human beings, or human types, in general, and thus its power is for learning. On the meaning of *katharsis*, see the note to 1341b 40 below.

pus set up when he was choral leader for Ecphantides.[235] Its rejection as unsuitable came later as a result of their experience with it, when they were better able to judge what was and was not conducive to virtue, as with the rejection on similar grounds of many old-styled instruments, such as Lydian and pear-shaped harps and others designed for their users to intensify pleasure in their listeners, and seven-cornered and three-cornered and angled harps[236] and all those requiring cunning of hand. And the legend told by the ancients about flutes has good sense in it, for they claim Athena invented flutes but threw them away. And while it is not bad to go on to say that the goddess did this out of disgust at the scrunching up of her face, the more likely reason is, however, that education in flute-playing offers nothing of value for one's thinking, and we give the credit for knowledge and art to Athena.

So we reject as unsuitable a professional education in performance on the instruments. And we apply the word "professional" to what is meant for competitions, because someone who pursues education in that spirit is not undertaking it for the sake of his own virtue but for the pleasure of his listeners, and pleasure of a debased sort at that, which is the reason we judge it not to be an activity suited to free people but one that is too menial. And the performers too end up becoming debased, because the goal which they make their end is a worthless one. For the spectator, who is unrefined, ordinarily produces a change in the music, and makes the professional performers themselves, who are attentive to him, be of a certain sort, even, on account of their movements, in their bodies.

Chapter 7

Further consideration needs to be given to the modes and rhythms, and also in relation to education, as to whether all modes and all rhythms should be used or distinctions need to be made, and then whether we are going to impose that same dividing line on the people working at them for

---

235 Ecphantides was an Athenian comic poet who lived about a century before Aristotle's time.

236 Pear-shaped and angled harps are conjectures that have been made in one place or another, not necessarily on reliable evidence, for the meanings of *barbitoi* and *sambukai*, respectively.

an education, or need some other one. Now since we see that music consists of melodic composition and rhythm, one must not fail to consider what power each of these has in relation to education, and whether music with a good melody or with good rhythm is more to be preferred. And since we regard many things on these topics as having been beautifully said by some of the present-day experts on music, and also by those who, coming to it from philosophy, happened to be experienced with musical education, we shall ₃₀ leave **30** those who want a precise account of particular matters to seek it from them; for now, let us make distinctions the way laws do,[237] speaking of them only in outlines.

Now we accept the dividing of melodies in the way some of those engaged in philosophy distinguish them, holding them to be adapted to character, action, or inspiration, while they hold the nature of the modes to be akin to each of these kinds, a different mode for a different type of melody, and we claim that one ought to make use of music not for one sort of benefit alone but for more than one, since it is for the sake of education and also for the sake of catharsis (and what we are now simply calling catharsis, we will speak of again with more clarity in the *Poetics*),[238] and **40** thirdly for a pastime, a relief, and a relaxation of tension. In light of these things, it is obvious that all the modes ought **1342A** to be used, though they ought not all to be used in the same

---

237 "Laws speak only of what is universal" (1286a 10-11 above).

238 The *katharsis* of fear and pity which Aristotle names in the *Poetics* as the goal of tragedy is never explicitly clarified in that work either. The primary meaning of the word is "cleansing." Centuries of interpretation have taken it to mean a purging of toxic feelings, a refining of crude feelings, a ritual purification of guilt in the tragic hero, an intellectual clarification, or a clearing up of moral confusion. The present translator finds deficiencies in all these interpretations, for reasons given in the introduction to his translation of the *Poetics* (Focus Philosophical Library, Focus Publishing/R. Pullins Company, 2006). The way in which Aristotle does add clarity to the notion of catharsis in the *Poetics* is by replacing it later in the work with various words for and descriptions of a state of wonder. The work of tragedy, according to Aristotle, is to arouse fear and pity in order either to cleanse the spectator of those feelings, leaving in their place a state of wonder, or to cleanse fear and pity themselves of those elements that stand in the way of a state of wonder. His understanding of wonder is itself in need of interpretation, but what is relevant here is that it is a disposition into which the work of art moves us. Music that educates does so by imitating and thus revealing dispositions of the soul; music that is cathartic arouses feelings in the listener which leave a new disposition in their wake.

way, but those best adapted to states of character for education, and those adapted to action and inspiration for listening while others perform them. For any passion, such as pity or fear, that comes strongly upon some people is also present in different ways in everyone to a lesser or greater degree, and this is also the case with inspiration. For with some people, who are susceptible to being overcome by that sort of motion that is transmitted by the sacred melodies, we

10   see that when they experience melodies that drive the soul into an ecstatic frenzy they settle down as though they had been given a healing and cathartic cleansing. So people susceptible to pity and to fear, and those susceptible to feelings in general, necessarily have this same experience, and so does everyone else, to the extent that each has such susceptibilities, and thus everyone comes to have some sort of cathartic cleansing and to have a pleasant sense that burdens have been lifted. And melodies adapted to action[239] bring a similar harmless thrill to human beings. Accordingly, those who perform music for the theater in competitions should be permitted to use modes and melodies of these kinds. But since there are two kinds of spectators, one kind free

20   and educated while the other is an unsophisticated collection of mechanical and menial laborers and others of that sort, competitions and spectacles should be put on for such people too for relaxation. And just as their souls are turned away from their natural condition, so too among modes and melodies there are deviant forms with strained intervals and chromatic tones; and what is akin in its nature gives pleasure to each sort of person. For this reason, license should be allowed to those who compete in front of this sort of spectator to use any such kind of music.

For education, though, as has been said, melodies that

30   depict character and modes of that kind should be used. As we said above, the Dorian mode is of this kind, but any other

---

239   Ross adopts this emendation of the manuscripts, which read "adapted to inspiration." In Bk. XIX, Chap. 48 of the *Problems*, a work attributed to Aristotle or to his school, the Hypophrygian and Hypodorian modes are mentioned as appropriate accompaniments for dramatic scenes, including those depicting military actions, and not for choral speeches. The fundamental tone of each is an interval of a fourth below that of the mode with the related name. One might imagine music that is stirring, but which contributes nothing to learning or to any cathartic effect.

mode ought to be acceptable to us if those who take part in philosophy as a way of life and also in education in music approve of it. But it is not a beautiful idea for Socrates in the *Republic* to leave only the Phrygian mode with the Dorian, especially since he rejects the flute from among the   **1342B** instruments. For the Phrygian has the same power among the modes that the flute has among instruments, since both arouse frenzy and passion. For all Bacchanalian revelry and all movement of that kind is accompanied by flutes the most of any instruments, while among the modes it finds what is appropriate to that in Phrygian melodies. Poetry makes this clear in the case of the dithyramb,[240] for instance, which is by general agreement held to be a Phrygian form. Those who specialize in this sort of knowledge cite many examples of this, and especially the fact that Philoxenus tried to   **10** compose his *Mysians* as a dithyramb in the Dorian mode and was unable to do so, but by the very nature of the thing fell back into Phrygian as the appropriate mode. As for the Dorian, everyone agrees that it is the most stately and that it most of all has in it the character of courage. Moreover, since we praise the mean between extremes and claim that one should pursue it, and the Dorian has this nature in relation to the other modes, it is obvious that Dorian melodies are more suitable for the younger generation to be educated in.

And there are two goals, the possible and the suitable, since people of each sort ought to take up things that are more possible and suitable for them. But these are also limit-   **20** ed by their ages; for instance, it is not easy for those who are worn down by time to sing in the strained modes, but nature prompts us toward the relaxed ones for those of such an age. And some who specialize in music make a beautifully apt criticism of Socrates on this point as well, because he would reject the relaxed modes as unsuitable for education, taking them to be intoxicating without the power of strong drink, which is rather a stimulant to Bacchanalian revelry, but as conveying a worn-down feeling. So one ought to take up modes and melodies of these sorts too with a view to the age that lies ahead, that of the elderly, and also, if there is any of   **30** the modes that suits the age of children because of an abil-

---

240 A type of hymn to Dionysus (Bacchus), chanted and danced in a frenzied style by a large chorus.

ity to hold together orderliness and education, as appears to be an attribute of the Lydian mode most of all, to take it up as well. So it is clear that the three things that should be made the standards for education are these: the mean, the possible, and the suitable.[241]

---

241 Some scholars have argued that this last paragraph should not be regarded as authentic, but as something tacked on by hands other than Aristotle's. It is, however, strikingly appropriate that Aristotle should end the *Politics* with a reminder that Socrates in the *Republic* painted a picture of a city that would sing in unison, while the true task of politics is to bring harmony out of a city's disparate members by means of education. (See 1263b 29-37 above.)

GLOSSARY

The word at the heart of the *Politics* is **city** (*polis*). It refers not to a place but to a group of people gathered together, not for practical purposes alone but as participants in an **association** (*koinônia*) in which the nature of each can come to completion. Nature determines the appropriate size of the political association in a range large enough to be self-sufficient but small enough for its members to know each other and work together. The old translation "city-state" suggested that the *polis* was a particular variety within the general class comprising all aggregates of ruling and ruled human beings, or even a primitive stage in the evolution of the modern nation state. Aristotle considers the city to be of a size and capacity that allows the full development of human nature.

Derivatives of the word *polis* fill the work, and one of them provides its traditional title, *ta politika*, things that pertain to the life of a city. The *Politics* includes a dialectical study of things that are learnable and knowable about **politics** (*hê politikê*), as opposed to those matters about which the best that can be discovered are the persuasive arguments he explores in the *Rhetoric*. Most of what is knowable about cities has to do with their **forms of government** (*politeiai*); a *politeia*, sometimes translated here as **constitution** or simply **government**, is what gives the city its identity. The form of government determines who is a **citizen** (*politês*), and a distribution of greater or lesser authority over the decisions of the city among all its citizens characterizes **political rule** (*hê politikê archê*). Most existing governments deviate in whole or part from political rule and from any other safeguard of the common good; the primary **deviant forms** (*parekbaseis*) are **tyranny** (*turannis*), **oligarchy** (*oligarchia*), and **democracy** (*demokratia*), each of which, in its extreme form, rules arbitrarily and remains in effect by force. The forms from which they deviate are, respectively, **kingship** *(basileia)*, a paternal rather than political form of rule, **aristocracy** (*aristokratia*), and **constitutional rule** (*politeia*), all of which govern by laws and remain in effect by consent. The last named form, usually translated elsewhere as "polity," applies the general name for a form of government to the particular case of a government that constitutionally divides specific governing functions among classes of citizens.

aristocracy (*aristokratia*)

Rule by persons elected on the basis of merit (1293b 10-12), or any government in which a public education is established with a view to the virtue of a human being as such (1293b 1-7), rather than to those virtues that make citizens useful in war and conquest (1333b 5-1334a 10).

art (*technê*)

Skilled know-how in any practical endeavor, grounded in some theoretical knowledge and allowing a person with experience and aptitude to achieve a reliable result. It is *technê*, and not *epistemê* (demonstrable knowledge from first principles, sometimes translated "science"), that is the likely implicit substantive in the phrase *hê politikê* that Aristotle uses for the study and practice of politics (1252a 7-23). On its other side, art is distinguished from *banausia*, the repetitive practice of a merely mechanical craft.

citizen (*politês*)

Anyone entitled to participate to any extent in the judging, ruling, and deliberative activities of a city (1275a 22-23, b 17-20). Citizenship requires a willingness and capacity to rule and be ruled at the same time (1277a 26-27, b 16-17).

constitutional rule (*politeia*)

The general word for a form of government, when applied to a mixture of democracy and oligarchy, and especially to one in which democratic elements predominate (1293b 33-36). Aristotle considers the more democratically inclined mixtures more stable and secure (1307a 10-20), and since, in a city that has grown large, democracy is the only viable form of government (1286b 20-22), the best attainable government at such a time would be a democracy which reserves some role in government to those with property of at least a certain value. Such governments, however, he considers to have been of rare occurrence (1293a 39-41), partly because powerful democratic and oligarchic cities tend to support sympathetic factions elsewhere (1296a 36-38).

democracy (*demokratia*)

Rule by the poor (1279b 40-1280a 4), who are incidentally virtually always the majority (1290a 30-b 20). Democracy is a deviant form of government (1279b 4-6) because it contains no protection for the rich against injustice by the poor (1281a 14-24); where such protection is established in law, there is constitutional rather than democratic rule (1279a 37-39). Aristotle regards it as characteristic of a democracy to choose ruling officials by lot (1317b 17-21) rather than by election.

education (*paideia*)

The whole endeavor to develop the human potential, rather than to transmit specialized skills. The common education that should be the concern of a city includes gymnastic training, instruction in reading and writing, and a study and practice of music (Bk. VIII). Music has the most important role in education, which is the formation of a capacity to make right judgments about character and action (1340a 14-28). This concern with character is the education that Aristotle says can make a city one out of many (1263b 36-37), and is the only way to help people attain the self-discipline that allows oligarchies and democracies, or mixtures of them, to be ruled at all (1310a 12-36).

form of government (*politeia*)

An arrangement of the ruling offices in a city (1278b 8-10) and hence its constitution, written or unwritten. The word occasionally refers to the thing so constituted, where it is translated simply as "government," and sometimes applies to the particular form of government which explicitly divides ruling functions among different classes of citizens, in which cases it is translated as constitutional rule.

justice (*to dikaion*)

The political good (1282b 16-17). Of the various senses of this notion distinguished in Bk. V of the *Nicomachean Ethics*, the one meant here is what is generally called distributive (*en dianomê*) justice, though no form of that modifier is used anywhere in the *Politics*. Here, Aristotle defines it as dividing (*diairein*) things equally among equals and unequally among unequals (1280a 11-13), and applies it primarily to the constitutional division of decision-making authority among different classes of citizens. This form of justice is also what Aristotle refers to as the reciprocal equality (1261a 22-32) that holds together the political association, and makes it different from the homogeneous aggregate of an alliance or a nation.

kingship (*basilea*)

Rule by one person (*monarchia*) when it is by consent and bound by laws. Aristotle regards it as an archaic form of government in Greece, one that prevailed at the time when villages first combined into cities, under the protection of one paternal leader and benefactor (1252B 19-20, 1285B 3-19), a type of rule that ceased to be accepted when cities grew in size and rivalries for leadership became common (1286B 8-13).

middle range or **middle group** (*meson*)

Citizens who are neither rich nor poor (1295B 39-1296A 5). Our phrase "middle class" is not inaccurate, but it has the wrong connotations if we understand it to refer to those who make a living by trading in goods or services. Aristotle has in mind primarily people who own small pieces of land. He considers mechanical and commercial trade to be inconsistent with the proper practice of citizenship, which requires some leisure (1328B 33-1329A 2).

oligarchy (*oligarchia*)

Rule by the rich (1279B 40-1280A 4), who are incidentally virtually always the minority (1290A 30-b 20). Oligarchy is a deviant form of government (1279B 4-6) because it contains no protection for the poor against injustice by the rich (1281A 24-28), restricting all ruling functions to those who meet a property qualification. The number of those who rule may vary with tighter or looser qualifications, and there may be any degree of reliance on law, from none at all in a confederacy of the powerful to a complete rule of law (1292A 39-b 10), but oligarchies in practice always seek to make the rich get richer; hence they are mirror images of democracies in which those who rule also confiscate the property of those they rule (1321A 40-b 1).

provisioning (*chrêmatistikê*)

In its most proper sense, skill at using landed property to supply the needs of the members of a household (1258B 12-20), but with the development of a currency and the expansion of trade, a second kind of provisioning arose, as a skill at making and increasing wealth without limit. The common translations of *chrêmatistikê* as "money making" or "skill at business" let a derivative meaning crowd out the primary one. The root word *chrêma* similarly began by meaning any useful or consumable thing, but came to refer, in the plural, simply to money.

slave (*doulos*)

A human being who is the property of another human being
(1254A 12-17). By nature, a human being can be a slave only if he
cannot foresee his own actions by thinking, but only by imagination (1252A 32), lacks any capacity for reason beyond grasping what
is said to him (1254B 22-23), and is therefore wholly incapable of
deliberation (1260A 12). Most slavery, imposed on people captured
in war, Aristotle considers unjust and disadvantageous to all concerned (Bk. I, Chap. 6). He mentions, but does not elaborate on, his
own recommendation that all slaves should be offered the chance to
earn freedom (1330A 32-33).

tyranny (*turannis*)

Monarchy in which subjects are ruled not as citizens or even
children would be but as though they were slaves of a master (*des-
potês*). Aristotle mentions mixed forms of kingship and tyranny, but
regards the word as defined primarily by its most extreme mani-
festations (Bk. IV, Chap. 10), in which the ruler's aim is to make his
subjects think small, distrust one another, and have no power to act
(1314A 26-29). When tyrannical rule is shared among a small group
of people, he calls it a confederacy of the powerful (*dunasteia*), which
is not captured by our word "dynasty" but is closer in meaning to
what we would call a "junta." Tyrannical rule, whether exercised by
one person, a small group, or even a democratic majority contemptuous of law, is the annihilation of a city, since it abolishes political
life (1272B 13-15, 1292A 15-21, 1293B 27-29).

usual path, usual course (*hê huphêgêmenê methodos, ho huphêgêmenos
tropos*)

The beaten path of popular or received opinion, the starting
point Aristotle invokes in Bk. I, Chap. 1, for the whole study of politics, and again in Bk. I, Chap. 8, for the study of property. The near-
universal translation of these phrases as "*our* usual procedure," or
words to that effect, gets their meaning exactly wrong. They indicate
departures from Aristotle's own conclusions in theoretical works
such as the *Physics* and *Metaphysics*. Similarly, at the beginning of
Bk. VII, Chap. 1, Aristotle announces that an argument based on his
popular writings (*exôterikoi logoi*), rather than on his *Nicomachean
Ethics*, will be sufficient for the purposes of political inquiry. Near
the end of the *Nicomachean Ethics*, where Aristotle introduces a transition to the inquiry in the *Politics*, he says that such a study must
recognize and include the unwritten laws, national character, and
inherited opinions and habits already present in people as it finds

them (1180A 34-b 7).

virtue (*aretê*)

Originally a general term for the excellence of anything as a fitting example of its kind, *aretê* used without qualification refers to human excellence, displayed primarily in a character that acts with courage, moderation, and justice, within a life guided by practical judgment. Aristotle regards virtue as the necessary and sufficient condition of happiness (1323B 21-23), and as the goal of all political association (1328A 35-41). The achievement of this goal is measured not by conquest and wealth but by the extent to which all citizens can live fulfilling lives in peace and leisure (1333B 5-1334A 10).

Summary of Contents

None of them should be ruled simply by commands; all have virtues that need to be fostered for the sake of the well-being of the city.

Book II Previous opinions about the best city

Chapters 1-5 The hypothesis Socrates adopts in the *Republic*, that the best city is the one with the greatest degree of unity, is mistaken. Too much unity destroys the political association just as much as does too little. Citizens have private interests that a well-governed city can harmonize by means of education.

Chapter 6 Plato's *Laws* elaborates a form of government constitutionally mixed out of elements of oligarchy and democracy, but too near to oligarchy.

Chapter 7 Phaleas advocated an equal distribution of landed property to all citizens as a cure for injustice, but he did not understand the nature of the disease.

Chapter 8 Hippodamus proposed a theoretical arrangement for a city and encouraged a perpetual amendment and improvement of laws on the model of progress in the arts, not understanding that any change for the better in political life brings with it a weakening of the habit of obedience to law itself.

Chapter 9 The Spartan government found a stable division of responsibilities among kings, elders, and a governing board chosen from the common people, but did not constitute any of those parts well. It has produced citizens with the virtues needed to wage and win wars, but not good at governing in times of peace. Its practices in regard to slaves, women, and inheritances are all unwise.

Chapter 10 The Cretan form of government is a more ancient version of that adopted by Sparta. The common meals are provided on a more communal basis in Crete, but the governing board of common citizens is even less well designed than Sparta's, and is periodically suspended and replaced by arbitrary rule by a few powerful people. The long survival of Crete's government is explained more by its remote location than by its policies.

Chapter 11 The Carthaginian government is better designed than the preceding two, by incorporating more aristocratic elements and assigning offices on the basis of merit. Its weaknesses come from its oligarchic elements. It has maintained an orderly and contented body of citizens by providing opportunities in colonies for those who want to get rich, rather than by education. Despite their flaws, the three distinctive cities discussed are all justly admired.

Chapter 12 Solon tempered a too-oligarchic Athenian government with a balance of democratic elements, but the populace gradually increased in power until it became virtually a tyrant, pandered to by demagogues. Particular measures introduced by Solon, and by a handful of lawgivers in other cities, may be worthy of imitation.

Book III Citizenship and political rule

Chapter 1 A citizen is not just anyone subject to and protected by a city's laws but only someone who participates in some way in making and applying those laws.

Chapter 2 Having citizens as parents may be the usual practical criterion for conferring citizenship, but it does not define what is conferred.

Chapter 3 A city is a composite thing determined not by its location, its walls, or even its constituents but by its form. The fact that a city is a democracy, an oligarchy, or of some other form determines the activities and roles of its citizens and makes the association of them be what it is.

Chapter 4 Citizens contribute in different ways to the well-being of their cities, which in turn have different forms of government, so the virtue of a citizen is not necessarily the complete virtue of a human being. A ruler always needs the intellectual virtue of good practical judgment, while the lives of those who are ruled can be guided by others. But political rule over free and equal fellow citizens is learned only by being ruled, and is potentially shared among them all.

Chapter 5 Not all those who make up the population of a city and make necessary contributions to it are citizens, and even where they are, not all can have lives that permit cultivation of the virtues of citizens.

Chapter 6 Cities exist because human beings are political animals who seek not merely to live but to live beautifully. Governments differ in form by the way offices, and particularly the offices of highest authority, are arranged. Since the political association is by its nature a sharing of ruling and being ruled among free and equal people, those forms of government are just and rightly directed to their ends in which ruling authority is exercised for the common advantage.

Chapter 7 Rightly constituted forms of government are kingship, aristocracy, and constitutional rule, according as the highest authority is held by one person, by few, or by the majority, but their rightness depends upon the virtue of the rulers, at least upon military virtue in the last-named form. When rulers lack virtue and seek their own advantage at the expense of that of others, these forms deviate into tyranny, oligarchy, or democracy.

Chapter 8 But in the deviant forms, it is incidental that the rulers are few or many. The true distinction between oligarchy and democracy is based on whether the ruling power is held by the rich or the poor.

Chapter 9 Oligarchs argue that those who have more wealth deserve more honor and authority, while democrats argue that those things should be shared equally among all citizens, since they are all equal in freedom. Each side is right in assuming that justice requires an equitable distribution of those things the city has the power to give, but each is wrong about what each citizen contributes to the good of the whole. A political association is not merely an alliance for the sake of mutual exchange, punishment of crime, and military defense, but a common choice to live a shared life. While the rich may contribute more of its material resources and the poor more of its necessary services, the possibility of happiness among its citizens depends on the use they make of whatever prosperity and freedom they achieve. The happiness of a city is lived out in actions, and the quality of those actions is a result of the virtues of all those who participate in them.

Chapter 10 But any assignment of the highest ruling authority is potentially unjust. A majority may oppress a minority and destroy the city just as much as the reverse; restricting authority to those chosen for superior character deprives the rest of full citizenship; and it is no solution to say the laws should be the authority, since laws themselves may be oligarchic or democratic in kind.

Chapter 11 It may be argued that the general populace, if it is not utterly corrupt, combines the virtues in its members in a way that overcomes their vices. In any case it is not safe for any city to deprive the largest part of its population of a role in governing. Executive and administrative authority need not be in the hands of the common people, but they may be assigned the power to select those who hold it and to review their actions. Ordinary people may not understand everything that goes into the decisions made by office holders, but they are capable of judging the effects of them. And the office holders will not be above the law, but will be capable of applying it to those particulars which cannot come under the notice of general laws. The laws will reflect the form of government, and can therefore avoid injustices of an oligarchic or democratic kind only if the constitutional division of authority here proposed prevents the enactment of laws that deviate from the common interest in either of those directions.

Chapter 12 The unequal restriction of the highest offices to certain citizens would be unjust if it were based on an inequality in appearance or height or any other attribute irrelevant to the performance of the jobs. If office holders are chosen on the basis of ability for their work and justice in their characters, the city will be practicing the distributive justice that matches honors and authority with fitness and merit.

Chapter 13 If one person is clearly superior to the rest in ability and virtue, he must either be excluded from the city or accepted as king for life.

Chapter 14 In practice, in certain cities, in barbarian nations, and in ancient times, kingship has usually been limited by law, and has been of four kinds: a permanent generalship, a traditional and hereditary tyranny, an elective tyranny, or hereditary kingly rule with ultimate powers over military, judicial, and religious matters. Full-scale kingship would be a fifth kind

Chapter 15 But it may not be good for any one person to have full-scale authority, since human beings, unlike laws, are subject to being swayed by passions. And granted that laws must be applied by human beings, a group of decent people would always be less liable to corruption than even the best sole ruler. This suggests that, wherever a number of people of exceptional virtue can be found, aristocracy is a better form of government than kingship. But over time, aristocracies have tended to degenerate into oligarchies, and then into tyrannies, making the populace stronger in relation to the decreasing number of rulers until democracies finally prevailed. Kingship is also inevitably flawed by the expectation that it will become hereditary, and by the necessity for a body of armed men to enforce its laws.

Chapter 16 The rule of law substitutes an orderly arrangement for an unpredictable human will, dispassionate intellect for corruptible judgment, and the mean for partiality. Laws can educate those who apply them about those matters laws cannot determine, and custom always gives them greater authority than the human beings who apply them. And since a king must always appoint others to be an extension of his eyes, ears, and hands, it is more suited to the nature of a political association for all the ruling functions to be shared and limited in the first place.

Chapter 17 Kingship is appropriate and advantageous only in a population in which one family is preeminent above all the rest in virtue and ability. Where such capacities are present in more than one family but lacking in all the rest, an aristocracy would be more natural, but any city that can sustain an effective army has the widespread capacity for sharing in ruling and being ruled that constitutes political rule among equals, no matter what differences of ability may be present among them.

Chapter 18 In all three rightly constituted forms of government, the virtue of a citizen is the same as that of a human being as such, and the best city can be any one among them which does the best job of educating its citizens and giving them scope for the fullest development of their lives.

Book IV The spectrum of democratic and oligarchic forms of government

Chapter 1 Since kingship and aristocracy are not ordinarily attainable, the study of politics ought to look at other forms of government suited to various kinds of people, the forms easiest to attain in various circumstances, the one form best suited to all cities, and the means by which existing forms might be improved and preserved.

Chapter 2 The worst form of government, the one that can least be said to be a form of government at all, is tyranny, the opposite of the best form. Second worst is oligarchy, which deviates from aristocracy by looking to wealth rather than to virtue.

Chapter 3 Every city has differing parts of its population, and forms of government differ in distributing the ruling power among these parts. Popular opinion ranks aristocracy and constitutional rule respectively as types of oligarchy and democracy. In fact the former two are well organized, while the latter pair form a spectrum running from the most tightly ruled oligarchies through the most slackly ruled democracies.

Chapter 4 The parts necessarily present in every city include farmers, mechanical workers, market traders, menial laborers, military defenders, wealthy philanthropists, and office holders. These groups may overlap in many ways, but it is impossible for the same citizens to be rich and poor. This is why popular opinion recognizes oligarchy and democracy as the two forms of government, based on an ascendancy of one or the other group. But democracies themselves differ according as the population itself predominantly pursues various ways of life, according as ruling offices are equally open to all or based on a low property qualification, and according as the primary authority rests on laws or on decrees. The last case allows demagogues to rise to power.

Chapter 5 Oligarchies differ according as offices are based simply on a high property qualification, or are in part chosen by election or inherited by the sons of those who hold them. In oligarchies too, as in democracies, the laws may or may not be the highest authority.

Arbitrary rule by a confederacy of powerful people is the oligarchic counterpart to tyranny and to democracies that rule by decree. And cities with oligarchic laws may have democratic customs or the other way around, especially if the form of government has changed.

Chapter 6 Democracies tend to place authority in the laws when most citizens cannot afford to take time off for frequent assemblies. In democracies that grow large and prosperous and pay fees for jury duty and assembly service, the poor end up having more leisure than the rich, and authority shifts away from the laws to the multitude itself. In oligarchies, the laws tend to have more authority when property qualifications for office are relatively low and the numbers of people taking part in administration correspondingly large. As the qualifications get larger and the numbers smaller, they begin passing the ruling offices on to their sons, and eventually disregard the rule of law altogether.

Chapters 7-8 Where the choice of ruling offices is based to any degree on virtue, along with any other restrictions to the rich or extensions to members of the general populace, it is appropriate to consider the government a form of aristocracy. But popular opinion misapplies the name of aristocracy to mixtures of oligarchy and democracy that incline more toward oligarchy, since education is usually the privilege of the rich, and people imagine that the rich have no reason to be unjust. Hence the name of constitutional rule, though it might have been applied to any mixture of oligarchic and democratic provisions, is reserved for those mixed governments in which democratic provisions predominate.

Chapter 9 Democracy and oligarchy can be mixed by taking elements from both, such as paying the poor for serving on juries and fining the rich for failing to serve; or by splitting the difference, such as having a moderate property qualification for service in the assembly, rather than none at all or a large one; or by intermingling parts from each, such as having office holders chosen by election rather than by lot, but with no property qualification. A well-blended constitutional government will seem to be both a democracy and an oligarchy, and neither. In Sparta, for instance, even the poor are educated, and even the rich use ordinary food and clothes. Such a government will be preserved if no part of the population wants a different form of government.

Chapter 10 Some forms of monarchy, which come into being in accord with law and by consent, but allow the monarch to rule without further recourse to law, are mixtures of kingship and tyranny.

Full-scale tyranny treats all subjects as slaves and looks only to the tyrant's own advantage.

Chapter 11 The best form of government for most cities and most human beings will be one that has a large number of citizens who are neither rich nor poor. Extremes of wealth and poverty, among other bad consequences, produce an unwillingness to both rule and be ruled. A large middle group gives stability to a city and reduces the likelihood of factional conflict. Where the middle group is small, a city is more likely to turn into an extreme form of oligarchy or democracy, each of which is a short step away from becoming a tyranny. The foreign policy of cities at the head of alliances adds to the pressure that forces other cities away from the middle range most advantageous to all their citizens.

Chapter 12 The stability of a government depends on a combination of the quality of life available to citizens who are better off and the proportion of the population to whom such a life is accessible. Lawgivers for both oligarchies and democracies ought always to include the middle group of citizens in positions of authority. No policies can succeed in the long run in holding together a badly mixed government.

Chapter 13 Trickery designed to make constitutional rule more oligarchic in practice imposes fines on the rich when they avoid government or military service, but no penalties on the poor. Trickery to make it more democratic in practice provides the poor with fees for jury and assembly service and food for military service, but no incentives to the rich. A well mixed government uses policies of both kinds to encourage all citizens to do their part. It is especially important to a city's stability for as many citizens as possible to serve under arms. Over the course of time, authority in cities has gradually expanded from those wealthy enough for cavalry service, to those who could provide and fight in heavy armor, to the growing numbers of people in the middle range.

Chapter 14 In an extreme democracy, the deliberative function belongs to all citizens on all matters, while officials do only preparatory work for their assemblies, but democracies may also delegate deliberation over some matters to officials and serve in assemblies by turns. In an extreme oligarchy, the deliberative function is restricted to a few self-chosen people who are not bound by laws; more inclusive participation, elections, and the dividing up of the deliberative authority among different groups incline an oligarchy in the direction of either aristocracy or constitutional rule. Fees and fines ought to be used to ensure the participation of both the poor and the rich in assemblies, and adjusted not to their relative numbers in the population but to balance their power. It is best, but opposite to current practice, for the general populace to have a veto power over proposals originating in a body of eminent citizens.

Chapter 15 Many people are chosen to perform administrative, religious, or other public functions on behalf of a city, but the ruling offices that involve decision making and the giving of orders need the most attention from the political art. In a large city, one person may be assigned a single job for a limited period; in a small city jobs may need to be combined and made permanent. And some functions are specific to certain forms of government, as pre-councils are to oligarchies and overseers of women and children to aristocracies. It is characteristically democratic for office holders to be chosen by lot from among all citizens, oligarchic for them to be chosen from among those meeting a property qualification, and aristocratic for them to be elected on the basis of merit; mixtures of these procedures may be more suited to constitutional rule.

Chapter 16 A city may have many different lawcourts to decide cases of various kinds, but those needing the most attention are the ones involving political matters, where decisions may lead to factional divisions and even changes of government. These include cases against public officials and on matters bearing on the constitution. As with office holders, judges may be elected or chosen by lot, from among all citizens or some designated group, and mixed procedures are possible.

Book V Factions and changes of government

Chapter 1 Factions seeking to change a government in whole or part, or take control within one, form when a number of people believe they do not have a role in ruling in proportion to what they deserve. Hence purely democratic or oligarchic governments are always short-lived, though democracies are relatively more stable, since they do not experience the internal rivalries common within oligarchic groups. Democracies with a large population in the middle range are the most stable of these sorts of governments, but the only effective means to preserve them is to have a mixture of strict equality in some matters and proportional equality in others.

Chapters 2-3 Many examples show the variety of conditions, attitudes, and events that lead to factions and precipitate changes of government. Changing conditions can sometimes alter governments without factional conflict, as when populations grow disproportionally or when votes come to be bought and sold. And factions can form on the basis of distinctions other than that between the rich and **the poor, since virtually any difference can become a division.**

Chapter 4 Small matters can grow into large divisions, as shown by many conflicts that have arisen out of private disputes between powerful people. And parts of a population can earn good reputations that lead to their having greater power in a city, or to envy among their opponents, or to their own arrogance; these causes can have major effects, particularly where there is not a large enough middle group to keep things in balance. And governments can be changed by deceit as well as by force.

Chapter 5 Democracies have most often been destroyed by the reckless behavior of demagogues. In the past, when demagogues usually had experience as generals, they themselves often became tyrants. In later times, when demagogues have been more likely to be persuasive speakers who pander to the crowd, they have tended to cause oligarchic backlashes.

Chapter 6 When oligarchies treat the common people unjustly, they can cause democratic backlashes or give rise to demagogues who become tyrants. Or oligarchies can split into rival factions, particularly when some of the oligarchs waste their own fortunes through dissipation. Oligarchs can also undermine their own governments by relying on mercenary soldiers, out of fear of the populace or even out of fear of one another. And sometimes change happens unnoticed in oligarchies if over the course of time a greater part of the population attains the property qualification originally set for participation in government.

Chapter 7 Aristocracies are destroyed when people are wrongly honored, or believe themselves wrongly dishonored. Constitutional rule cannot be lasting if the mixture of provisions in its constitution fails to achieve an appropriate balance. Aristocracies are particularly liable to crumble imperceptibly after small changes, since they depend most on stable traditions. And all forms of government can be changed by outside interference.

Chapter 8 All governments are preserved by being on guard against small departures from the laws, which can breed a habit of lawlessness, by treating people well and not relying on trickery to make it appear so, by limiting terms of office, by reacting to external threats and internal divisions when they are in their early stages, by making periodic adjustments in property qualifications, by avoiding any large sudden elevation or diminution of the power of any citizen, and by keeping power balanced in the hands of opposing groups.

Most of all, the laws should aim at keeping office-holding from being profitable, so that people will be attracted to offices for the sake of honor and to avoid being ruled by worse people. Democracies ought to avoid any policies that impoverish the rich, and oligarchies ought to seek ways to enrich the needy.

Chapter 9 Those who hold ruling offices should have an attachment to their own form of government and share its prejudices about what is equitable, as well as having great ability for their work. In positions of military authority, ability is the more important qualification; in those with authority over money, qualities of character are more important. The only safeguard against a lack of virtue in the officials is for those attached to the present government to be stronger than those who want it to change. But democracies and oligarchies can also be destroyed by those who are too strongly attached to their prejudices; they are deviant forms of government, which can deviate only moderately from the mean before their policies become self-destructive. There is no substitute for education: the children of oligarchs need to learn that ruling is not a license for luxury, and those of democrats need to learn that freedom is not a license to do whatever one pleases.

Chapter 10 Kings have generally arisen from among prominent people, have sought honor, and have been guardians of both the landowners and the common people. Tyrants have generally started out as demagogues, have sought money, and have mistreated both the rich and the poor. Hence kingships have been destroyed for the same reasons as aristocracies, and tyrannies for the same reasons as oligarchies and democracies. Many examples show that monarchs of both kinds have incurred hatred or contempt because of their private lives, that eventually led to their downfall. These feelings are even more likely to be aroused against hereditary monarchs. Kingships were more enduring than tyrannies, but they no longer come into being.

Chapter 11 The longest-lasting kingships have been those that willingly surrendered parts of their authority. Tyrannies have extended their duration by measures designed to make their subjects think small, distrust one another, and have no power of action. But just as kings have been overthrown when they became tyrannical, some tyrants have preserved their power by becoming kingly and seeking to be respected rather than feared. This approach not only makes the tyrant's rule last longer, it makes it more worth having for him and more advantageous to all concerned.

Chapter 12 The most moderate tyrannies have been the longest-lasting, but tyrannies are still the shortest-lived of all governments. The pattern of transformations described by Socrates in the **Republic**, dead-ending in tyranny, does not reflect experience, since no form of government is of a single variety or subject only to a single form of destruction. Tyrannies can turn into governments of any other form, and also into tyrannies in other hands.

Book VI How democracies and oligarchies can be made more effective and enduring

Chapter 1 Differing ways of setting up the parts of each form of government can be adapted to a particular city's circumstances, and can be combined with measures of an opposite tendency to avoid the excesses that cause factional backlashes.

Chapter 2 The assumption underlying democracy is that each person should have an equal say in ruling, and all should be free of restraint. Democracies seek equality by making all offices open to all for short terms filled by lot, and by paying fees for holding office and for participation in juries and assemblies. They seek freedom by reserving all, or the most important, decision making to the assembly of all citizens. Any hereditary positions of honor surviving from ancient forms of government are stripped of their powers.

Chapter 3 But while the poor believe the authoritative opinion is that of a numerical majority, the rich believe it is the opinion that represents the major part of the wealth of the city. A truer equality than either sort alone would be achieved by a constitutional procedure for counting both the number of citizens on each side of a vote and the proportion of the city's assessed property they represent. A procedure for resolving split decisions, perhaps by lot, would need to be included. Any constitutional means of combining both kinds of majority into a single result is superior to expecting either sort alone not to produce a tyranny of one group over the other.

Chapter 4 The most successful democracies have been those in which the greatest part of the populace is engaged in farming. If no profit is to made from office-holding, people prefer to stick to their own work. And if offices are elected on the basis of a property qualification or merit, but are subject to review by the people as a whole, the government will generally be well administered. People engaged in farming or herding lead disciplined and healthy lives, and are capable of serving effectively in times of war. A predominantly town-based population lacks those virtues, more readily takes part in assemblies, and can quickly become a mob. Demagogues seek to relax laws about citizenship to increase this population; the common people should outnumber the rich and the middle group together, but when their number becomes too large the city becomes unruly and the democracy loses the support of its prominent citizens.

Chapter 5 Democracies have been brought down by policies of taxation and confiscation, by lawcourts biased against the rich, by frequent assemblies with fees for attendance, and by handing out public funds to the needy. They are strengthened by public aid and incentives that permit the needy to buy land or set up trades. Wealthy citizens with good sense will always be willing to assist the poor with capital that lifts them out of poverty and into productive work.

Chapter 6 The most successful oligarchies are those which use higher and lower property qualifications for offices of higher and lower authority. The more people they bring into the government from the middle and lower groups in the population, the stronger they themselves will be in relation to those they rule. The tighter the property qualifications become, the more unstable the government itself becomes.

Chapter 7 Terrain that can be defended by cavalry and heavy-armed infantry alone is most favorable to oligarchy, since these forces consist only of those who can afford the equipment. Where light-armed troops may be needed, the oligarchs should train their sons to take part in this kind of fighting while young, to avoid arming and training a force exclusively drawn from the populace, which could turn against its rulers. An oligarchy that wants to be lasting needs to seek ways to bring competent people from among the populace into the government. The highest offices, reserved for those with the most property, should customarily involve expenditures on the public behalf out of the private wealth of those who hold them. Oligarchs in practice seek to make themselves still richer, but their rule would be more secure if they were content with power and honor.

Chapter 8 All cities require officials for policing the marketplace, the town, and the countryside in various ways, for holding and distributing revenues, and for maintaining legal records. The functions of carrying out punishments and guarding prisoners incur hostility, and should be divided among many people for short terms; young citizens can be rotated through these duties, with various officials in charge of them by turns. Command of the military requires persons of experience and trust, as do oversight of the treasury and calling and presiding over assemblies. Other officials are needed to oversee religious observances, and prosperous cities where many people have leisure may also have overseers of various kinds of public recreation and private behavior.

Book VII Characteristics of the best city

Chapter 1 All would agree that the best life must include external goods, but is not possible in the complete absence of the virtues of character and intellect. The disagreement is over their relative contributions to happiness, with most people believing that any trace of virtue is sufficient, while external goods ought to be sought without limit. A little reflection on ends and means will show that even for the sake of a life of enjoyment, an orderly character and moderate possessions are best, and these same conditions are the basis for living a life of action and for being part of a community in which people do well and get along well.

Chapter 2 Opinions about the ends sought by the best city vary in the same way as opinions about what makes one human being happy. It should be obvious that a form of government that permitted each person to achieve the greatest happiness of which he was capable would be the best. But those cities whose laws have had a guiding purpose have aimed at conquest and mastery of other cities, and this sacrifices one understanding of the highest virtues to make possible another. If war and conquest are not ends in themselves but are for the sake of something else, a lawgiver must think about how to foster the means without undermining the end.

Chapter 3 Those who believe that the best life is free of all involvement in politics are mistaken. Happiness is well-being in action in all aspects of life. But no worthwhile end can be attained by unjust means, and a city need not dominate its neighbors to be active. For a city and a human being, the best life involves internal as well as external activity.

Chapter 4 Every city needs to have appropriate material to work with, especially in its supply of human inhabitants. But the greatest city is not the largest, but the one whose people are best capable of contributing to its work, and in fact all cities with good laws have controlled the size of their populations. The best size for a city is one that permits it to be self-sufficient, but also permits all the citizens to know enough about one another that decisions can made intelligently and not haphazardly.

Chapter 5 The best size for a city's territory is one that produces enough resources to support a life that is neither frugal nor luxurious, but gives the citizens sufficient leisure to live in freedom and moderation. The terrain should be easy to defend but hard to invade, and allow for ease of movement internally.

Chapter 6 A city ought to have sufficient access to the sea to be a market for itself but not for others. A port at a short distance from the town is best, so that the city can better control its population. A naval force is necessary to provide flexibility in defending the city and to discourage potential attackers, but the large number of rowers this requires should be supplied not by an increase in the number of citizens but from those who live and work on the land outside the city; the fighting force on sea as well as land should be made up of full citizens.

Chapter 7 A population needs to be spirited enough to resist foreign domination and to feel an attachment to one another, but also thoughtful enough to be capable of ruling and being ruled. The best city needs not only the right size of population, but the right blend of qualities in its temperament.

Chapter 8 Citizenship should extend to everyone who is part of the common life of the city, but not to everyone who produces necessities used by the city. Every city requires things provided by farmers, artisans, soldiers, land owners, priests, and those who make decisions on the its behalf.

Chapter 9 In the best city, all citizens must have sufficient leisure for the formation of virtue and for participation in political activity; the work of farmers and skilled artisans is not compatible with this requirement. The four remaining indispensable activities listed in the last chapter should be shared among all full citizens, in the sense that each should own some property, and should serve in the military when young, hold offices requiring judgment in the middle years of life, and take on priestly functions in old age.

Chapter 10 Hence the best city would consist of two distinct classes of people, an arrangement that was common among prominent ancient cities and has not been improved upon by any other arrangement subsequently tried. In addition to the private property owned by the citizens, some land should be held in common by the city, but the produce of all the land should be shared among both classes at common meals. Each private estate ought to be divided, with one part near the center and the other in an outlying area, so every citizen will have a stake in defending both the town and the borders. It is best for all the farming to be done by slaves, but for all slaves to be offered a way to earn freedom.

Chapter 11 For health, a city should be sheltered from north winds but open to the east; a lack of fresh-water sources can be made up for by the construction of reservoirs. Dwellings should be laid out in clusters, to combine ease of access within and security from without. The placement of fortifications should vary with the form of government, but no city can afford to do without well-maintained walls.

Chapter 12 Guardhouses at the walls are convenient places for common meals, as are temples within the city. Two distinct open areas ought to be provided, one reserved as a place of assembly and recreation in the central area on high ground, the other nearer the port for a marketplace and for the daily business of government. Both at meals and in recreational activities, the ruling officials should mingle with older citizens to benefit from their experience, and with younger citizens to have a beneficial effect on their characters.

Chapter 13 Much of the equipment necessary for the best city depends on luck and chance, but the need for these external things is minimized, and the happiness to be gained by the use of them is maximized, in citizens who have attained virtue. And while the capacity for virtue is built on nature, it is habit and reason that determine whether it will be attained. Hence the job of a city that aims at providing its citizens with the greatest opportunity for happiness must include education.

Chapter 14 Since all citizens will need to be ruled when young, and be capable of ruling when older, a single kind of education will be appropriate for them all. Such an education should make them fitted for leisure as well as business, peace as well as war, and for activity that is an end in itself as well as for actions that are necessary and useful. But in the rare past cases in which a public education has been provided at all, this has been aimed only at making citizens useful for war and conquest, and events have proved that such cities come to ruin when they are not at war.

Chapter 15 The whole education of the whole human being for peace and war, for necessary work and leisure activity, must instill all the principal virtues of character and intellect. In the natural development to maturity of a human being, the rational capacity is the last to become fully at work, but the first stages of the formation of character by habituation should begin early in childhood, and exercise to foster health and fitness of the body can begin earlier still.

Chapter 16 In fact, if the laws are to encourage the best bodily condition of the citizens, concern for this needs to begin before birth. Marriages should take place when women are about eighteen and men are about thirty-seven, and pregnant women should take daily walks and eat a healthy diet. The ages prescribed for marriage would also promote lifelong harmony between the spouses and between generations. Defective infants should not be raised, and conception that takes place after a certain number of births ought to be ended by abortion early in pregnancy, before the embryo develops the power of perception. Adultery should be discouraged, and if it occurs during optimal child-rearing years it should be a bar to holding office.

Chapter 17 Infants should have a diet rich in milk, with little or no addition of wine; it is good to follow the custom of many barbarian nations that start a training to endure cold weather right in infancy. Up to the age of five, children should get lots of exercise through play, and up to the age of seven, care should be taken that they not hear or see anything indecent. Religious observances that involve such things should be open only to those who have reached an age near adulthood when their education should have made them less impressionable. Children get comfortable with the sorts of things and people they are first exposed to, and these should never include vice or malice. At the age of five, they should begin to be spectators at the lessons of older children, and start such lessons themselves at seven. The manner of their education should change at adolescence, and continue to the age of twenty-one.

Book VIII Education of citizens

Chapters 1-2 The best safeguard for any form of government lies in the character of its people, and this needs to be made a common concern in the early life of its children. There is no agreement in practice about whether education of the young should include any training in useful activities or any instruction in exceptional kinds of knowledge; both are suitable as long as they are not pursued with the aim of mastering specialized knowledge or skills. A civic education should always look to the whole development of a free human being.

Chapter 3 The things most often taught the young are reading and writing, gymnastic activities, and music. Reading and writing are rightly included for their usefulness in all aspects of life, and gymnastic training to develop strength and health and to prepare the way for the development of courage. Music is commonly taught for the sake of pleasure, but this may be misunderstood. Life involves necessary work, and needs pleasant amusements as a relaxation of stress, but pleasures of that sort are instrumental to the kind of work that is itself instrumental to necessities. There is a deeper and more enduring pleasure inherent in the satisfying use of leisure, for its own sake, by a free human being, and the teaching of music should aim at developing the capacity for activity of that kind. The drawing lessons that are sometimes given to the young are also valuable to help give them an eye for beauty.

Chapter 4 Gymnastic training ought not to be aimed at competitive athletics or at fierceness in war. No rigorous workouts should be imposed until a few years beyond adolescence. A lighter regimen in early life is healthier, and provides a truer preparation for courage.

Chapter 5 And music too is a preparation for the formation of virtue, and not just a source of pleasure. While the visual arts can indicate feelings and states of character, rhythms and melodies directly embody states of the soul in a way that we take on as we listen. Music in the various modes can make us feel mournful and grave, softer and sympathetic, moderate and settled, or ecstatically inspired. In the young, a habituation to appropriate feelings in various situations can lead to the development of character, and the use of music sweetens discipline with pleasure.

Chapter 6 For the sake of becoming better listeners, the young ought to learn to make music themselves, but not with the aim of professional skill. Playing a flute or a harp is more complicated and specialized than necessary for the education of all citizens, but everyone can learn to sing.

Chapter 7 Contrary to the opinion of Socrates in the **Republic**, a city ought to welcome the use of all musical modes, since even frenzied and passionate music has a cathartic and calming effect. And every city ought to provide the kinds of music that everyone, including the uneducated and the elderly, can enjoy. And while the stately and moderate Dorian mode ought to play the primary role in early education, children should be exposed to any kind of music that is found suitable for depicting human character.

INDEX

abortion 1335b

administrative offices 1299a-1300b, 1321b-1323a

adultery 1335b-1336a

aid to the needy 1320a-b

Amasis (and the footpan) 1259b

animal meant for a city 1253a, 1278b

Antisthenes 1284a

Archilochus 1328a

aristocracy 1279a, 1286b, 1293b, 1294a, 1295a, 1306b-1307b

association 1252a, 1260b, 1276b

Athens 1268a, 1275b, 1284a, 1291b, 1300b, 1302b, 1303b, 1304a, 1305a, 1307b

Babylon 1265a, 1276a, 1284b

barbarians 1252b, 1255a, 1257a, 1285a, 1327b, 1336a

beautiful, the 1278b, 1281a, 1281b, 1291a, 1311a, 1323b, 1325a-b, 1326a, 1331b-1332a, 1337b-1338b, 1339b-1340a, 1340b

bodyguards 1285a, 1286b, 1311a

bribery 1270b, 1271a

Carthage 1272b-1273b, 1293b, 1316a, 1320b

cavalry 1270a, 1289b, 1297b, 1306a, 1321a

citizenship 1274b-1278b, 1283b-1284a, 1292b-1293a, 1319b, 1332b-1333a, 1337a

commerce 1258b, 1327a

common meals 1263b-1264a, 1265b, 1271a, 1272a, 1294b, 1329b-1330a, 1331a

confederacy of the powerful 1272b, 1292b, 1293a, 1302b, 1306a,